THE NEAR EAST

ARTHUR COTTERELL

The Near East

A Cultural History

HURST & COMPANY, LONDON

First published in English in the United Kingdom in 2017 by
C. Hurst & Co. (Publishers) Ltd.,
41 Great Russell Street, London, WC1B 3PL

Printed and bound in Great Britain by Bell and Bain Ltd, Glasgow

Distributed in the United States, Canada and Latin America
by Oxford University Press, 198 Madison Avenue, New York,
NY 10016, United States of America.

A Cataloguing-in-Publication data record for this book
is available from the British Library.

ISBN: 9781849047968

This book is printed using paper from registered sustainable
and managed sources.

www.hurstpublishers.com

For Yong and Alan

CONTENTS

LIST OF MAPS

All of the maps were drawn by Ray Dunning.

PREFACE

During a recent Mediterranean cruise that sailed as far east as Israel, a couple of passengers asked if I could recommend a book on the whole area. As I had already suggested how much we owe to the Sumerians, whose cities in southern Iraq marked the beginnings of civilization on the planet, this request was hardly surprising. When I told them that there were accounts of the peoples who had shaped the Near East—the Sumerians, Babylonians, Assyrians, Hittites, Trojans, Syrians, Jews, Persians, Greeks, Romans, Byzantines, Arabs, Franks and Turks, to name only the best known—one passenger commented how strange it was that for such an important location there was no account written for the general reader.

He went on to say that trying to understand the Near East was not unlike negotiating the London Underground without a map indicating the relationship of its various lines. And he added how confusing it had been in Bethlehem to hear the complaints of local Christians about Muslim refugees pushed outside Israel's defensive barrier, when both the Christians and the Muslims were plainly Palestinian Arabs. It seemed to him that, along with the Jews, they were engaged in a family quarrel over the same religion. What he might have added was how from ancient times belief had been a Near Eastern preoccupation.

It struck me then how nothing was available between academic studies on the one hand and tourist guides on the other, a publishing gap which this cultural history endeavours to fill by offering an outline of the Near East's development from the genesis of civilization itself in southern Iraq until modern times. While any book covering such an incredible story of human endeavour can never hope to be more than introductory, there is a possibility that the general reader will obtain an overall view of the critical events that have determined the course of Near Eastern history, as well as their impact on the rest of the world. At the very least, this cultural survey should be more informative than the standard layout of the London Underground, especially through the maps and illustrations so expertly prepared by Ray Dunning.

INTRODUCTION

In the first century after the birth of Christ, the Roman author Pliny remarked how many plants which were not native to Italy had been imported from the eastern Mediterranean. He even went on to say that the arrival of such useful plants was one of the benefits of Pax Romana. That their Latin names were generally of Greek derivation, however, did not blind Pliny to the fact that the Greeks had either obtained these plants, or learned the technique of cultivating them, from further east. Although he states that Roman generals used to parade exotic trees in their triumphs, Pliny was more interested in ordinary specimens such as the cherry. Introduced from Asia Minor, this fruit tree had spread to the Roman province of Britain by the time Pliny wrote his *Natural History*.

What Pliny signalled was the indebtedness of the western Mediterranean to the ancient Near East. Besides the impact of the peach, plum, apple, carob, walnut, pistachio, olive, vine and cereals on its agricultural economy, new knowledge of grafting also transformed the tending of trees. Behind the western transfer of plants stood the last Ice Age, which ended around 9,000 years ago. The Near East was much less affected than Europe, with the result that it acted as a reservoir from which species eliminated in Europe during periods of glaciation could be brought back, either through human agency or natural diffusion. Just how severe the Ice Age was can be gauged by the survival of the rabbit, the sole indigenous animal of the Iberian peninsula. The Romans would take rabbits as far north as Britain.

The emergence of civilization in southern Iraq a few millennia after the Ice Age is not then so surprising when the geographical advantages of Mesopotamia, 'the land between two rivers', are taken into account. It comprises in fact a vast alluvial plain that had once been the bed of a single river, whose narrower remnants today are the Tigris and the Euphrates. With such fertile soil and a regular supply of river water, all that was required to guarantee a food surplus capable of sustaining the first urban society was an agricultural revolution. This achievement belonged to the Sumerians, whose great foundation of Uruk was the world's earliest city.

Though unaware of this pivotal event in the late fourth millennium BC, the three competitors for power in the western Mediterranean still sensed their own cultural indebtedness to the Near East. They all appreciated how the most valuable things had originated there. The Etruscans, Rome's northern neighbours, claimed to have migrated from famine-stricken Lydia around 1200 BC. The Carthaginians, the toughest opponents of the Romans, had quit the Phoenician port-city of Tyre four centuries afterwards. Their foundation of Carthage in present-day Tunisia soon dominated seaborne commerce, with trading posts as far west as Spain. Its ships even reached Britain in search of tin, an essential ingredient in the manufacture of bronze. Not to be outdone, the Romans believed that they descended from the Trojans. At Carthage, the Trojan hero Aeneas heeded the divine command of Juno and, abandoning Queen Dido to a funeral pyre, he sailed on to Italy in order to fulfil his destiny as the founder of the Roman nation.

With the aid of modern archaeology, we are able to follow in Chapter 1 the ancient transformation of the Near East. For our knowledge of its antiquity rests upon the spectacular finds resulting from excavation over the past century and a half. Apart from revealing the existence of completely forgotten powers such as Hatti and Mitanni, both located in the northern part of the Near East, the exploration of ancient sites has turned up texts that illuminate the early history of the entire region.

Near Mosul in northern Iraq, examination of a mound associated with the city of Nineveh resulted in the recovery of the library owned by the Assyrian kings, a treasure trove for approaching the world's first civilization. Surviving documents throw light on the Sumerians, whose own cities were founded 2,000 years before Nineveh fell in 612 BC to a combined assault of the Babylonians and the Iranian Medes. The destruction of this Assyrian stronghold ushered in the final era of the ancient Near East, that of Persian rule.

It was the Sumerians who shaped the consciousness of ancient Near Eastern peoples. Translation of one royal text from Nineveh caused a sensation in 1872 because it related the Babylonian version of the Flood, a story thought to have been biblical in origin. When scholars discovered that this myth went all the way back to Ziudsura, the Sumerian Noah, they realized that here were some of the oldest ideas to survive anywhere on the planet.

In Chapter 2, the genesis of civilization itself in Sumer is explored, as well as its most significant invention: writing. This stroke of genius eased communication in the world's earliest cities, but even more it set down in a permanent medium the ideas that informed their operation. Without cuneiform script we would neither possess poetical works like the amazing *Gilgamesh* epic, nor be aware of how profound was the Sumerian concern with premature death. In about 3000 BC, the inhabitants of Uruk hit upon the idea of creating hundreds of pictograms, plus signs for numbers and measures; these were pressed into clay tablets with a reed stylus to record events, decisions and opinions.

The realization that it was possible to capture language in written form travelled along the trade routes, so that cuneiform script became the means of communication throughout the ancient Near East. The archive of correspondence unearthed at Amarna, the palace-city built by the reforming pharaoh Akhenaten in the 1340s BC, shows how this script was employed when he wrote to his Syrian, Hittite and Assyrian counterparts. That ancient Near Eastern inventiveness later replaced cuneiform with the alphabet, which the Greeks borrowed from the Phoenicians during the eighth century BC, only serves to underline the crucial role that this part of the globe has played in the development of civilization.

Chapter 3 looks at the world's first great empires: Akkad, Babylon, Hatti, Assyria and Persia. Their influence was both far-reaching and long-lasting. The earliest mega empire was established by the Persians, who controlled territories as far apart as Thrace and India. It was the military ambitions of Xerxes, who ruled the Persians from 486 to 465 BC, which caused the intense conflict with the Greeks. His invasion of the Greek mainland in 480 BC was answered in 334 BC when Alexander the Great crossed to Asia Minor with an army of nearly 40,000 men. Once Persia was overthrown, Alexander recruited Asian troops and advanced as far east as India, but his generals could not hold onto his conquests after Alexander's sudden death from fever in Babylon, and so a revived Persia confronted his Greek successors and then the Romans in the eastern Mediterranean. The seesawing struggle between Europe and Asia lasted well into the medieval period, with the Crusades and the Ottoman occupation of the Balkans.

In ancient times, this international conflict had already acquired religious overtones, because the multiplicity of deities derived from the Sumerian pantheon were largely replaced by the monotheism of Jewish belief, through its powerful offshoot of Christianity. What Christians retained in Jesus, though, much to the consternation of Muhammad, was the Sumerian notion of a dying-and-rising god.

Chapter 4 delves into the religious beliefs of ancient Near Eastern peoples. Only recently has it been realized how influential were Sumerian ideas about divinity, not only here but also in adjacent areas such as Greece. Oceanus and Tethys, the primeval couple in Greek mythology, could easily have come straight from the Babylonian epic *Enuma Elish*, which was composed before the death of Nebuchadrezzar I in 1105 BC. By then, the Babylonians had adopted the Sumerian religious outlook lock, stock and barrel. According to the Sumerians, human beings were created for no other purpose than to serve the gods and furnish them with food and shelter. In the Sumerian story of the Flood there is no mention of sinfulness as in the biblical account: instead, the storm god Enlil inundated the surface of the earth in order to stop the racket that people were making below stairs. He found sleep quite impossible, so plague, famine and flood were in turn used to reduce the numbers then overcrowding the cities. Warning of the final disaster was given to Ziudsura by Enki, the Sumerian water god.

In each city a temple dedicated to a major deity shaped the lives of the inhabitants. City skylines were punctuated with ziggurats, multi-floored towers belonging to individual gods and goddesses, although their cult statues were often housed in a temple at the base. During the so-called Babylonian captivity, Jewish exiles seem to have been inspired by Marduk's 90-metres-high ziggurat to invent the Tower of Babel. In Genesis the reason given for confounding language was Yahweh's fear that the tower's top would eventually reach heaven. Afterwards its builders 'could not understand each other's speech' and the project was left unfinished.

In spite of unease amongst the Jewish prophets, there is little doubt that the Temple in Jerusalem, like its Mesopotamian equivalent, was viewed as the earthly abode of Yahweh, the place where he listened to psalmists singing as well as the prayers of his worshippers. But no divine image was ever installed in the Temple similar to Marduk's statue at Babylon, which was made of wood and overlaid with silver and gold. Elected champion of the gods, the titanic exploits of Marduk as recounted in the *Enuma Elish* explain his elevation as the foremost Mesopotamian deity. Single-handed, he defeated the threatening forces of chaos and created the world.

The biblical lands are the focus of Chapter 5. Before Israel existed, Yahweh chose from the peoples of the ancient Near East a certain individual, whom he instructed to take possession of Palestine. This man was Abraham. Only the Jews really managed to turn their beliefs into a national religion while, at the same time, perfecting the ancient Near Eastern tendency toward monotheism. Was Abraham himself a monotheist? He hailed from Ur, where the moon god was credited with the determination of destiny. Was perhaps the experience of Moses crucial? In Egypt he would have been aware of Akhenaton's attempt at religions reform. Or were the prophets, confronted by the brute force of Assyria, the inventors of a divine plan? Whatever the answer, we encounter a distinct mode of thought when the Jews address themselves to the question of divine omnipotence.

Unsympathetic though Yahweh's cult was to mythological events that included other deities, the Jews were still troubled over the use of idols, notwithstanding the stern prohibition of 'graven images'. Bronze figures are known to have represented Yahweh in the northern kingdom of Israel during the twelfth century BC. Struggles over the use of images have regularly convulsed what are now termed the Abrahamic faiths: Judaism, Christianity and Islam. Within Christianity there have been periods of severe iconoclasm under the Byzantine and Carolingian emperors, and more recently during the Protestant Reformation. It was of course unavoidable that the Jews would become entangled with West Semitic beliefs once they moved into the Holy Land. The prototype of Mount Zion was indeed Mount Zaphon, the home of the gods worshipped at Ugarit. Texts recovered from Tell Ras Shamra, the site of this port-city on the Syrian coast, reveal striking parallels between Yahweh and Baal, the local weather god. Both are linked to storm clouds, as Moses dramatically discovered for himself on Mount Sinai when he learned of the Ten Commandments.

The ancient era concludes in Chapter 6 with the Greeks and the Romans, who in turn controlled much of the Near East. After the early death of Alexander in 323 BC, the Macedonian commander Seleucus took charge of the region and showed respect for its traditions. This policy was continued by his eldest son, Antiochus I, who embellished Marduk's temple as well as others around Babylon. Yet Seleucid culture remained fundamentally Greek and expressed itself most of all at the gymnasium, to which Jews among others flocked. Naked athletics posed a serious embarrassment for Jewish participants, who made great efforts to hide the fact of circumcision. An uprising led by the priest Judas Maccabeus in 160 BC against the influence of Seleucid culture was ultimately successful, although he did not live long enough to witness the Jews gaining their independence.

The extinction of the Seleucid dynasty in 64 BC drew Palestine into the Roman sphere of influence. Yet its conversion into a province failed to bring peace to Judea, as it was now called, and a series of disastrous revolts culminated in the emperor Hadrian's expulsion of the Jews. Upon the ruins of Jerusalem, the Roman colony of Aelia Capitolania was built exclusively for non-Jewish residents. By then the devastated city had already exported Christianity to the Roman empire, which in 312 succumbed to this new religion through the conversion of Emperor Constantine. Roman domination of the eastern Mediterranean, however, left the Greek cultural heritage largely untouched and Constantine's Christian capital of Constantinople was filled with Greek speakers. Even the New Testament used this language, as indeed did the Hebrew Bible. The decline of spoken Hebrew had long necessitated the use of an Aramaic translation in synagogues; popular since the Persian empire, Aramaic would have been the tongue spoken by Jesus.

Chapter 7 brings the historical narrative into the medieval era. It is entitled A World Crisis for the good reason that this is what the rise of Islam appeared to mean for the Near East, since Muhammad's mission literally brought its ancient culture to an end. In about 610, this Arab merchant had begun to experience visions in which the archangel Gabriel told him to proclaim that 'there is no God but Allah'. Even though Muhammad drew upon Near Eastern religious traditions, the deity he worshipped was unmistakably an Arabian one, whose direct message must owe something to a desert encampment, ringed at night with nothing but stars. Within twenty years the Prophet became the leading chieftain of Arabia, but to the Arab tribes was given the task of world conquest. Despite first Damascus in Syria, and then Baghdad in Iraq, acting as Muslim capitals, the original civilization of the Near East was lost until modern archaeologists discovered its ancient glories.

What Muslim scholars discovered themselves, however, proved no less amazing in the neglected works of classical Greece. Baghdad became a beacon of enlightenment during the Middle Ages. There was nothing dark emanating from Constantinople, but Islamic culture was then at its apogee, improving agriculture, encouraging trade and industry, promoting the sciences, philosophy, literature, art and architecture, and even founding such distant cities as Cordoba in Spain, with most of the amenities of modern life. Because society in Cordoba was so tolerant and easygoing, one of its most famous sons was the Jewish philosopher Maimonides, in Arabic Musa ibn Maymun. His ideas touched a nerve throughout the Islamic world, and especially the proposition that 'happiness consisted in knowledge of the deity'. Another resident philosopher was Ibn Rushd, better known in Europe as Averroes. At the request of the caliph Abu Yakub, he summarized in 1168 the works of Aristotle.

Western Europe had to wait until the fruits of Muslim and Jewish scholarship filtered through to Christian thinkers. Yet the rediscovery of Aristotle's works posed an immense challenge for medieval Catholicism until St Thomas Aquinas succeeded in his *Summa Theologica* in satisfactorily ordering both human and divine affairs. But his rigorous logic was not enough to save his own body from decapitation and boiling at the monastery of Fossanuova. Its monks were determined to keep his bones as holy relics when he died there in 1274.

Umayyad and Abbasid caliphs presided over the Muslim florescence, but the first signs of trouble were already apparent. The Prophet's death had led to a poor compromise over the leadership of Islam, with the assassination of three of the four men who were appointed as caliphs to succeed him, including his son-in-law Ali ibn Abi Talib. Not even the first dynasty set up by the Umayyads at Damascus could stem Arab violence; in 750 its family was slaughtered, with the sole exception of Abd al-Rahman. Fleeing westwards to Spain, he seized power at Cordoba where he ruled for more than three decades. But Abd al-Rahman showed that he had learned from the Damascus bloodbath, since he had the assassins sent after him killed and their severed heads returned to his Abbasid enemies.

As the revenues of Iraq, the home province of the Abbasids, were critical to the new caliphate, the capital was shifted to Baghdad, which became the largest city in the world outside China. Within little more than a century the Arabs had transformed themselves from desert dwellers into the owners of a metropolis, and encountered all the difficulties of urban life that the north African scholar, Ibn Khaldun, would later cite as an explanation for the decline of the first Muslim empire.

Power struggles fatally weakened Abbasid rule, its most serious breach expressing itself in the sectarian conflict between the Sunnis and the Shia. Whereas the former Islamic sect accepted the caliphate as a legitimate institution, with the Abbasids fully entitled to exercise religious as well as secular authority, the latter held that only the heirs of the fourth caliph, Muhammad's son-in-law Ali ibn Abi Talib, were the true successors of the Prophet. It is a quarrel that continues in the Near East today.

Chapter 8 marvels at the stubborn resistance of the Byzantines, the name by which the Greek-speaking successors of the Romans in the eastern Mediterranean are known. They called themselves Romans. Long a bastion for Christian Europe, the Byzantine empire was almost always ready to fight, and often fought for its life. During much of its history

Byzantine provinces were essentially military districts garrisoned by soldiers and governed by generals. The army ruled the roost and might well have rolled Muslim power back from Syria and Palestine had not its offensives been blunted by the arrival of the Oghuz Turks, a nomadic people from the Central Asian steppe. They established the Seljuk empire, named after a prominent Oghuz family. Yet the Oghuz were not the earliest Turks to have travelled westwards, because the Abbasids used Turkish slave-soldiers in a fashion reminiscent of Sumerian practice. But it was the Seljuk leader, Alp Arslan, who achieved what no other Muslim general had done. At the battle of Manzikert in 1071, he broke the Byzantine border defences and opened Asia Minor to Turkish settlement. The Byzantine emperor Romanus IV Diogenes was taken prisoner and his army dispersed. Oghuz expansion might be viewed as a continuation of nomad raiding, except that Alp Arslan regarded the establishment of the Seljuk empire as a holy war, a Sunni assault on Christians and Shia Muslims alike.

Within twenty years of Alp Arslan's death in 1073, the Seljuk empire disintegrated but Palestine remained firmly in Muslim hands, much to the disappointment of Christian Europe. A consequence of this situation was the Crusades, a holy war sponsored by Pope Urban II. Yet the Crusades were never the same as jihad, the endless struggle that Muhammad had prescribed against those who refused to acknowledge Allah, since the Christian call to arms arose from a specific complaint, the barring of pilgrims from the holy places of Jerusalem. Having just backed action against Muslims in Spain, the pope transformed a Byzantine request for military assistance into a campaign of religious revivalism, personally preaching in 1095 a crusade that sent more than 50,000 individuals eastwards.

Given the wide-ranging Christian attack on Islam's Mediterranean frontiers from the eleventh century onwards, it is hardly surprising that many Muslims saw the Franks as a dire threat to Islamic civilization as a whole. Although the conquest of Sicily and al-Andalus rang alarm bells, this anxiety did not last long, because the Crusader states in the Near East were soon swept away. Yet the dramatic rollback of Christian power owed less to Muslim heroics than European exhaustion: these states were simply too far away from western Europe. There was, however, no coordinated Muslim counter-crusade: rather jihad remained an ideal, a convenient rallying cry for leaders gathering troops for a border campaign. The Frankish threat failed to generate a militant Islam, although it did harden attitudes towards Christians living under Muslim rule.

The main beneficiary of the turmoil was the Ottoman empire, named after its founder Osman. In Chapter 10, the course of this last great Near Eastern empire is traced from the early fourteenth century until the early years of the twentieth century. The Ottoman caliphs concentrated their attentions on Hungary and the Hapsburgs, looking to the Balkans for permanent acquisitions, so that they shifted the emphasis from crusading to power politics. Those who ruled the empire, following Mehmed II's final defeat of the Byzantines, were more concerned with strengthening Ottoman power than fighting for Sunni domination. In the 1540s, when Suleyman the Magnificent announced that he was the caliph, the rightful successor of Muhammad, his motive had nothing to do with religious enthusiasm. He knew that his assumption of divine leadership could not disguise the presence of a large non-Muslim population that, in most of the empire's European provinces, actually comprised the majority.

At its height, Ottoman authority extended from Algiers to Basra, from Budapest to Mecca, with a population of about 26 million. But the subjects of the Ottoman caliphs had short lives: in the final decades of the nineteenth century the average lifespan was forty-nine years. Famines were a recurrent feature of the empire's history and, coupled with not infrequent wars, they tended to keep population figures low.

The collapse of Ottoman power at the close of the First World War brings us to the Near East's modern era. The failure of a modernization programme had been compounded by the Ottoman decision to side with the Central Powers. Although a treaty of alliance with Germany was signed prior to the outbreak of hostilities, the Turks had no wish to enter the conflict until Bulgaria and possibly Romania joined the alliance. Defeat at the hands of the Russians in the Caucuses was only the start of Turkish troubles, which in 1915 saw seaborne landings on the Gallipoli peninsula narrowly repulsed, and two years later the British capture of Jerusalem. Chapters 11 and 12 chart this chaotic period, which witnessed the end of the caliphate and Ataturk's remarkable establishment of modern Turkey. A fierce nationalist, Ataturk believed that the future lay with a secular nation-state in which religion played a minimum role and gradually became the private concern of each citizen.

Many rejected such a vision. And some of Ataturk's emulators in the second half of the twentieth century struggled to achieve a political accommodation of modern times similar to that of Turkey. Worse still, a large number of Arab countries succumbed to dictatorial rule. Arguably the World Wars, and in particular the Second, introduced to the modern Near East what Muslim traditionalists feared most in the Western outlook, as is made clear in Chapter 13. Yet their worries hardly compared with the reaction to the founding of the state of Israel.

Decolonization and Jewish immigration have complicated present-day politics, just as the Gulf Wars added an incredible degree of instability to Iraq. Chapter 14 shows how the Islamic State of Iraq and Syria has thrived on the confusion, its militant members making short work of archaeological sites in the name of Allah. Bulldozers and dynamite wrecked Nimrud in 2015 and further damage is to be anticipated at other locations in northern Iraq and Syria. It is justified by Muhammad's condemnation of images after he purged the Ka'ba of idols. Respect for the sacred black stone of the Ka'ba, supposedly restored by Abraham and Ishmael, most likely derives from pre-Islamic worship of prominent rocks. Whereas Abraham's younger son Isaac became the founder of the Jewish nation, his older brother Ishmael founded the Arab tribes. Originally Muslims prayed in the direction of Jerusalem but, after Jews living in Arabia rejected Muhammad's claim of divine inspiration, the direction was changed to Mecca. Today pilgrimage to the Ka'ba provides a common aspiration for Muslims worldwide. Sadly one of the most visited places today is the vast cemetery at Najaf, south of Baghdad. It is the busiest burial ground in the whole of the Near East.

PART 1

LOST CIVILIZATIONS

The Ancient Near East

1

DISCOVERY

AN ARCHAEOLOGICAL REVELATION

The man-made ziggurat could not fail to recall to the Sumerian the highlands where once his fathers lived and the true nature of the gods he worshipped, bidding him to lift up his eyes to the hills from which came his help.

Leonard Woolley, on the ziggurat at Ur

The nineteenth century was the great era of archaeology. Since then methods of excavation have been refined, with science adding an extra dimension to our understanding of the past, but the realization that beneath the soil of modern Iraq were traces of the first civilizations on the planet resulted from the enterprise of such individuals as Paul-Emile Botta and Austen Henry Layard. In 1842 it was the discovery of Dur-Sharrukin, 'Sargon's fortress', by Botta that inaugurated Assyrian archaeology. The village of Khorsabad, some 15 kilometres north-east of Mosul, where Botta was the French consul, had been the site of the Assyrian capital from 721 to 705 BC, when on the sudden death of King Sargon II it was moved to Nineveh, on the outskirts of the city of Mosul itself.

Three years later Layard began his excavations at Nimrud, nearly 30 kilometres south of Mosul. This ancient city was known to the Assyrians as Kalhu, the biblical Calah. On his way to Sri Lanka, where he hoped to find suitable employment, Layard caught sight in 1840 of the tells, the pyramidal mounds marking the locations of ancient settlements. Mesopotamian cities were constructed with mud and clay: unlike wood, these building materials do not decompose; and unlike stone, they cannot easily be reused. As a consequence, a crumbling mud-brick wall tended to be pushed over and levelled to create a new floor, which was stamped flat. New bricks were then introduced to erect another structure, so that over the years this practice raised considerably the height of a settlement. This is also how ziggurats may well have evolved: renewing old temples on their platforms would slowly raise the main shrine ever higher. Ur's stepped ziggurat, the best preserved of any ancient Mesopotamian city, was regularly repaired and even rebuilt on two known occasions. One reason for the ziggurat's state of preservation was that its mud-brick core boasted an outer skin of baked brick, more than 2 metres thick and set in bitumen mortar. Some of these stronger bricks are stamped with the names of the kings who commissioned them. The ziggurat's structure consists of three superimposed levels, each of which diminishes in size like a wedding cake. Its outer face is decorated with buttresses and recesses, while drainage holes ensure that moisture cannot accumulate in its core.

For the Sumerians a ziggurat functioned solely as the residence of a city god. It was where the cult statue of each deity was placed. In Babylon, however, the sanctuary of its god Marduk doubled as a vantage point in time of war, which probably explains the reason for the damage done to this great structure when the army of the Assyrian king Sennacherib sacked the city in 689 BC. It is clear that the ziggurat was wrecked beyond repair, as later Assyrian kings had to spend many years rebuilding it from the foundations up. After further damage in 484 BC during a Babylonian revolt against their Persian overlords, the ziggurat languished until Alexander the Great cleared the site for yet another reconstruction, but his successors never completed the task in spite of the respect shown by the Seleucid dynasty for Mesopotamian religion.

ASSYRIA

Layard tells us: 'These huge mounds of Assyria made a deeper impression upon me, gave rise to more serious thoughts and more earnest reflection, than the temples of Balbec and the theatres of Ionia ... My curiosity had been greatly excited, and from that time I formed the design of thoroughly examining, whenever it might be in my power, these singular ruins'.

Instead of continuing on his journey to Sri Lanka, Layard managed to get some funds from the British ambassador in Istanbul and commenced excavations at Nimrud. But a shortage of money still obliged Layard to have recourse to tunnelling. This shortcoming, however, pales into insignificance when compared with the wanton destruction visited upon the site by Islamic State militants in 2015. Then bulldozers and dynamite were used to wipe out Nimrud's archaeological remains, which were seen as no more than 'symbols of the infidel'.

It is more than fortunate that Layard's pioneering excavations caused the removal from Nimrud of so many priceless treasures. Today the colossal sculptures and bas-reliefs that he unearthed are among the glories of the British Museum. What Layard had discovered was the palace of the Assyrian kings prior to the reign of the usurper Sargon II, who favoured

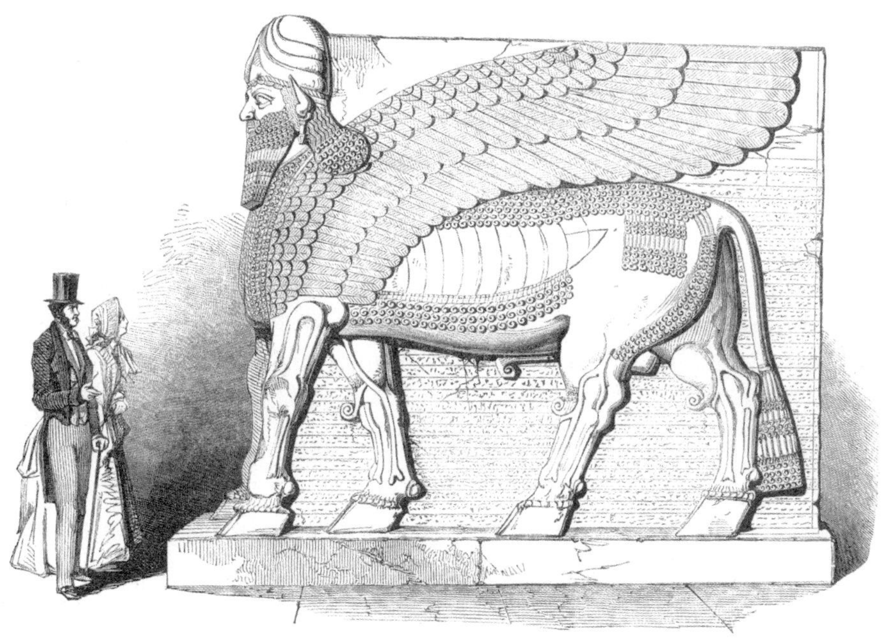

One of the Assyrian winged bulls that Layard sent to the British Museum

Dur-Sharrukin. How central Nimrud was to the Assyrian empire can be grasped from the ceremonial name of the palace entrance; it was called:

> Justice Gates, which fairly judge the rulers of the four quarters of the world, when they come bearing tribute from the mountains and the sea to their King, their Lord.

King Ashurnasirpal II had expanded Nimrud as the administrative centre of a growing empire during the early ninth century BC. He built a temple for Ninurta, a warrior god from earliest times in Mesopotamia. A Sumerian myth recounts how Ninurta, returning from battle in his chariot, still full of sound and glory, was persuaded not to disturb the storm god Enlil, notorious for the premium that he placed on sleep. So Ninurta put away his weapons, stabled his horses and crept into Enlil's temple at the city of Nippur. More inclined to warfare than the Sumerians, the Assyrians placed immense emphasis on Ninurta's violent character, since they regarded the shedding of blood as an expression of his divine will.

On huge stone reliefs placed in Ninurta's temple, Ashurnasirpal praised the god for being 'the perfect warrior unequalled in battle' and also advertised the treatment that he personally meted out to his enemies. Not only did the Assyrian king 'stand on the necks of his foes' and 'with their blood dye the mountains red like wool', but more precisely he 'cut off noses, ears and extremities' of captives, 'gouged out eyes', 'burnt prisoners', 'slashed the flesh of rebels' or 'flayed them alive'. One disloyal ruler had his skin 'draped on the city wall of Nineveh'.

Massacre, pillage, wholesale resettlement—these were instruments of Assyrian domination. What allowed the Assyrian king to behave without restraint was the prowess of his army, which increased in size from 60,000 regular troops during Ashurnasirpal's reign to an incredible strength of 200,000 at the turn of the seventh century BC. From military scenes depicted on the bas-reliefs, Layard gathered that he had located the nerve centre of the Assyrian empire.

Although the massive defensive towers in the south-east corner of Nimrud were not explored until the 1950s, there could be no question about the correctness of Layard's view. At first believed to be another palace, this complex was finally called Fort Shalmaneser after an inscribed brick of Shalmaneser III was discovered in one of its outer walls. The son of Ashurnasirpal, Shalmaneser continued to campaign on a grand scale, pushing the Assyrian frontier as far west as Palestine. From clay tablets unearthed in the fortress, it is clear that this was a military complex: they comprise among other things muster rolls, inventories of weapons, and dockets for fodder. On one tablet there are details about a unit consisting of deported foreigners noted for their horsemanship.

Layard's discoveries at Nimrud were greeted in Britain with enthusiasm, because they confirmed the aggressiveness of the Assyrians in the Bible. According to the prophet Isaiah, Assyria was chosen by Yahweh to punish the sinful Jews. It would be 'the rod of mine anger, and the staff in their hand is mine indignation'. So angry was the Jewish deity with 'an hypocritical nation' that the Assyrian monarch was given 'a charge, to take spoil, and take the prey, and to tread them down like mire in the streets'.

Once the Nimrud bas-reliefs went on public display in the British Museum, Layard was financed by the Treasury so that excavations could

The Assyrian king Shalmaneser III receiving tribute.
Symbols of the gods are shown before him

resume. Impressive winged lions with human heads had already been shipped to Britain before Layard left Nimrud in 1851, never to return. Even though others took up the challenge of excavating the site, Layard's discoveries at Nimrud as well as Nineveh had made him, and Assyriology, household names. His books became best-sellers on station bookstalls.

Much greater excitement would occur in the 1870s, when some of the clay tablets which Layard had sent back from Nineveh were translated. He discovered them in the library of King Ashurbanipal, the last effective ruler of Assyria. During his reign from 668 to 627 BC, Ashurbanipal assembled a huge collection of 22,000 clay tablets, which now form the most prized portion of the British Museum's cuneiform archive. Fully aware of the find's significance, Layard wrote that 'we cannot overrate their value. They furnish us with materials for the complete decipherment of the cuneiform character, for restoring the language and history of Assyria, and for inquiring into the customs, sciences, and we may perhaps even add, literature of its people'.

Understanding the tablets in the royal library was far from easy since Akkadian, the language in which most of the texts were written, was long extinct. That it was a Semitic tongue was obvious to the English and French scholars who tried to unravel its structure and meaning. Instrumental in the final stage of decipherment was Henry Creswicke Rawlinson, an English East India Company official once resident in Baghdad. It was he who recommended that George Smith, an Assyrian enthusiast employed by a London printer, should join him at the British Museum in sorting out the clay tablets from Nineveh.

In 1872, Smith made his great discovery when he translated a part of the 'account of the Deluge'. So excited was he by this unexpected revelation that Smith immediately started to throw off his clothes. Yet Smith was careful to choose a very public platform from which to announce the find: the winter meeting of the Society of Biblical Archaeology. Even Prime Minister Gladstone was in the audience. Everyone was baffled that a clay tablet belonging to an ancient ruler could refer to the biblical Flood. More startling still was the realization that the Babylonians, whose version Smith had translated, wrote of the Flood mentioned in Genesis long before the Jews arrived in Palestine. The only possible explanation was that the Jews had reworked a Mesopotamian myth to demonstrate Yahweh's power.

Overnight Smith's translation was news and in 1873 *The Daily Telegraph* paid for him to go to Nineveh, where it was hoped that he might find more of the Flood story. Sorting through the rubbish heaps left by Layard and his successors, he soon recovered a clay tablet which included the order to construct the Ark, but it did not belong to the *Gilgamesh* epic, a fragment of which Smith had translated at the British Museum, but to an even earlier mythological composition about Ziudsura, the Sumerian Noah. Smith never knew this, since during a second trip to Nineveh in 1876 he died of dysentery. He left a wife and several children, for whom an annuity was granted by Queen Victoria.

SUMER

Even though the Sumerian cities of Ur, Uruk and Eridu had already been surveyed, they failed to deflect public attention from the Assyrian palaces. Serious excavation in southern Iraq had to await the twentieth century, when first H. R. Hall and then Leonard Woolley began to uncover Sumerian civilization. Hall's exploratory excavation at Ur, on behalf of the British Museum, prepared the ground for the amazing discoveries of Woolley in the 1920s. At Tell el Obeid, some 5 kilometres west of Ur,

The lintel from Ninhursag's temple at Tell el Obeid

Hall had found a temple dedicated to the goddess Ninhursag, with a lintel over the entrance which featured a winged lion and two stags.

The Pennsylvania and British Museums dispatched Woolley to Ur in 1922, and he ended his excavation there in 1934, having established the most accurate picture of any ancient Mesopotamian settlement. The city temple belonging to the moon god Nanna, Woolley reported, was 'immensely old ... By 2300 BC, the temple had been completely rebuilt several times, and the temple with which Abraham was familiar was perhaps the fifth to occupy the site.' Woolley noted how there were lists of 'the various functionaries attached to the temple, besides priests, ministers of state, a choirmaster, a controller of the household, a master of the harem, and directors of livestock, dairy-work, fishing and donkey-transport. Numbers of women-devotees were attached to the temple and employed in weaving.' The size of the establishment reflected the deity's status. Woolley concluded that Nanna was 'lord of his city; he controlled its destinies as did the temporal ruler'.

Painstaking work on the site ensured that the development of Ur was fully understood. Its well-preserved ziggurat, for example, reveals at least two stages of construction. Perhaps originally built by the Sumerian governor Ur-Nammu around 2112 BC, along with the adjacent temple for Nanna, the ziggurat was restored by Nabonidas, who ascended the throne at Babylon in 556 BC. The king's mother was a devotee of Sin, as Nanna became known in the Akkadian language, and Nabonidas even made his own daughter high priestess of the moon god at Ur.

The most surprising find at Ur occurred in 1932, when Woolley uncovered an early royal graveyard. Despite the absence of any hint of human sacrifice in Mesopotamian texts, it was transparent that 'the Sumerian king went to his tomb in the company of soldiers, courtiers and women, who, like the vases of food and drink set in his grave, should minister to his needs and pleasures in another world'. Woolley describes how: '[on] the sloped approach which led from the ground surface to the bottom of the grave-shaft ... stood six soldiers of the guard wearing copper helmets and great cloaks of heavy felt. Their bones, their helmets and their spears were found lying in order ... Then just inside the shaft proper, standing as they had been backed down the slope, come two wagons, clumsy four-

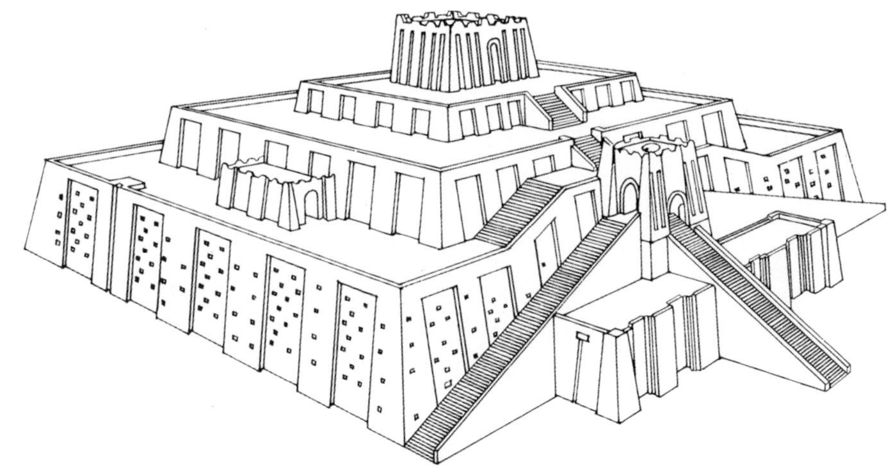

The ziggurat at Ur

wheeled affairs each drawn by three oxen ... Against the masonry chamber (which contained the dead king's body) were nine ladies of the Court, wearing elaborate head-dresses of stone and gold; round the forehead was a wreath of beads and gold leaves which held a veil; in the ears were grotesquely large ear-rings of gold in the form of crescent moons ... In front of these was a mixed crowd of people, men and women, less richly dressed, the subordinate attendants of the Court. Along the walls ... were two rows of servants, women on the left, on the right men wearing headbands of beads and silver-chains, and carrying daggers in their belts'.

The orderly arrangement of the fifty-nine people accompanying the king in his burial chamber, 5,000 years ago, suggests that they were volunteers. Conspicuous consumption perhaps, but wealth and rank counted for nothing in the Sumerian underworld, and so early rulers obviously tried to take with them the necessities for a luxurious afterlife. As there is no trace of human sacrifice after this period, it appears that the practice was short-lived. The depressing notion of a shadowy existence in 'the house of dust' was common in the ancient Near East until the Persians introduced the idea of a last judgement and the resurrection of the dead. For the Jews, Christians and Muslims alike, this final reckoning of accounts had immense appeal.

One of the chariots depicted on the Standard of Ur

Among the artefacts recovered by Woolley from Ur was the so-called Standard of Ur. Notwithstanding damage to its edges, the inlaid standard allows us to see the king and his court dining; servants bringing food for the feast; a war scene in which heavily armed men with spears advance behind a line of skirmishers; and four-wheeled chariots, each drawn by four asses, crushing the bodies of fallen enemies. The Sumerian chariots represented are not really battle-worthy: they lack spoked wheels and effective harnessing. The genesis of the war chariot is still a matter of dispute, but light, bent-wood, fast horse-drawn vehicles would seem to have been an ancient Near Eastern invention.

BABYLON

Archaeological recovery of Babylon's past also followed in the wake of the discoveries in Assyria. Despite the finds being less spectacular than those found in Sumerian cities, the excavation of Babylon led to the recovery of another civilization of great sophistication. How else could the city of Babylon have been so renowned for its Hanging Gardens? Together with the city walls, they were once regarded as one of the seven wonders of the world.

The choice by the ancient Greeks of seven as the number of amazing sights, like so much else in their culture, came from the Near East. In the Akkadian language, seven or *kissatu* meant totality, the number of the heavens, the number of spells that had to be recited for them to work, and the number of garments and ornaments that the great Sumerian goddess Inanna had to shed when she descended to the underworld in order to challenge her sister Ereshkigal's deadly power. Even though the remains of the Hanging Gardens have never been satisfactorily identified, the city of Babylon was excavated by German archaeologists under the direction of Robert Koldewey, starting in 1899.

Koldewey's decision to excavate Babylon could not have happened at a better time, because Berlin felt that it ought to have a collection of Mesopotamian antiquities equal to those on display in Paris and London. The Kaiser himself took an interest and donations poured in to support the excavation. Seeking to advance German interests in the Near East, the Kaiser had visited Turkey in 1889 and enjoyed a warm welcome from Abdulhamid II, through whose empire a German-financed and German-built railway was attempting to link Berlin with Baghdad. The French and the British were understandably concerned about the project, which they correctly surmised would bring the Ottomans into the German camp in the event of a European war.

Not that Koldewey and his team of excavators dwelt on politics. Instead, they grasped with both hands the chance of exploring ancient Babylon, and their thorough excavation uncovered royal palaces, a splendid processional way and the so-called Ishtar Gate. Using glazed-brick fragments from the city, along with new bricks specially designed to match them, the Germans were able to piece together the lions, dragons, bulls and floral features which once decorated the walls of the gateway and the processional avenue. The reconstruction made the Berlin Museum famous, although it did not win the instant acclaim that had greeted French and British exhibitions of monumental Assyrian sculpture half a century before.

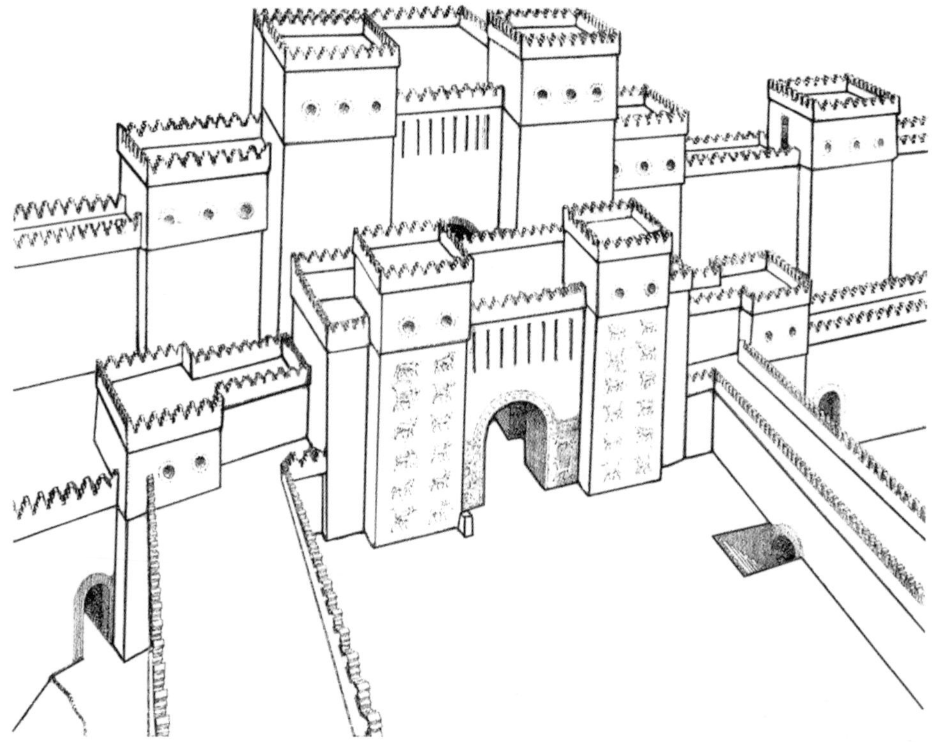

The Ishtar Gate at Babylon

Some aspects of the German excavation were disappointing, however. Works of art were few and far between, and even finds of inscriptions were small in number. By the Ishtar Gate stood the palace extension built by Nebuchadrezzar II, next to which this king is supposed to have constructed the Hanging Gardens, shortly after his accession in 604 BC. So determined a builder was the king that a vast labour force was put to work producing mud bricks which, under the supervision of royal architects, became palaces, temples, gateways and city walls, on a scale that deeply impressed his subjects as well as visiting envoys. In particular, Nebuchadrezzar's partiality for blue-glazed bricks made these new buildings resplendent in sunlight. Proud of these achievements, the king lists them in a cuneiform inscription but without mentioning the Hanging Gardens. It looks therefore as if Greek and Roman historians confused Assyrian gardens with Babylonian ones, and especially the great garden laid out by the Assyrian king Sennacherib at Nineveh. A stupendous work of engineering was required to supply this royal garden with water, as the remains of a 50-kilometre-long aqueduct of stone testify today.

At Babylon, Koldewey had tentatively identified a vaulted building with the Hanging Gardens. He speculated that a 'mechanical hydraulic machine ... which worked on the same principle of our chain pump' continuously drew water from a well beneath this structure. The remains of thick walls of stone also seemed to point to a garden of some kind having been planted on a higher level, but Koldewey said 'that the identification bristles with difficulties will surprise no one who has more than once had to bring ancient statements of fact into accordance with the discoveries of the present day'.

A snake-dragon from Babylon

After the First World War, discoveries in the upper reaches of the Euphrates showed how urban civilization had spread far from Uruk, the first city built in 3200 BC by the Sumerians in southern Iraq. Trade had played a role in this development as the ancient city of Mari demonstrated during its excavation in the 1930s. Situated close to the Euphrates in Syria, Mari was discovered when tribesmen dug into Tell Hariri, seeking a stone that could be used to mark a tribesman's grave. A headless statue brought French archaeologists post haste from the Louvre, because the Treaty of Versailles had awarded France control of Syria. Their excavation of Mari recovered some 20,000 clay tablets from the palace archive, mainly dating from the reign of King Zimri-Lim. Sometime before 1800 BC this monarch's passion for horses had prompted an official to advise caution. 'My lord should honour his position as king,' he wrote, 'and not ride with horses.' A cart drawn by mules was both safer and more dignified. In the Mari archive there are references to the stabling and feeding of imported horses, but this concern for animal welfare bears no comparison with the training manual written by Kikkuli, who was in charge of the chariot horses belonging to the king of Mitanni in the fourteenth century BC.

An unidentified king of Mari

The respect accorded to the 'words of Kikkuli, master horseman of the land of Mitanni' cannot be gainsaid. His training scheme included the feeding, washing, exercising and manoeuvring of chariot horses. What ancient Near Eastern rulers sought from his training manual was a foolproof method of preparing their chariotry for war. They could not afford to commit such a valuable military asset to battle unless they were certain of its quality, and especially the readiness of the chariot horses for the swiftness of such encounters. This was why Kikkuli emphasized continuous training, day and night: it allowed a charioteer to develop a close and trusting relationship with his team of horses. The confidence inspired by Kikkuli was not dissimilar to that felt by a fighter pilot for his Spitfire during the Second World War. The aeroplane's easy handling gave the Royal Air Force the edge in dog fights over southern England throughout the summer of 1940.

MITANNI

Completely forgotten until Assyrian records mentioned its existence, the kingdom of Mitanni once stretched from the Mediterranean to the Zagros mountains in northern Iraq. Its civilization was an amalgam of Hurrian and Indo-European cultures. The Hurrians spoke a language which has no recognized affinity with any other ancient Near Eastern tongue except Urartian. As the kingdom of Urartu arose in the old Mitannian heartland, albeit several centuries after Mitanni fell, it is tempting to assume a degree of cultural continuity here. The forward policy of the Assyrian king Shalmaneser III was responsible for pushing the Urartians northwards: they moved their capital to Tushpa, modern Van in eastern Turkey.

The great majority of the personal names in Mitanni were Hurrian, suggesting that they comprised most of the kingdom's population, but some were Indo-European. They can be identified by the fact that they are compounded with the names of Indo-European deities or by their interest in horses. For example, Biridasura means 'possessing many horses' and Sattawaza, meaning 'winner of seven prizes', celebrates horse-racing, while King Tushratta's name probably meant 'having a terrifying chariot'. Detailed knowledge of Mitanni's history is still frustrated by the absence of written records, although at Nuzi, an Assyrian city near present-day Kirkuk in northern Iraq, clay tablets have been excavated with indications that intermarriage between the Indo-Europeans and the Hurrians was commonplace. For a time Nuzi had been a Mitannian vassal state.

An interesting insight provided by the clay tablets recovered from Nuzi is the fact that carpenters enjoyed a status not much below that of charioteers. This is hardly surprising in light of the importance of bent-wood

An Assyrian chariot pursues fleeing enemies while a bird of prey contemplates its dinner

technology in the manufacture of chariots, the world's first war machine and the reason for Mitanni's triumph on the battlefield. That the Mitannians perfected chariot warfare is not at all unlikely, since at Lchashen in present-day Armenia barrow graves were found to contain very early examples of horse-drawn transport when, in the 1950s, a hydroelectric scheme lowered the level of Lake Sevan. Undisturbed but waterlogged, the twenty-three vehicles show an incredible range of types, from four-wheeled wagons with solid wheels to light-spoked passenger carriages and chariots. The accepted date of the Lchashen finds is 1500 BC, but the recovery of wheels with twenty-eight spokes, mortised at their outer edges into a felloe of two half circles of bent wood, is testimony to an established tradition of advanced carpentry.

HATTI

The rise of two great powers—a revived Assyria and a new Anatolian kingdom named Hatti—prepared the way for Mitanni's downfall, steadily squeezed as it was between both of them. Assyria had regained its independence in the 1360s BC and began a long series of campaigns against Mitanni itself. Egypt's friendly attitude towards Mitanni cooled and the pharaoh welcomed Assyrian ambassadors at his court. But even worse, the Hittites in central Asia Minor began to push eastwards. Except for their mention in Deuteronomy as one of the peoples whom Yahweh ordered the Jews to destroy, the Hittites—as the people of Hatti are known—remained almost as mysterious as the Mitannians until the early twentieth century.

The biblical Hittites lived in Syria with a capital at Carchemish, having quit Asia Minor around 1150 BC. Before this move, their power base was the natural stronghold of Hattusha, near the town of Boghazkoy in central Turkey. Light was first shone on the kingdom of Hatti by the recovery in 1887 of Akhenaten's diplomatic correspondence at Amarna, the palace city which was abandoned on this pharaoh's death in 1332 BC. Virtually all of the four hundred clay tablets in its archive were written in Akkadian and dealt with Egyptian holdings in Syria and Palestine. Amazingly there were letters from the Hittite king Suppiluliuma as well as the Mitannian king Tushratta. Yet it was the excavation of Hattusha itself, undertaken by the German archaeologists after 1906, that finally illuminated the Hittite kingdom because 10,000 clay tablets located there comprised the royal archive. Only those written in Akkadian could be read, including a translation of Kikkuli's famous horse-training manual, but decipherment eventually proved that Hittite was an Indo-European language, indeed the earliest one ever to be written down.

Professor John Garstang of Liverpool University did much to bring the Hittites to public notice. Garstang's own excavations in northern Syria unearthed a late Hittite palace, but his ambition of excavating Hattusha was dashed when the Kaiser's personal intervention secured the concession for Berlin University. Yet the decipherment of the Hittite language was the work of a Czech scholar by the name of Bedrick Hrozny, who proved that most of the Hattusha clay tablets were inscribed in the Indo-European tongue. The centrepiece of Hrozny's decipherment was a single sentence in a set of regulations drawn up for temple staff. It read: 'Then you will eat bread and drink water.'

The Lion Gate at Hattusha

Rather like the political situation that prevailed in Mitanni, it would appear that a group of Indo-European warriors dominated the Hattian population. Whilst they would have employed local speech to communicate with their subjects, for official purposes scribes wrote in Hittite, or Nesite as it was called. Because the royal succession in Hatti remained the prerogative of a small number of families throughout Hittite history, mastery of Indo-European Nesite must have been a prerequisite for membership of this narrow elite.

Translation of the Hattusha archive came as a revelation to classical scholars, for in Hittite mythology there were obvious parallels in the ancient Greek myths. The Greek monster Typhon clearly owes something to the dragon Illuyanka, who temporarily incapacitated the Hittite storm god Teshub by removing his heart and eyes. The son of the earth goddess Gaia, Typhon did the same to Zeus by 'cutting the tendons from Zeus' hands and feet'. Typhon's daring assault on the supreme Greek god indicates how the Hittites and Mitannians acted as a conduit for Sumerian

Zeus about to hurl a thunderbolt at Typhon

religious ideas, because the Sumerian warrior god Ninurta had to see off a challenge from Azag, the equally monstrous offspring of Ki, mother earth. With tempestuous winds and floods, Ninurta defeated the serpentine Azag, but not before their duel had set the world ablaze.

UGARIT AND EBLA

Strife among the leading Hittite families weakened their rule in Asia Minor and forced the transfer to Syria. An urgent request for grain addressed to the city of Ugarit, just before the migration took place, is a sign of how desperate the situation became. A loyal ally of the Hittites, Ugarit was neither a major power nor a mere city-state. Its territory on the headland of Ras Shamra, north of modern Latakia in Syria, was far from small and backed by thickly wooded mountains. Rich in timber, grain, wine, oil and livestock, Ugarit was renowned for its metalwork and textiles. As a trading port, it acted as an intermediary between the islands and shores of the eastern Mediterranean and the lands stretching eastwards to the Euphrates.

In 1929, the accidental discovery of a tomb at Tell Ras Shamra led to a series of excavations by French archaeologists. An entire city was uncovered with palaces, temples and houses, plus an archive of clay tablets in a script which turned out to be alphabetic in nature. The earliest exclusive use of an alphabetic system of writing, the Ugaritic language used thirty highly simplified cuneiform signs. The tablets themselves were extremely varied in content and included not only mythological tales but lists of deities and the offerings they received, details of commercial and administrative matters, and even private correspondence. They were composed between 1400 and 1200 BC. What is most fascinating about these texts happens to be the way that Ugaritic scribes anticipated styles of composition in the Old Testament, and in particular Psalms. The fundamental difference is content: whereas the Jewish petitioner relies on prayer, the Ugaritic one promises in Mesopotamian fashion a physical sacrifice.

Inland from Ugarit another West Semitic city caused a stir when, in 1975, its archive of over 14,000 clay tablets was discovered by Italian archaeologists. Its name was Ebla, probably meaning 'white rock' after the limestone outcrop on which the city was built. Excitement arose at the mention of Abraham and David in the city's archive, with the result that the excavators, Paolo Matthiae and Giovanni Pettinato, found themselves the focus of media attention.

A tablet in the Cypro-Minoan script excavated at Ugarit

Professor Matthiae was unhappy about the concentration on the Bible, but there was little he could do to damp down speculation. One reason for his annoyance was that Ebla represented a typical Semitic settlement, its pantheon as indebted as other ancient cities to the Sumerians. Although their West Semitic names are not the same as those in Mesopotamia, the connection between Eblaite and Sumerian deities was transparent in the recovered texts. Thus the plague god Namtar, whom Enlil ordered to reduce the size of the noisy Sumerian population just before this sleepless deity came up with the final solution of the Flood, became Resheph, while the sun god Utu was worshipped as Shapshu, a variation of Shamash, the Akkadian divine name.

TROY

An incidental outcome of the translation of the Ugarit and Ebla archives was the realization that ancient Near Eastern religious ideas had spread to Cyprus, Crete and Troy. According to Homer, Apollo was the only god who consistently sided with the Trojans: he showered the Greek camp with plague-tipped arrows and guided the arrow which hit Achilles' heel. As he was not a hunter like his twin sister Artemis, the bow that Apollo wielded against Agamemnon's host must have been acquired from Resheph in Cyprus, where the plague god was worshipped by the Phoenicians, and more importantly was identified by them with Apollo. And it is quite likely that the name of the mythical serpent killed by Apollo at Delphi, Python, derives from the West Semitic word for a poisonous snake.

The excavation of Troy depended upon the German archaeologist Heinrich Schliemann, the indefatigable pursuer of the Trojan War. No account of nineteenth-century archaeology would be complete without reference to his excavations at Troy from 1871 to 1874, and then again in 1878–9 and 1882–3. He deserves most credit for correctly locating at present-day Hisarlik the site of the Trojan capital, a city called Wilusa by the Hittites. It was actually inhabited with only short breaks from the fourth millennium BC onwards. A destruction level dated to around 1250 BC rather neatly corresponds with Homer's timing of the Trojan

A Greek coin with Apollo slaying Python

War. Schliemann's penultimate dig at Hisarlik followed his spectacular discovery of a golden mask at Mycenae in a shaft-grave, just inside the Lion Gate. In 1877 he informed the Greek king that he had 'gazed upon the face of Agamemnon'. Inspired by this find, Schliemann returned hot foot to Troy, where he recovered enough artefacts to fill nearly an entire gallery in the Istanbul Museum, although Schliemann was allowed to keep for himself a third of the gold and silver ornaments, goblets and vases unearthed.

The London Illustrated News reported the display of these finds in South Kensington and wondered about the size of Troy: '[Because] the extent of Troy encompassed by its wall is very small, and it cannot possibly have contained more than 4,000 or 5,000 inhabitants; but, small as it was, it was larger than Athens under the Kings, which was confined to the Acropolis until Theseus added the twelve surrounding boroughs to it. At Troy also there must have been straggling suburbs, where the inhabitants flocked into the Acropolis at the approach of the enemy ... Such are the views of Dr. Schliemann'.

It might well have been Schliemann who discovered the Minoans, the name which Arthur Evans gave to the earliest people with a city culture in Europe. Problems over the purchase of Knossos discouraged the German archaeologist, and it was not until 1900, after the end of Turkish rule in Crete, that Evans was able to start excavating the Palace of Minos there. Evans had always held that the Mycenaean finds were far older than the Trojan War and may have told Schliemann as much on their meeting in Athens in 1882. However, it is more likely that he concentrated upon the seals he saw in Athenian antique shops, because their maritime motifs—such as the octopus—pointed to an Aegean provenance. When an antique dealer said that all the seals he sold came from Crete, where Cretan woman valued them as charms, Evans set off in quest of the island's 'golden age' which he was certain lay 'beyond the limits of the historical period'.

CRETE AND CYPRUS

The islands of Crete and Cyprus were essentially offshoots of the ancient Near East, places where its culture ignited the flame of civilization. But excavation of the Palace of Minos was a more formidable task than anyone imagined. The labyrinthine ruins were so extensive that Evans decided to make it his life's work, and in 1906 he built next to the site the Villa Ariadne as a permanent headquarters for the excavation. During the Second World War the villa was the residence of Heinrich Kreipe, the commander of the German forces occupying Crete. Nearby he was kidnapped in 1944 by British and Greek volunteers and, to the delight of the Cretans, smuggled to Egypt as a prisoner of war.

It did not take Evans long to appreciate the antiquity of this first European civilization, which revealed 'nothing Greek—nothing Roman'. In vain, Evans sought an outside stimulus to explain its unexpected development. Unaware then of the pivotal role played by Ugarit in the westward transmission of ancient Near Eastern culture, Evans looked instead to Libya and Egypt. Despite preserving the story that Europa, the mother of

A snake-priestess from the Palace of Minos

King Minos of Knossos, had been abducted from Phoenicia by Zeus, the ancient Greeks were equally baffled by the origins of the Minoans. Their myth about Minos' construction of the labyrinth to house the Minotaur, a bull-headed man fed annually with seven girls and seven boys from Athens, was either a garbled account of the bull games or a misunderstanding of ancient Near Eastern creatures with a bull's head on the body of a man. Rather than someone confused by its composite form, the bull-man was from earliest times in Mesopotamia a reliable guardian against demons.

But the ancient Greeks would have been less surprised by Minoan reverence for snakes, which is preserved in the statuettes of snake-goddesses or snake-priestesses found by Evans at Knossos. There was, however, little religious anxiety about snakes in the ancient Near East other than the threat posed by chaotic sea serpents, the coiled dragons Tiamat and Lotan. A snake god by the name of Latarak was even worshipped at the city of Nippur, where he acted as the guardian of the great temple belonging to Enlil, the Sumerian storm god. And in Syria and Palestine the snake seems to have been associated with both gods and goddesses, except among the Jews who blamed the serpent for enticing Adam and Eve to eat the forbidden fruit. This singular story may have been intended to disparage Baal, the West Semitic equivalent of Enlil, since the fertility aspect of his cult involved snakes.

Just as baffling for the ancient Greek settlers were the cultural traditions they encountered in Cyprus. The city of Enkomi, near modern Famagusta, exported copper to Ugarit as early as the fourteenth century BC and appears in both Hittite and Egyptian records as Alasiya. It made use of a still undeciphered script which is not unlike the so-called Linear A of the Minoans; hence its name, Cypro-Minoan. The strangeness of ancient Cypriot worship was exposed by Swedish archaeologists in the early 1930s at the small village of Agia Irini on the northern coast of the island. The village priest, while digging in a field belonging to his church, chanced upon a terracotta statue, one of thousands, some life-size, placed around an altar as votive offerings. This long-forgotten shrine, dedicated to an unidentified deity who was believed to reside in a cult stone sometime before 1000 BC, remains as mysterious as the rest of pre-classical Cyprus. Whatever the divinity once worshipped in Agia Irini, there was a great deal of concern with the bull-cult, for many of the votive figures are bulls or men wearing horned headdresses. Bull-men are relatively rare in ancient Cyprus, but the respect shown to bulls is obvious in a statuette discovered at Meniko, near modern Nicosia. Two attendants stand each side of a handsome bull with their arms folded on their chests as a sign of worship. This sixth-century BC statuette was possibly dedicated to Baal in a Phoenician sanctuary.

It had long been the custom in ancient Mesopotamia to place statues in temples. For the Sumerians they were supposed to represent the donor and to ask the deity to grant a long life. This effort to secure divine protection was not sought from the chief gods but lower-level deities. In spite of the votive statues creating a personal relationship between the donor and the deity, the Sumerians often removed and ritually buried them away from a temple, possibly on the death of the donor.

Votive statues from Agia Irini

Greece was of course never insulated from the ancient Near East. After the Greek conquest of Minoan Crete around 1450 BC, the influence of its culture, already

Cadmus killing the serpent of Thebes

long-established in this island, was bound to impact on the Greek outlook. And before any settlement took place in Cyprus, Greek trading ships had also sailed as far east as the city of Ugarit. But contact became intense during the expansion of the Assyrian empire, when King Tiglath-Pileser III conquered Syria in 732 BC and installed compliant rulers. A critical factor in the spread of Mesopotamian ideas was the Assyrian practice of resettlement, which for the first time brought people from Assyria and Babylon into northern Syria and southern Asia Minor. Not to be overlooked, too, is the presence of Near Easterners in mainland Greece itself. Legend declares that the Phoenician prince Cadmus founded the city of Thebes, having abandoned the search for his sister Europa, whom

Zeus had abducted from Tyre. Told by the oracle at Delphi to forget about Europa and instead find a cow marked on her flank by a moon-shaped sign, and build a city at the first place she should choose to lie down and rest, Cadmus proceeded to Thebes in central Greece. But as the Phoenician was about to sacrifice the cow, an enormous serpent attacked and devoured some of his men before Cadmus could slay it.

The killing of the serpent by Cadmus was an exact parallel to Apollo's takeover of Delphi. Again we are back to the Sumerians, whose reverence for Ninurta rested on the firm belief that this warrior deity battled against terrible snake-dragons. In addition to founding Thebes, the ancient Greeks remembered that Cadmus had introduced an alphabet of sixteen letters. A curious coincidence is that Europa, Cadmus' sister, is now thought to be a West Semitic goddess of the night, since her name relates to the verb 'to set'; hence the coinage of Europe, the continent where the sun sets.

PART 2

THE ANCIENT NEAR EAST

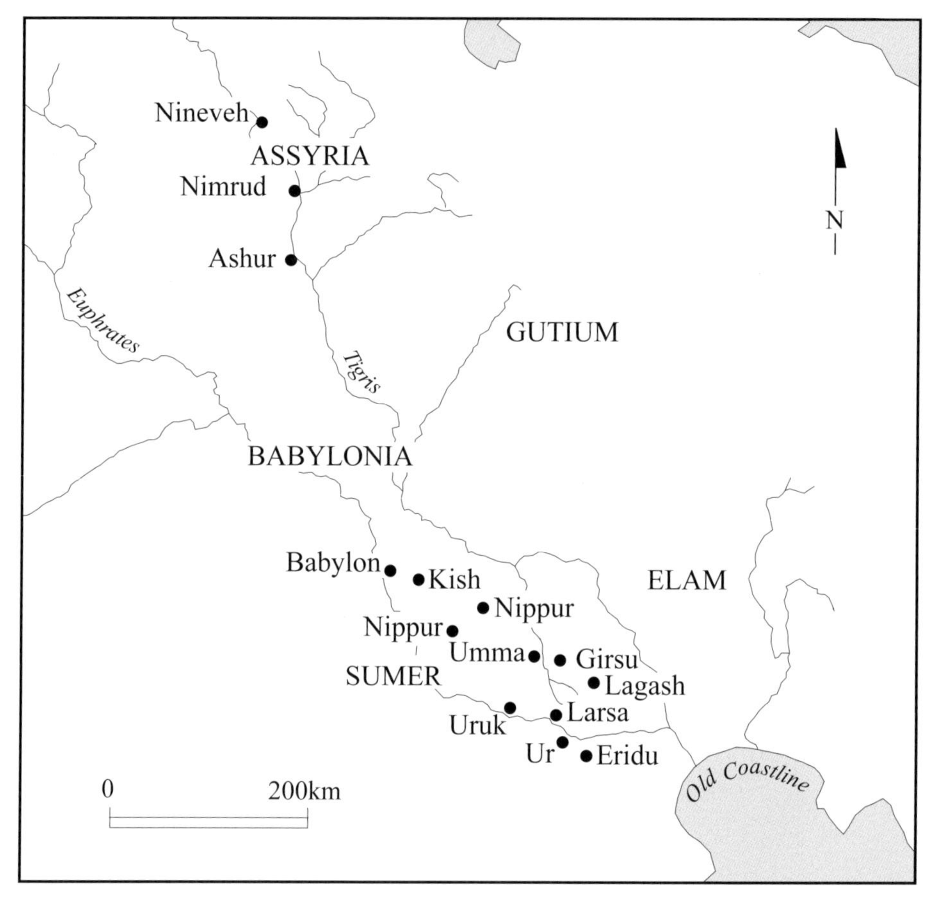

Ancient Mesopotamia

2

SUMER

THE CRADLE OF CIVILIZATION

The king's speech was very grand, its meaning very deep. The messenger's mouth was too heavy; he could not repeat it. Because the messenger's mouth was too heavy, and he could not repeat it, the king of Uruk patted some clay and put words on clay; before that day, there had been no putting of words on clay.

From an early Sumerian epic

There are certain moments in the history of the world when something irrevocable happens. One of these events, and arguably the most decisive, was the foundation in 3200 BC of Uruk, the first city to appear on the planet. Its builders were the Sumerians, a still comparatively obscure people who settled in what is now southern Iraq during the fourth millennium BC. For a turning point in human development was undoubtedly reached with the coming together at Uruk of all the factors that were necessary to sustain urban life. After its emergence as a fully-fledged city, which had between 50,000 and 100,000 inhabitants, Uruk pointed to the future: most human beings would henceforth be shaped by societies that drew their inspiration from large settlements. This fundamental cultural shift was possible because the Sumerians achieved an advance no less impressive than the mechanization of modern agriculture, thereby creating a food surplus that was sufficient to allow cities to flourish.

Underlying such an increase in productivity were the geographical advantages of Mesopotamia, 'the land between the rivers'. Impressed by the flow of both the Euphrates and the Tigris, the ancient Greeks gave this name to the region without realizing that these two rivers were the remnants of one gigantic water course. The rich alluvial land upon which the Sumerians settled was in fact the enormous bed of an extinct river.

Fed by snowmelt from the Taurus mountains of Asia Minor and the Zagros mountains of eastern Iran, the Euphrates and the Tigris were prone to chaotic flooding in their lower reaches, a circumstance which must stand behind the story of the Flood. Over one hundred kilometres from the Persian Gulf the rivers merge to form the Shatt al-Arab, a marshland that separated the southernmost Sumerian cities from saltwater. Dramatic changes in water levels and currents have caused the rivers to meander, so that ancient cities once situated on river banks are now far from them. Exactly where the ancient coastline met the Euphrates–Tigris outflow is uncertain, but the Sumerians refer to vast swamps, full of towering reeds and tortuous channels, the natural habitat of fish, fowl and other game. As soon as the waters could be canalized and the land irrigated, Sumer became a veritable paradise.

Instrumental in this far-reaching transformation was the water god Enki, who flooded the rivers with life-giving power, while Ennugi acted as the deity responsible for dykes and canals. Although Ennugi assisted his father, the storm god Enlil, in flooding the world so as to reduce the number of noisy Sumerians overcrowding the cities, it was the water god who warned of the coming catastrophe. Having sworn not to divulge Enlil's decision, Enki let the Sumerian Noah, Ziudsura, know by the sound of wind blowing through a reed wall. So Ziudsura was told to 'build a boat and put on board the seed of all living creatures'. The ingenious device of the reeds may be explained by the location of Enki's cult centre at Eridu, a city close to the marshes.

Despite its survival in fragments, the Sumerian story of the Flood provides an outline of the events that were fully expressed in the later versions of the Babylonians with Atrahasis or Utanapishtim, and the Jews with Noah. For Ziudsura heeded the command of the reed wall in preparation for the deluge. Then the Sumerian tablets relate how: 'all the windstorms and the gales arose together, and the flood swept over the land. After the flood swept over the land, and waves and wind had rocked the boat for seven days and seven nights, Utu the sun god came out, illuminating sky and land. Ziudsura made an opening in the huge boat and hero Utu entered the huge boat with his rays. Ziudsura the king prostrated himself before Utu, and sacrificed oxen and offered innumerable sheep'.

As soon as Ziudsura's vessel touched ground, we are told, 'many animals disembarked' and as a reward the gods An and Enlil granted Ziudsura 'eternal life like a deity'. These all-powerful deities then settled Ziudsura in the distant land of Dilmun, here a legendary location but most probably the island of Bahrain.

A remarkable sequel to the story of the Ark was Irving Finkel's translation of a Babylonian tablet brought into the British Museum by a member of the public. Badly damaged though the tablet was, Finkel was amazed to discover in 2009 that it contained instructions for the vessel's construction: an absolute revelation was its circular shape. Drawing upon traditional shipbuilding skills in southern India, a replica of the Ark was made there and tried at sea.

The famous Ark tablet which Irving Finkel translated in 2009 at the British Museum

Mesopotamia became an attractive place for settlement only after the end of the Ice Age. A definite change to a cooler, less humid climate that was capable of supporting a wide variety of wild animals and edible plants acted as a magnet for migrants. Nothing is known, however, about the arrival of the Sumerians. As they believed that they had travelled in a westerly direction, the discovery of the Indus civilization in the 1920s has encouraged the idea of the Sumerians being earlier occupiers of north-western India. Yet it is just as likely that they moved into the Euphrates–Tigris river valleys from

Iran, as did other peoples attracted to their agricultural potential, although there is also the possibility that the Sumerians always lived in Iraq and moved south as conditions turned dryer. The Sumerian language, the earliest ever to be written down, sheds no light on origins because it is unlike any other. Apparently tonal, Sumerian was an agglutinative language without the inflections common to Semitic tongues, so that sentences were built up by the addition of syllables. Even the name by which the Sumerians are called is Babylonian, since it means the people who lived in Sumer, southern Babylonia. They named their own country Kengir, 'the civilized land': it stretched from the sea to the city of Nippur, around one hundred kilometres south of present-day Baghdad.

URUK: THE WORLD'S FIRST CITY

The urban revolution at Uruk did not happen overnight. It lasted for well over a century but the consequences were a complete transformation of the economy as well as the structure of society. Driving this profound alteration was a temple priesthood. Although powerful secular leaders eventually came to dominate Sumerian cities, all the evidence suggests that Uruk evolved as a city from being first and foremost a religious centre. Disputes between temples and palaces were to become commonplace, but the piety of the Sumerian people ensured that the city gods always got their due.

Uruk is the setting of the Babylonian epic about Gilgamesh, a legendary Sumerian king whose name may have been Bilgames. The city's earliest rulers fascinated later poets, much as the heroes of the Trojan War did the Greek epic poet Homer. They were the favourite subjects of court entertainment, their adventures retold to king after king. In the *Gilgamesh* epic, Gilgamesh's father is Lugalbanda, an antediluvian ruler who appears in the so-called Sumerian King List. The eight monarchs named before the Flood reigned for a total of 72,000 years, an invention comparable to the extended genealogy in Genesis. Of these early rulers only the king of Uruk was of royal birth, which suggests that this city hosted the first Sumerian dynasty.

The long period on the throne attributed to Lugalbanda makes it difficult to fix precise dates for him and Gilgamesh, although their reigns are now thought to lie somewhere between 2800 and 2500 BC. It is not impossible that Gilgamesh conquered Uruk as an outsider, and then pretended that his father was a famous king of the usurped dynasty. We cannot be sure. But there is no question that Gilgamesh built the city wall, because he had to coerce the inhabitants into undertaking the task. Its length ran for an unprecedented 9.5 kilometres and its strength relied on at least nine hundred towers. According to the epic:

> There was nobody among the kings who could compare with him. Two-thirds god, one-third man, Gilgamesh was destined for fame.

The so-called Sumerian King List

Gilgamesh's divine inheritance derived from his mother Ninsun, a goddess whose name translates as 'lady wild-cow'. Her cult was associated with wild cattle, the untamed animals still roaming on the fringes of the Euphrates–Tigris valley. But a profound anxiety about his mortal inheritance forced Gilgamesh to seek out a means of securing immortality during his lifetime.

The wall that Gilgamesh constructed enclosed an area of 5.5 square kilometres, which was twice the size of the original city. But it did not take many years to fill up and for suburbs to spring up outside the city wall. Uruk's expansion resulted from population growth as well as resettlement from nearby villages. A general drift from the countryside to the cities was the pattern during Sumerian times. It seems likely that two cult centres in Uruk once belonged to separate settlements which amalgamated to form the city. They were dedicated to An, the personification of heaven, and the fertility goddess Inanna, sometimes called Ninanna, 'mistress of heaven'. The remoteness of An explains his later displacement by the storm god Enlil, whose temple was at the city of Nippur. It

An alabaster mask of Inanna

also explains the popularity of Inanna at Uruk, where her escapades delighted its inhabitants. Enlil was known as Kurgal, 'the great mountain', but his awesome power manifested itself in the thunderstorm.

With the decline of the Sumerians at the close of the third millennium BC and the rise of Babylon under Semitic kings, centre stage was occupied by Marduk, the divine saviour celebrated in the *Enuma Elish.* Although this Babylonian epic was not written down until the reign of Nebuchadrezzar I, who died in 1105 BC, Marduk had already ceased to be a god of magic and incantation and assumed the leadership of the Babylonian pantheon. In spite of Marduk's identification with Enlil, the Babylonian champion made short work of both An and Enlil, since An was flayed and his head cut off, while Enlil had his eyes plucked out. A growing brutalization in myth reflected the intense competition between Mesopotamian cities, once their gods came to embody more and more of their political aspirations.

There was no palace at Uruk when its two temples triggered the city's development. Here for the very first time men and women tried to live peacefully together in a densely populated community. They found ways to thrive through customs that were eventually recorded in the earliest law codes. Utterly unique was the role played by the priests who served An and Inanna; they provided a theological justification for the communal effort required in the fields and pastures surrounding the city. Like human beings, the Sumerian gods and goddesses had to be sheltered and fed, so meat, beer, bread, vegetables and fruits were laid out for them several times each day. Inanna's closeness to humanity is evident in a life-size alabaster mask that once fitted on a wooden statue of the fertility goddess. We are fortunate that five months after the mask was stolen from the Iraq Museum in 2003, it was recovered from a Baghdad garden. The asking price had been US$25,000.

The status of temples, and their importance in city life, caused them to be awarded special names. They usually begin with e, the Sumerian word for 'house'. Thus in Uruk, the temple of Inanna and An was Eanna, 'house of heaven'; in Nippur, the storm god Enlil dwelt in Ekur, 'mountain-house'; and in Babylon, Marduk enjoyed Esagila, 'house of the eminent peak'. Noteworthy is the use of the Sumerian language to describe Marduk's cult centre as well as his ziggurat, Etemenanki, 'house-support of the universe'. The religious legacy of Sumer was immense.

Among the various functions of Eanna was an economic one. The remains of a foundry have been excavated as well as waste from pottery kilns. Most telling of all for Uruk's administration were documents recording transactions written in an archaic script. At this stage of economic development, the capital at the disposal of the temple was not monetary, but an accumulation of raw materials, above all food. Keeping track of such assets naturally encouraged some form of record keeping, no matter how primitive it initially was. From these tentative steps towards literacy evolved the cuneiform script, the world's first system of writing. The Sumerians had no doubt that putting words on clay represented a critical advance for civilization.

Cuneiform is named after *cuneus*, the Latin word for wedge, since the characters of the script were formed by pressing wedges or marks into a clay tablet. In less than half a millennium, cuneiform was transformed into a subtle means of communication, albeit only available to professional scribes. For us their writings inaugurated history: they are the irreplaceable documents that allow access to attitudes and actions dating from long-forgotten times. Without cuneiform, the Sumerians, Akkadians, Babylonians and Assyrians would be beyond our comprehension. Archaeology teaches much about the ancient world, but texts alone illuminate its findings.

Sumerian kings soon came to appreciate that in the priesthood there was a restraining influence upon their conduct, not least because the first duty of every monarch was ensuring the satisfaction of the gods by means of support for the temples in which they dwelt. Rarely was the divinity of

An early administrative tablet from Uruk

a king asserted in Mesopotamia, unlike ancient Egypt, but a formula accepted that kingship 'came down from heaven' and inscriptions maintain that the assembly of the gods chose and invested each monarch. In Sumer the temporal ruler was essentially viewed as a steward managing the gods' estates.

The divine estates at Uruk, as in other Sumerian cities, were based on two elements: barley and sheep. The reason for the choice of barley as a staple was its fast growth and its tolerance of saline soils. In comparison with wheat, barley could tolerate both pests and poor drainage. Rich alluvial soil and river water meant that the effective management of agriculture produced large surpluses, which were used for supporting infrastructure projects, including the digging of irrigation canals and the enhancement of temples. The cultivation of long fields was closely connected with the introduction of a plough pulled by oxen. Long furrows reduced the number of turns required to prepare a field, saving an enormous amount of time and assisting channel irrigation. But even more, the invention of the seeder-plough minimized the loss of seed when compared to scattering seed by hand. A funnel placed the seeds individually inside the furrow. It is reckoned that the seeder-plough increased the barley yield by fifty per cent. The increase in productivity accounts for the extra grain which sustained rapid urban development, because there was now enough food in Uruk to allow specialists the time needed to perfect their arts and crafts, without worrying about the next meal. In addition to the advance in sowing, animal traction also speeded up threshing through a sledge fitted with flint blades and pulled by an ass.

The origin of agriculture rested entirely with the gods, whose dwelling was a hill around which the first human beings lived. Conscious of the need for food, the gods created Sheep and Grain, and gave them to the Sumerians according to a famous debate between these two sources of sustenance. We learn how: 'Sheep being fenced in by her sheepfold, they gave her grass and herbs generously. For Grain they made a field and gave

The funnel of a seeder-plough is clearly depicted in the bottom panel

her the plough, yoke and team. Sheep standing in her sheepfold was a shepherd of sheepfolds brimming with charm. Grain standing in her furrow was a beautiful girl radiating charm; lifting her raised head up from the field she overflowed with the beauty of heaven'.

Both Sheep and Grain had fulfilled the wishes of the gods, filling storerooms with cereals and wool. 'Wherever they directed their steps, Sheep and Grain added to the riches of the household with their weight.' As in other Sumerian myths, though, Sheep and Grain started a quarrel after drinking too much beer. They argued about their relative worth and the gods were asked to decide which was the more valuable. Eventually the water god Enki announced 'of the two, Grain shall always be greater', in recognition perhaps of the dependence of Sumer on barley. In another epic about the natural order, Enki is credited with putting agriculture on a regular basis, when 'he organized ploughs, yokes and teams'.

A seal showing the Sumerian sun god Utu rising behind mountains, while Inanna stands on the left and Enki on the right, with the Euphrates and the Tigris pouring from his shoulders

It was also Enki's supply of water for the irrigation system that sustained this agricultural revolution. A rise in the sea level of the Persian Gulf kept river levels stable, even though climatic conditions were steadily reducing the flow of both the Euphrates and the Tigris. Irrigation was of course a godsend in Sumer, where rain hardly fell. It was believed that Enki presided over Abzu, a vast underground reservoir of sweet water which appeared in rivers and canals. Mesopotamia's fertile soil combined with the use of river water to reduce the amount of land required to feed an individual with barley. Families were able to grow vegetables and figs for their own consumption too. Yet intensive irrigation was not without its problems since it led to the salinization of the soil. Near the marshes salinity was so severe that land became completely barren, indicating how critical drainage was in maintaining healthy soil because salts rise to the surface when the ground is moist. In ancient China the problem of salinization was solved through the construction of terraced fields and the digging of field drains. Even though this involved a great deal of labour, Chinese farmers compensated for this loss of time by the liberal application of fertilizer. Although animal manure was never wasted, they discovered that 'night soil', or human waste, when in liquid form acted as a powerful fertilizer. Not only did its high proportion of nutrients, and especially potassium, stimulate plant growth, but even more the solid element was useful in mulching the soil and retaining moisture. In ancient Mesopotamia there was hardly any use of fertilizer.

TEMPLES AND PALACES

With the rise of kings in Sumer it might be anticipated that priests would lose power, but this never happened for the good reason that the Sumerians were a deeply religious people. Although conflicts did take place when rulers encroached upon temple property, the usual solution to such a dispute was a compromise which gave no offence to the city deities. So closely were cities associated with their gods that cuneiform employed the same sign for the name of the city and its resident deity. The exulted position of Nippur best illustrates priestly authority. Even though this Sumerian city was never powerful enough to be ruled by its own king, the presence of Ekur, Enlil's own temple, conferred immense prestige upon its inhabitants. As the storm god Enlil once installed in his temple there both Sumerian and early Babylonian kings, the city remained the focus of royal interest for centuries. Only with the rise of Marduk at Babylon did the ritual connection with royalty begin to wane, as later Babylonian monarchs looked to Esagila, the great temple of Marduk at Babylon, for an assurance of their legitimacy.

Apart from keeping the city gods contented, priests were always consulted by rulers over future plans. Without seeking the advice of diviners about the attitude of the gods, no king would dare to take a diplomatic decision or start a military expedition. The *nam*, or 'destiny', of any action rested entirely with the gods, which was why it was so important to learn exactly what they thought. The Greeks and Romans also adopted the Mesopotamian practice of examining the entrails of animals in order to determine the will of the gods. In Greece and even more in Rome, the observation of victims was done by whoever had the need of divine advice: a civil or military magistrate, someone elected or appointed to political or military tasks. But no priest was involved, for only the Etruscans used specialist interpreters before undertaking new enterprises. On the outskirts of Piacenza in 1877, a farmer dug up a bronze liver covered with comments in the Etruscan language. Possibly a teaching aid for trainee diviners, this stylized sheep's liver has explanations of future events that are very close indeed to those recorded in the ancient Near East.

Another divine gift was the difficult art of brewing barley. Although alcohol was associated with the gods in virtually all ancient cultures, and wine was embraced by mainstream Christianity and incorporated into its most sacred rituals, climatic conditions in Sumer made *kas*, or beer, the universal beverage. Since vines could be readily grown in the hills of Assyria, large quantities of wine were shipped down the Tigris for a number of Sumerian rulers, who developed a taste for this expensive drink. Around 2340 BC the king of Lagash established a cellar 'into which wine was brought in great vases from the mountains'.

Most Sumerians were satisfied with beer, as indeed were their gods. A hymn to the goddess Ninkasi celebrates the brew that exhilarates the drinker, 'making the liver happy and filling the heart with joy'. Enki's daughter Ninkasi was charged with preparing beer each day for the gods: it was seasoned with honey, dates, figs, anise and cinnamon. At Uruk, the consumption of beer varied according to social status, with 2 litres being the daily intake of most inhabitants, except for priests and temple staff who were allocated 6 litres per day. Quite likely this greater volume had some connection with worship, since libations were made regularly to gods and goddesses. Not all the beer would be poured on the ground as a libation though: trance-like votive statues indicate that intoxication may well have been a means of approaching divinity. Drinking alcohol was also connected with warfare: beer was actually brewed in the temple of the warrior god Ningirsu at Girsu, as an adequate supply of beer was deemed necessary before a battle. Once Girsu ceased to be an important city during the period of the third dynasty of Ur, Ningirsu's myths were attributed to the other Sumerian warrior god, Ninurta.

The exploits of Ninurta fascinated the Sumerians as much as the labours of Herakles did the ancient Greeks. It seems likely that the model for the semi-divine Greek hero's adventures was in fact those of this energetic Sumerian god, as they both took special delight in bringing back terrifying trophies. A Sumerian epic describes how, among other examples of his prowess, Ninurta 'hung the Six-headed Wild Ram, the Warrior Dragon, the Bison, the Terrible Lion, and the Seven-headed Serpent' on his chariot 'which inspires awe'.

Prior to an abundance of wine during Greco-Roman times, there was no prejudice against the drinking of beer. Yet the Greeks and the Romans thought that beer really suited barbarians, a cultural attitude which lingers in some parts of southern Europe today. In the *Gilgamesh* epic, the wild man Enkidu is introduced to civilization by two things: a sexual encounter with a prostitute from Uruk and plenty of beer. After consuming 'seven kegs', Enkidu 'relaxed, cheered up, his insides felt good, his face glowed'. So the wild man quit the steppe and came to the city of Uruk, where Enkidu became the boon companion of King Gilgamesh.

It was the death of Enkidu that shook Gilgamesh, who wept over his friend's 'corpse for seven days and seven nights, refusing to give it up for burial until a maggot fell from one of his nostrils'. Unwilling to accept that death was the inevitable end to life, Gilgamesh sought out his ances-

Gilgamesh's companion, the wild man Enkidu

tor Utanapishtim, the sole survivor of the Flood. On the way, he was not dissuaded from his quest by a barmaid, who told Gilgamesh that he should eat and drink, making merry day and night, celebrate festivals, bathe and wear new clothes, look at the child holding his hand, and enjoy the embrace of his wife, because 'these things alone are the lot of human beings'.

The Sumerians never believed that death entirely extinguished the individual: one continued to lead a shadow existence afterwards. As an unburied person flitted about like a ghost, it was imperative that a proper interment occurred so that he or she could reach the land of no return, though this was a depressing place as Enkidu revealed when, out of a hole in the ground, his spirit issued 'like a puff of smoke'. He told Gilgamesh how 'the house of dust' was totally different from the world, since princes acted as servants and earthly rank counted for nothing at all. Even worse was the suffering of the childless dead, for nobody bothered to make any offerings to them. Other spirits with surviving children and grandchildren were the fortunate ones, since the Sumerians never forgot their forebears. Yet the most terrible fate in the underworld, Enkidu informed Gilgamesh, was that of those who have lost limbs or other body parts because their disfigurement persisted for eternity in the afterlife. This ancient revulsion towards the burial of a corpse in an incomplete state has by no means disappeared in the modern Near East.

A tablet of the *Gilgamesh* epic, discovered at Ur, throws a sharp light on the horror of a premature death. On his deathbed, Enkidu vented his fury on the prostitute who had introduced him to civilization at the very moment he was being carried off by a grim man with 'hands like a lion's paws and claws like an eagle's talons'. He cursed her and said:

May the lee of the city wall be where you stand!
May briar and thorn tear your cheek!
May ruined houses be your abode!
May the rabble of the street crowd your brothel!
May there be brawls in your tavern!

The standard version of the epic's text omits this passage, but the Ur tablet reveals the utter despair which overwhelmed Enkidu when he realized that he could never match the achievements and reputation of Gilgamesh. Their friendly rivalry had been brutally cut short. Quite where this singular episode fits into the epic remains a mystery, but it leaves us in no doubt about the Sumerian fear of an early death.

Enjoying a drink was much less straightforward for Jews and Christians, and of course anathema for Muslims. After the Ark grounded on Mount Ararat, 'Noah began to be a husbandman and planted a vineyard. And he drank the wine, and was drunken; and he was uncovered within his tent.' In Genesis, Noah's cultural role is obscured as the founder of agricultural technique through a marked ambivalence about wine. Outside the Bible, the sinfulness of Noah is even more obvious, because he was said to have entered a wine-making partnership with Satan, who poured on the roots of the vine the blood of a slaughtered lamb, lion, pig and monkey. In this manner Satan explained the effect of alcohol: before a man tastes it, he is as innocent as a lamb; after imbibing moderately, he feels as strong as a lion; after swallowing much, he resembles a pig; and becoming drunk, he behaves like a monkey, talks gibberish, cavorts, and is obscene.

It should perhaps be noted that alcohol was safer to drink than water because the process of fermentation killed off most of the harmful bacteria. Without the habit of boiling water, which in China was necessary for making tea, the ancient Near East had no chance of matching its large population. Waterborne diseases were so prevalent in Mesopotamia that the plague god Namtar needed to be continually appeased with enormous offerings.

The first king named in the Sumerian King List is Etana, who probably ruled the city of Kish at the very beginning of the third millennium BC. In the course of time the authority of Kish waned and it was conquered by Uruk, whose kings were celebrated by Sumerian bards. Notoriously lacking in metals, the alluvium of southern Mesopotamia obliged the early Sumerians to reap the great expanses of barley they had sown with clay sickles, crescent-shaped tools with sharpened internal edges. It was indeed the absence of metals, stone and wood which stimulated long-distance trade. Such an exchange of goods can be traced to prehistoric times but, with the development of cities, these imports became an absolute priority. This is the context of the Enmerkar epic, which records the dispute between Uruk and Aratta, as yet an unidentified city in central Iran. The quarrel began when King Enmerkar of Uruk sought to embellish his city with precious metal and stones, but the fabulously wealthy city of Aratta refused to open trade relations in order to supply them. Worshipped though she was in both cities, the goddess Inanna favoured Uruk and told Enmerkar to inform Aratta of her partiality. Still reluctant to oblige either the king or the goddess, the ruler of Aratta posed a series of baffling challenges to Enmerkar before he would consider doing any business at all. Having found the solution to each challenge in turn, Enmerkar finally invented writing so as to make his position clear.

At the end of the epic, the king of Aratta 'took from the messenger the tablet upon which the spoken words were mere wedges, and looked at the tablet in the light of a brazier'. Realizing that the storm god Enlil had given Inanna his full backing, he accepted with 'his brow darkened' that 'the people of Aratta had the task of trading in gold and lapis lazuli' so that these products would 'pile up in the courtyard of Eanna', the temple of Inanna at Uruk. A surviving marriage hymn of Inanna actually mentions the use to which the goddess put these precious metals and stones. It relates how: 'a man brings to the maiden Inanna, he brings a heap of stones to choose from. He gathers the lapis lazuli from the top of the heap. The goddess chooses the buttocks beads and puts them on her buttocks. She chooses the head stones and puts them on her head. Inanna chooses the lumps of translucent lapis lazuli and puts them on the nape of her neck. She chooses gold and puts it on her hair and over her ears. She chooses burnished bronze and puts it in her ear lobes'.

Besides the question of trade, which had clearly spread well beyond the Tigris–Euphrates valley, an intriguing feature of the epic is Enmerkar's invention of writing, because it shows how Sumerian was then the international language. Anyone who was anybody understood the speech of Sumer, long before it was ever written down. But there is still something missing from this story about international commerce, since it remains unclear whether Sumerian trade was in the hands of merchants, as later on in Assyria, or whether each city-state procured the raw materials it required through some central agency. Were traders in effect the servants of temples and palaces? At present we simply have no idea.

In epics about Gilgamesh and Dumuzi, another legendary king, there is a more pronounced metaphysical element. Even though Gilgamesh's pursuit of immortality was in vain, this king of Uruk traversed the entire cosmos, reaching the western mountains where the sun sets. There he persuaded a gigantic scorpion-man and his wife to let him pass; travelled through a dark tunnel which ended in a wondrous garden where the sun rises; roamed the deserts beyond this paradise; and crossed the waters of death to the house of his ancestor Utanapishtim. Made immortal by the gods after the Flood, Utanapishtim warned Gilgamesh that, as he could not resist sleep, there was little chance of avoiding death itself. Moved by pity, Utanapishtim's wife asked her husband to give Gilgamesh a parting present, and Utanapishtim revealed the existence of a herb of eternal life at the bottom of Abzu. But as Gilgamesh made his way back to Uruk with the miraculous herb which he intended to consume as he grew older, he went to sleep by a water-hole. Smelling the wonderful perfume of the leaves, a serpent stole up and swallowed the lot. At once the snake gained the power to slough its skin and Gilgamesh, seeing what had happened, realized that death was now his certain fate.

For Dumuzi, on the other hand, the experience of death became an annual event, a consequence of the challenge thrown down to Ereshkigal, 'the mistress of death', by his wife, the goddess Inanna, 'the impetuous lady' who journeyed to the land of no return in order to assert her power of fertility there. At each of its seven gates, Inanna was obliged to shed a garment or ornament until she stood naked before Ereshkigal. For three days Inanna was left hanging lifeless on a stake, until Enki sent two sexless beings to revive her with the 'food and water of life'. But after her miraculous recovery, the goddess could not shake off a ghastly escort of

The divine lovers, the goddess Inanna in bed with Dumuzi

demons as she wandered from city to city. They refused to depart unless a substitute was found. So Inanna returned home to Uruk, took offence at King Dumuzi enjoying himself at a feast, and let the demons take him away to Ereshkigal's underground realm.

Thereafter Dumuzi's fate was spending half the year in the land of the living, the other half with the dead. Thus he became the ancient Near East's original dying-and-rising god, the prototype for deities such as Adonis, the victim of a wild boar. An alternative version of this Greek myth has Adonis handed over to the underworld goddess Persephone for safekeeping; but, impressed by his good looks, she refused to return him to the world of the living. When Aphrodite, a goddess with close links to Inanna, protested to Zeus, he decided that Adonis should spend a third of every year with each goddess and the remaining third with himself. For Muhammad the death and resurrection of Christ placed the Son of God firmly within the same Sumerian tradition.

At Uruk there is compelling evidence that the king acted as an intermediary between the city and the city goddess through the New Year rite of a sacred marriage. In a temple set within a beautiful garden the ruler impersonated Dumuzi, a high priestess Inanna. One text has the king of Uruk boast how he 'lay on the splendid bed of Inanna, strewn with pure plants ... The day did not dawn, the night did not pass. For fifteen hours I lay with Inanna.'

The fertility goddess was the awaking force that stirs desire in people and causes ripeness in vegetation. A ruler's enjoyment of 'the sweetness of her holy loins' was regarded by the Sumerians as vitally important because this sacred coupling guaranteed a city's survival. It is tempting to see their joy during the festival as recognition that a new seasonal cycle was about to begin, marked by the return of Dumuzi from the underworld to Inanna's 'ever youthful bed'.

THE THIRD DYNASTY OF UR

We know so much about Sumer thanks to King Shulgi, the second king of the third dynasty of Ur. During his reign from 2094 to 2047 BC, Shulgi expanded a training scheme for scribes in order to exercise greater control over the city's economy. Inadvertently, he ensured the preservation of Sumerian literature.

King Ur-Nammu, Shulgi's father and the founder of the third and last dynasty at Ur, was particularly active as a builder, his most important work being a city wall and rampart of mud-brick construction. The safety of Ur depended upon such defensive measures, because the Sumerians were under increasing pressure from incoming Semites. For two humiliating defeats marked the city's history. The first defeat was at the hands of a Semitic ruler by the name of Sargon, during whose long reign from 2330 to 2274 BC the city of Akkad came to dominate most of the ancient Near East.

The second humiliating defeat of Ur in 2004 BC was the result of an Elamite invasion. Before this final catastrophe, however, Sumerian culture enjoyed its swan song. The city of Lagash came to the fore as a political force, especially under King Gudea, whose piety found expression in the rebuilding of temples, the composition of hymns and the carving of statues. Almost life-size statues of Gudea in hard black dolerite were beautifully

One of the statues of King Gudea

carved and inscribed with his acts: they were placed in the temples he patronized. Fortunately the records that this energetic ruler kept of his building activities provide details of how a temple was constructed and consecrated. They tell us how the warrior god Ninurta showed himself in a dream to Gudea as a huge man with a divine crown on his head, wings like a bird, and the lower part of his body resembling 'a flood wave'. He ordered the king to build him a temple and, in a second dream, an architect actually drew on a tablet its plan. After Gudea had the two dreams interpreted, he set to work and completed the project in record time; the temple was opened with a splendid feast during which social distinctions were deliberately set aside, as all were equal in the presence of divinity. Hymns were sung and goodwill prevailed so that no strife would mar such an auspicious occasion. That is one reason why joyful music along with alcohol were always part of Sumerian worship; the other reason was the obvious delight of the Sumerians in the here and now. Not long after Gudea's death in 2122 BC, King Ur-Nammu founded the third dynasty at Ur.

Whereas kings of Akkad had assumed the herculean task of controlling 'the four quarters', and in particular the trade routes to the Mediterranean and Iran, both Ur-Nammu and Shulgi concentrated on Mesopotamia itself. Yet the success of father and son in restoring prosperity to the Sumerians led them to contemplate the assumption of divine honours. Ur-Nammu seems to have been deified and Shulgi was sorely tempted to follow his example. This appears to have been the reason behind the composition of *The Curse of Akkad*, which claimed that it was the sacrilege of King Naramsin which had brought about Akkad's downfall. Having extended his authority into Syria, Naramsin decided to crown his achievements, as a divine monarch, by rebuilding Enlil's temple at Nippur. It involved the total demolition of the temple and the laying of entirely new foundations. The thoroughness of the project certainly offended Sumerian sentiment, because in *The Curse of Akkad* an angry Enlil invited the Gutians to invade Akkad in retaliation.

The semi-nomadic Gutians descended from the mountains of Iran and terrorized both Semites and Sumerians. Although they overran much of Mesopotamia, the cities of Uruk and Ur somehow escaped their attention. That the Gutium invasion took place nearly a century after the end of Naramsin's reign did not stop the priests at Ur from using the event as a dire warning to Shulgi. They composed *The Curse of Akkad* as a warning to this king about the danger of overstepping the mark. Unlike Akkad, Sumer had little sympathy for deified rulers.

Ironically for Ur, it was yet another invasion from Iran that ended its final days of glory. Despite the construction shortly before 2050 BC of 'a wall in front of the mountains', the Elamites were not to be denied the loot of Ur. A lament tells us how at Ur 'water no longer flows in weed-free canals, the hoe does not tend fertile fields, no seed is planted in the ground, on the plain the oxherd's song goes unheard, and there is never the sound of churning'. Such outpourings of woe developed in Sumer to commemorate the periodic destruction of its cities. They were the fore-runner of *The Book of Lamentations*, in which the Jews expressed their anguish over the loss of 'their inheritance to strangers' and their 'houses to aliens'. Yet nothing similar to the Jewish admission of sinfulness as a cause of their sorrow ever features in Sumerian compositions, for it was the departure of the city gods which ensured that the ancient ways 'changed for ever'.

Following the withdrawal of the Elamites from Sumer, the king of Isin emerged from the new fortifications which had saved his own city, and annexed the territory of Ur. Notwithstanding the pretentions of the Ur III dynasty, its royal tombs never approached the megalomania of the earlier ones uncovered by Woolley in 1932. They were much smaller and contained no human sacrifices. But the Elamites still broke into their chambers and removed the grave goods.

Another settlement arose on the site of Ur, but this city never flour-ished as before. One reason was undoubtedly a shift in the course of the Euphrates, which today flows some 12 kilometres to the east of the ruined city. As Woolley puts it: 'Gradually the inhabitants moved away to other homes, the houses crumbled, the wind sweeping across the now parched and desiccated levels brought clouds of sand which they dropped under the lee of the standing walls, and what had been a great city became a wilderness of brick-littered mounds rising from the waste'. He might also have pointed out that, at the time of Ur's terminal decline,

The Elamites would not have found in the Ur III Dynasty cemetery anything as valuable as this gold helmet, which Woolley uncovered in 1922

Sumer had virtually disappeared anyway. For in 1750 BC King Hammurabi conquered Larsa, the last independent Sumerian city, which gave Babylon absolute authority over the whole of southern Mesopotamia. By then Sumerian-speakers constituted a minority. All that was left of ancient Sumer was its culture, which amazed the Babylonians as much as the Assyrians. Like Latin in medieval Europe, Sumerian retained a privileged position as a scholarly language because it had been the vehicle of the ancient Near East's first advanced culture, whose remarkable ideas were avidly translated into Semitic Akkadian. Sumer had, after all, invented civilization.

3

THE FIRST GREAT EMPIRES

The Assyrian came down like a wolf on the fold,
And his cohorts were gleaming in purple and gold;
And the sheen of their spears was like stars on the sea,
When the blue wave rolls nightly on deep Galilee.

'The Destruction of Sennacherib' by Lord Byron

Mesopotamian kingship originated with leadership in war. When an attack threatened a Sumerian city, a young nobleman was chosen to lead the community in battle and was granted absolute authority during the emergency. By getting involved with justice, a few of these temporary kings managed to hold on to some of that power afterwards. They broadened their appeal by defending the underprivileged members of society.

Fundamental to a Sumerian king's position was a large retinue of unfree retainers, in part recruited from captives whose lives the king had spared. This military tradition lingered into the medieval period with the recruitment of Turkish slave-troops by the Abbasid caliphate and ex-Christian slaves by the Ottomans. As one astute Arab put it: 'Better an obedient slave than a hundred sons. Whilst the latter desire the father's death, the former prays for his master's glory.' Slaves even formed the bodyguard of Muslim rulers. Like these lifelong soldiers, the Sumerian king owned his retainers body and soul: they ate with him and did his bidding in war as well as peace.

Because cities in Sumer expanded around temples, the nuclei of all significant foundations, the Sumerians expected their rulers to maintain good relations with the priesthood. As we saw in the previous chapter, the city of Uruk had no palace at all when in 3200 BC it emerged as the world's first city. For the highest authority in the Sumerian universe was the assembly of the gods. It met, when occasion arose, in the forecourt of Ekur, the storm god Enlil's temple at Nippur. The decisions of the divine assembly were believed to include the choice of kings. As the Sumerians were from the beginning organized into a number of city-states, consisting of a city with surrounding villages and countryside, the idea of a unitary state was slow to develop. The Sumerian King List names kings of different cities, but after the Flood it tends to mention single rulers in chronological order, ostensibly with each one governing Sumer as a whole. But it seems unlikely that the various city-states willingly forfeited the independence they had enjoyed in antediluvian times. A case in point is the so-called Stele of the Vultures, now in the Louvre. Commemorating the victory of King Eannatum of Lagash over the neighbouring city of Umma, which probably occurred around 2450 BC, the stele demonstrates how professional warfare had become: a solid phalanx of infantry

Sumerian infantry depicted on the Stele of the Vultures

armed with metal helmets, large shields and thrusting spears advance over the bodies of dead enemies.

When one ruler became particularly powerful, there was peace and disputes between Sumerian city-states were adjudicated rather than settled by brute force. Thus King Uruinimgina of Lagash was able to introduce laws, which stand at the head of a long series including Hammurabi's famous law code at Babylon. Uruinimgina deplored the confiscation of temple properties and he instituted regulations in which the interests of the gods were paramount. Driven from Lagash, Uruinimgina continued to rule from Girsu before being taken prisoner by the Semitic king of Akkad, where he died. Even though the exact location of Akkad remains undiscovered, this ancient city was certainly situated in Babylonia. For the Sumerians its rise as an imperial power meant the beginning of the end of their distinctive cultural identity.

AKKAD

Considered to be the first super state in the ancient Near East, Akkad's foundation was the achievement of Sargon, who ruled from 2340 to 2274 BC. Yet Sargon's background remains obscure: he was said like Moses to have been found in a basket floating down the Euphrates and raised at the royal court of Kish, where he became the king's cupbearer. Another legend claims that he was loved and protected by Ishtar, the Semitic name for the great Sumerian goddess Inanna. Whatever the circumstances of his seizure of power at Kish, which he rebuilt perhaps intending to make the city his capital, Sargon was a Semite and therefore took the Akkadian title *sharru kenu*, meaning 'legitimate king'. In the Old Testament this was transformed into Sargon.

King Sargon created his empire through an army of bowmen and light-armed spearmen, whose mobility overcame the compact infantry formations favoured by the Sumerians. One of his earliest inscriptions mentions the rout of an army from Uruk, the first of many recording Akkad's spread of conquests. Another inscription boasts that Sargon fed 5,400 troops daily, who made him 'victorious in thirty-four battles'. His far-flung campaigns were not primarily driven by a desire for territorial

King Sargon of Akkad

aggrandizement; rather they aimed to secure the overland trade routes which passed through Akkad. Sargon's concern with trade explains his efforts to ensure that seagoing vessels could sail upriver from the Persian Gulf and moor in the harbour of his capital. Inscriptions mention ships arriving from Bahrain, India and Egypt. Long-distance trade with the Indian subcontinent is shown in the archaeological discoveries which have been made in Meluhha, as the Indus valley was called by the Akkadians.

Throughout the territories brought under his direct control, Sargon installed Akkadian-speaking governors who were backed by garrisons. As aware of his religious duties as earlier rulers, he appointed his daughter Enheduanna as high priestess of the moon god Nanna at Ur. Sumerian was still spoken in this city, but Nanna had already become Sin, the deity's Akkadian name. Enheduanna composed hymns in the Sumerian language as well as an autobiographical poem in which she tells us how she prayed to Sin when rebels took control of Ur. Since the moon god did nothing to help, Enheduanna appealed to the warlike aspect of Inanna's complex nature instead, and this goddess responded with such frightening swiftness that the rebels fled from the city in panic.

By this time, the land of Sumer had been reorganized as an imperial province, a move designed to break down the old boundaries of the city-states. Into Akkad flowed revenue from tribute as well as trade—warehouses next to the city quay were filled with precious metals, plus tin, copper and timber—so that its rulers could afford a costly system of government. Whereas the kings of Sumer based their power primarily on revenues derived from agriculture and animal husbandry, the Akkadian kings obtained most of theirs from commerce, and especially taxes on the trade of luxury goods. If the situation required force, though, Sargon and his successors were prepared to fight for booty or the imposition of tribute. They were very much the precursors of the Assyrians, who looked upon the profits of war as their divinely approved entitlement. A fellow usurper such as the Assyrian king Sargon II greatly admired the example that the first Akkadian ruler had set in the ancient Near East.

The rebels who troubled Enheduanna at Ur had tried to shake off the harshness of Sargon's rule. Their local uprising was followed by a more widespread rebellion on the accession of his son Rimush: it was suppressed with such severity that the Akkadians were thereafter regarded as merciless opponents. Large numbers of Sumerians were killed or deported to forced labour camps, where many also died. For the first time in the history of the ancient Near East, thousands were slaughtered in battle or as prisoners of war. It was therefore something of a relief when Rimush was murdered in a palace conspiracy and was succeeded by his brother, Manishtusu. The new king's interest was international trade, which he stimulated by friendly and unfriendly means. His army actually invaded central Iran in search of valuable materials and products, unlike the king of Uruk who had relied upon divine persuasion to get the city of Aratta to supply him with gold and lapis lazuli.

This surge of wealth may have wrecked Akkad in the longer term because its fourth king, Manishtusu's thirty-seven-year-old son, Naramsin, came to see divinity as his due. Not long after he ascended the throne in 2291 BC, there was a widespread revolt that almost succeeded in toppling Naramsin; but, against all the olds, the new king reasserted imperial authority with almost superhuman strength. In his inscriptions, Naramsin readily proclaimed himself as a peerless conqueror, to whom the cities of Syria submitted one by one. Shortly after this triumph, he adopted the title of 'king of the four quarters' or, more literally, 'of the four seas', for the world was then thought to be a great island entirely surrounded by the sea. To celebrate this new authority he did two things. First, he began to rebuild Ekur, the temple of the storm god Enlil at Nippur, whose inhabitants were exempted from compulsory labour and military service. The reconstruction of the temple may not have progressed beyond the laying of new foundations during Naramsin's reign. Bricks with this king's name as the builder have been unearthed there, but they may have

The divine king Naramsin depicted on the Victory Stele

been made under him and only laid by his son Sharkalisharri, who finished the project.

Naramsin's second decision was no less controversial, when he assumed divine honours. No Mesopotamian king had ever dared to do this before him. The horned helmet he is shown wearing on the so-called Victory Stele is unambiguous: such a headdress was always reserved for gods and goddesses. Carved in pink limestone, the stele celebrates Naramsin's defeat of the Lullubi, a troublesome tribe in the Zagros mountains. The stele's unusually dynamic composition highlights the achievement and glorifies the Akkadian king as a deity. A sun at the top of the stele beams approval of this newly won status for a king who led his army 'where no other ruler has gone before him'.

Naramsin was careful, however, in justifying his divine elevation in terms of popular demand, claiming that the people of Akkad beseeched the great deities to allow the worship of their king as a god, because he had not only saved the Akkadian empire but enlarged it as well. The great gods and goddesses are said to have agreed to this unusual request so that a temple was built in the king's honour. As far as we can tell, Naramsin died around 2213 BC, still a hero in the eyes of the Akkadians. His son Sharkalisharri, whose name means 'king of all kings', was crowned in the Sumerian city of Nippur, where the reconstruction of Enlil's temple was still in progress. During his reign, however, the Akkadian empire contracted drastically and Sharkalisharri was killed by his courtiers, an action which inaugurated a period of anarchy.

The Sumerian King List pointedly asks, 'Who was king? Who was not king?' The last ruler of all was Shuturul, 'the mighty one, the king of Akkad', a grandiose title which belied the fact that he dominated no more the environs of his city. Shortly after Shuturul's death Akkad itself seems to have perished. The decline and fall of Sargon's dynasty was believed by the Sumerians to be the result of Naramsin's arrogant assumption of divinity. According to *The Curse of Akkad*, later composed in Ur as a warning to the Sumerian king Shulgi not to hanker after divine honours himself, an enraged Enlil called upon the semi-nomadic Gutians to descend from the Zagros mountains and punish Akkad.

Whilst an epic hero such as Gilgamesh was prepared to disobey the gods, he never sought divinity for himself but rather immortality like his ancestor Utanapishtim, the survivor of the Flood. Slaying Enlil's forester Huwawa in the cedar forest was one thing, for which a newly discovered fragment of the *Gilgamesh* epic suggests that he and Enkidu expressed their regret; but setting up a temple, as Naramsin did for his own worship, was quite another.

Despite former Sumerian kings being elevated to a quasi-divine status after their deaths, including Gilgamesh's own father Lugalbanda, the idea that a living ruler could become a divinity was unacceptable in Sumer. Such a lack of respect for the gods was bound to invite retribution. Among the Semites the distinction between the human and the divine was even more pronounced, which made Naramsin's action so extraordinary. Yet even Gilgamesh's perpetual challenge to the divine order eventually backfired: the gods' displeasure caught up with him when his close friend Enkidu suffered an early death. It was a fear that haunted Gilgamesh throughout his life, as he could not but notice how 'the dead outnumber the living'.

BABYLON

As far as the Sumerians were concerned, the avenging Gutians brought a time of terror, their hit-and-run tactics earning them the epithet 'fleet snake of the mountains'. In Sumer, though, there were fewer Gutian raids so that Sumerian dynasties revived at Lagash as well as Ur. Yet on the horizon there was already another superpower in the process of replacing Akkad: it was Babylon. The start of Babylonian history is traditionally dated to the fall of the third dynasty of Ur in 2004 BC and the arrival from the Syrian desert of the Amorites, a large group of Semitic-speaking nomads. They spoke a language that was related to Akkadian and later developed into Ugaritic, Hebrew and other West Semitic tongues. The Amorites captured a number of city-states where they established new dynasties and then gradually settled down and adapted to Mesopotamian ways. One of these dynasties in Babylon became supreme under King Hammurabi, who ruled from 1792 to 1750 BC. Even though Assyria had just emerged as a powerful state, Hammurabi captured its capital of Ashur and, learning that King Zimri-Lim of Mari was reluctant to pay tribute in full, he then marched up the Euphrates and captured Mari, burning the great palace there to the ground.

The column on which King Hammurabi's law code was recorded

To his subject city-states in the upper Euphrates and Tigris river valleys, Hammurabi was a distant overlord. As long as Babylon received a regular flow of tribute, which included textiles and wine, they were largely left to their own devices. Quite late in life, Hammurabi promulgated a law code which served as a model for at least a millennium. Carved on an elegant stone column 2.25 metres high, the code's settlement of disputes and crime bears witness to the Semitic custom of 'an eye for an eye and a tooth for a tooth', since this tougher approach replaced the system of fines used by the Sumerians, who preferred to recompense physical injury with an appropriate payment, although murder and robbery were always punished by death. One case addressed by Hammurbi's code is about the consequences of shoddy workmanship. It states: 'If a master-builder did not build a house properly so that it collapsed and caused the death of the owner of the house, this master-builder shall be put to death. If the collapse caused the death of the son of the owner, they shall put the son of the master-builder to death'.

Apart from the punishment here exactly matching the crime, there is no reference to the owner's wife or daughter. That they are not mentioned in any examples of domestic violence either—'If a son has struck his father, they shall cut off his hand'—seems to suggest that Babylonian women inhabited some kind of legal limbo. But the legacy of Hammurabi's harsh law code still informs attitudes in the Near East: turning the other cheek is not the usual response to a modern insult.

Laws concerning women focus upon marriage. They cover dowries, divorce and the plight of wives whose husbands fail to return after a campaign. It was acceptable that, in the absence of a husband captured by the enemy, a wife could move into the house of another man. If the husband returned, however, his wife would have to go back to him, leaving behind any children she may have had with the other man. Remarriage was never a problem for the Babylonians. There were also laws which allowed the children of enslaved women to become legitimate: some of these mothers bore surrogate children for married women.

Cultural continuity between Sumer and Babylon was the defining feature of this period of Mesopotamian civilization: as a saying asked, 'The scribe who does not know Sumerian, what kind of scribe is he?' What the Babylonian kings were particularly keen to draw upon was Sumerian omen literature. An important collection of texts relates how 'a malformed birth' constitutes an ominous message from the gods. Almost invariably found written on clay tablets, a single omen concerning an abnormality in a fish has survived written on the two sides of a bronze dogfish. A missing fin is explained as 'the destruction of a foreign army': the oracular fish dates from the sixth century BC and the rebirth of Babylonian power under Nebuchadrezzar II.

Although Babylon's supremacy ultimately rested upon its armed forces, Hammurabi also attended to irrigation. In the thirty-third year of his reign, we are told, the Babylonian king 'made abundant water reach Nippur, Eridu, Ur, Larsa, Uruk, and Isin and returned Sumer and Akkad to their former prosperity'. Either the supply of water from the north had been diverted elsewhere, or the dykes were in need of urgent repair. The eclipse of Hammurabi's dynasty occurred in 1595 BC, when a raid by the Hittite king Mursili I resulted in the sack of Babylon. Curiously, Mursili withdrew to Asia Minor immediately after the destruction, and the Kassites took advantage of the power vacuum to seize control. Some Kassites remained in Iran, where they are mentioned in Assyrian texts as late as the seventh century BC, but most of these hill-people moved to Babylon and adopted the Akkadian language.

In 1155 or 1152 BC, the Elamites overthrew the long-lasting Kassite dynasty. That the greatest king of the next royal house, Nebuchadrezzar I, was remembered for his chastisement of the Elamites only serves to show how cherished the Kassites had been in Babylon. Nebuchadrezzar, the usual spelling of Nabu-kudurri-usur, is based on a later Hebrew corruption of the name given to Nebuchadrezzar II in the Bible.

Nebuchadrezzar I was the fourth king of the new Isin dynasty, and ruled Babylon for twenty-two years. By carrying off the cult statue of Marduk, the Elamites had utterly humiliated the Babylonians. A first attempt to return the city-god's statue to its rightful place in the great temple of Esagila was thwarted by an outbreak of plague in Nebuchadrezzar's army. Having received favourable omens for a second attack on Elam, however, the Babylonian king advanced in sweltering heat at the height of summer, and the unexpected timing of the attack caught the Elamites by surprise. In a great battle which 'blotted out the light of day', the Babylonian chariotry decided the outcome and in triumph Nebuchadrezzar bore the cult statue home.

So it happened, a chronicler relates, that 'the great god Marduk relented his anger against his land and returned to protect it once again'. It may be that the crushing victory over the Elamites encouraged Nebuchadrezzar to declare that Marduk was the supreme Mesopotamian deity. In Esagila, the Babylonian monarch participated in an annual ritual of renewal, a reaffirmation of his entitlement to rule. To this impressive ceremony the gods and goddesses of other major cities were brought as witnesses, until political unrest towards the end of Nebuchadrezzar's reign caused a temporary halt to the practice, because it was too risky for their cult statues to be conveyed to Babylon. Before his death in 1103 BC, Nebuchadrezzar raised the first ziggurat at Babylon, opposite Marduk's temple.

The earliest mathematical texts date from this time, anticipating among other things Pythagoras' theorem by a thousand years. Yet calculations of all kinds, such as estimating the number of days required to complete a task or determining the size and shape of fields, show how the Babylonians were perfectly capable of solving the mathematical problems of daily life. Pythagoras dwelt on Samos, an island off the coast of Asia Minor, before his emigration to Italy in 531 BC. Like Thales, who lived close by in the coastal city of Miletus, he would have encountered ancient Near Eastern ideas. Thales was one of the Seven Sages, according to the ancient Greeks, and made his name through accurately predicting a solar eclipse in 586 BC; in all probability he made use of Babylonian astronomical tables. Cosmology has always been highly speculative, but in the case of Thales the practical nature of his interests was very marked, since they encompassed navigation, economics, engineering and geography, besides astronomy. And the prime importance that Thales attributed to water, whose movements he believed were the cause of earthquakes, depended entirely upon the Mesopotamian conception of the land floating on a cosmic ocean.

It may be fanciful to suggest that the silting of the Meander river, which empties into the Aegean at Miletus, confirmed Thales' belief in the power of water, because the process of alluviation seemed to turn water into earth. Ships' captains grumbled about their grounded vessels as the river gradually filled up with waterborne sediment. Thales was celebrated by the ancient Greeks as the source of rational enquiry because he first suggested that natural processes, rather than divine action, might be behind the shaping of phenomena.

At first there were only minor skirmishes between the Babylonians and the Assyrians, who dwelt to the north of Babylon, but during the ninth century BC Assyria enjoyed a revival of power and serious hostilities broke out. Tiring of an arm's-length method of domination in Babylon, each Assyrian king assumed Babylonian sovereignty until King Sennacherib decided to impose puppet rulers instead. When one of these, in fact Sennacherib's own son, was seized by the Babylonians and handed over to the Elamites, an enraged Sennacherib not only invaded Elam but in 689 BC sacked the city of Babylon as well.

While Sennacherib's successors attempted to make amends through a gigantic building programme in Babylon, hatred seethed in Babylonian breasts and ultimately sparked a major rebellion, which King Ashurbanipal put down with some difficulty. Yet this did not stop the Assyrian monarch from sponsoring a major restoration programme in Babylon, which included Maduk's temple, the Esagila. A votive statue recovered from its ruins shows Ashurbanipal in traditional form, carrying a basket of clay on his head. Within a couple of decades, though, a Chaldean leader by the name of Nabopolassar achieved full Babylonian independence. He was crowned in 625 BC.

The Chaldeans were a group of Semitic tribesmen who had originally settled along the Persian Gulf and had attempted to infiltrate Babylon for many years. In alliance with the Medes, Nabopolassar broke Assyrian power, so that Babylon won not only control of Assyria proper but also inherited the Assyrian empire. It was Nabopolassar's son and successor, Nebuchadrezzar II, who consolidated Babylonian rule; his most famous campaigns were those conducted in Palestine against successive Jewish rebellions. When Jerusalem fell around 586 BC, an exasperated Nebuchadrezzar transferred a large number of Jews to Babylon, an event known for ever after in Jewish history as 'the exile'. During the Jewish sojourn, Babylon was transformed into the greatest city in the ancient Near East,

A votive statue of the Assyrian king Ashurbanipal carrying a basket of clay in Babylon

with such magnificent buildings that it was titled a wonder of the world. The Chaldean dynasty came to an end in 539 BC, when the Persians occupied Babylon.

HATTI

Hatti was an ancient name for the area around Hattusha, the Hittite capital, located some 120 kilometres east of modern Ankara. Its inhabitants were subjugated by the Hittites, probably at the end of the third millennium BC. Although Hattili may have survived as a language right down to the collapse of Hittite power, the newcomers spoke an Indo-European tongue called Nesite.

King Hattusili I effectively established the Hittite kingdom, extending its influence into Syria, from where he brought back scribes to start a

The restored defences of Hattusha, the Hittite capital

cuneiform archive at Hattusha. The next Hittite king, Mursili I, also campaigned in Syria and even went on to capture Babylon. After looting the city, the Hittite king Mursili withdrew homewards with his army, no doubt savouring this extraordinary triumph, but apparently not intending to annex Babylonia. Back in Asia Minor, a whole series of palace murders ensued, including his own. Conflict among the ruling class would in the end so weaken Hatti that Hattusha was abandoned and the remnant of the kingdom moved to Syria.

The Hittites faced two determined enemies: Mitanni and Egypt. Mitanni was completely forgotten until discoveries in the nineteenth century revealed its name and location; it was the home of the Hurrians, the Horites in the Bible. Mitanni's civilization was the product of two distinct ethnic groups: the Hurrians and the Indo-Aryans. Although the language of Mitanni was Hurrian, an obscure non-Indo-European tongue, there is no doubt of the presence of an Indo-European vocabulary in Mitannian texts. In addition, the Mitannians are known to have worshipped Indra, Mitra, Varuna and the Asvins, the twin horse-headed gods of ancient India. As the upholder of the moral order, Varuna was always invoked in peace treaties. He was in fact one of the oldest Indian deities, an uncreated god who ruled the sky at night, when his star-like presence was a cause of wonder. Later he lost this role and became associated with seas and rivers. But for the Mitannians he remained an essential buttress of society, because he was 'the binder of those who do wrong'.

How non-Hurrians came to occupy a prestigious position in Mitanni remains a matter of debate. There is no dispute, however, about the fact that these Indo-European speakers were outstandingly competent charioteers, who assisted the Mitannian kings in expanding their territories from the upper Euphrates and Tigris valleys to the shores of the Mediterranean, where they encountered both the Hittites and the Egyptians. We know a great deal about the Mitannian chariotry from Kikkuli's famous manual for training horses. Emphasis is placed on a regime of exercise and feeding that would increase the range and speed of chariot horses. At the end of a seven-month programme, these horses were capable of trotting long distances without tiring, and of pulling a chariot at top speed for over a kilometre.

The application of bent-wood technology to chariot construction, the improvement in manufacture of the composite bow, the advances in methods of training chariot horses and in developing tactics of manoeuvring the chariot to best advantage together produced nothing short of a military revolution. Once Hatti and Mitanni had demonstrated the effectiveness of the chariot, the first war machine ever invented, the spread of chariotry became general in the ancient Near East as well as Egypt. Initially chariot warfare served Mitanni well, but the revival of Assyria and the eastwards expansion of Hatti proved irresistible. After King Tushratta was murdered in a rebellion, his son Mittiwaza fled to the Hittite court. The restoration of Mittiwaza and his marriage to a Hittite princess turned Mitanni into a puppet state, a convenient buffer for the Hittites against the rising power of Assyria.

Yet the Hittites discovered that the Egyptians were not so easily overcome. As Egypt claimed suzerainty over Syria, an inevitable clash between the Hittites and the Egyptians occurred in 1274 BC, outside the Syrian city of Kadesh. There the young pharaoh Ramesses II was surprised by 3,500 chariots in a trap cleverly laid by King Muwatalli II of Hatti. Only a series of desperate counter-attacks, led by Ramesses in his own golden chariot, prevented an utter rout. In the swirling chariot battle, the Egyptian archers held off their opponents until an allied relief column arrived to distract Muwatalli's chariotry.

A Hittite king and queen pouring libations for the gods

According to the Egyptian account of the battle, fighting ended when the Hittite charioteers and chariot warriors abandoned their vehicles on the bank of the Orontes river, and 'plunged like crocodiles face first into its waters'. Although the Hittite infantry had not taken part in the battle, King Muwatalli decided that he could not risk further combat without his chariotry now that the Egyptians were reinforced. As Ramesses pointed out afterwards, the Hittite king had stripped his land of silver in order to swell his forces with mercenaries. The Hittite army at Kadesh totalled 47,500 men, including the complement of 3,500 chariots.

After the foundation of Hattusha, the Hittites had expanded their influence in Asia Minor and beyond, with even the petty kingdoms in Cyprus acknowledging Hittite overlordship. The Hittite empire comprised a network of vassal states, whose rulers enjoyed considerable local autonomy but were committed by oath to the Hittite king, their obligations being spelt out through personal treaties. Of these obligations the key one involved the military assistance the Hittites could call upon in time of war.

Exactly where Troy fitted into the politics of Asia Minor is still unclear. There were obviously contacts between the Hittites and the Trojans, not least because King Tudhaliya I overran the Aegean seaboard in the fourteenth century BC. The kingdom of Wilusa, as Troy was known to the Hittites, suffered a number of attacks including the one by the ancient Greeks, whose relationship with the Trojans alternated between commercial cooperation and military conflict. Two reasons have been advanced for this fluctuating state of affairs: disputes over the use of the Hellespont by Greek merchant ships, whose captains were probably required to pay a toll; and competition over the rich fishing grounds lying off the Trojan shore. It is quite possible that such mundane matters as trade and fishing triggered the Trojan War, rather than the desire of an outraged husband to seek revenge and recover his beautiful queen.

Parallels between Indian and Greek epics indicate a shared mythological heritage, which was recast to suit the different historical experiences involved in the occupation of Greece and India. Well might a Mycenaean king have led a Greek expedition against Troy, but the Trojan War has been absorbed into a story of divine rivalry, of gods and goddesses set-

A part of the city wall at Troy

tling their personal disputes by backing either the Trojans or the Greeks. Yet even with Helen, the human cause of the conflict, we are dealing with a goddess rather than a wayward queen. Hatched from an egg, this daughter of mighty Zeus was a fertility goddess, whose cult may have encompassed abduction as well as rescue. Helen's mother was Queen Leda of Sparta, whom the great god visited in the form of a swan.

ASSYRIA

Not until the Hittites crushed Mitanni in the fourteenth century BC, and two centuries later Hittite power itself disintegrated under the impact of the Sea Peoples, was there scope for the Assyrians to pursue imperial ambitions of their own. The reasons behind the great migration of the so-called Sea Peoples are still not really understood, but cities were set on fire in Greece, Asia Minor, Syria and Palestine. Assyria fought off migrants who tried to enter the Euphrates valley, while Ramesses III turned back most of the Sea Peoples in two hard-fought battles on the borders of Egypt. In 1182 BC the pharaoh defeated them on land as well as water.

Assyria was centred on the confluence of the Tigris and one of its major tributaries. The rolling hills of Assyria supported both herders and farmers thanks to a regular rainfall, in contrast to the dryness of Babylonia and Sumer. Unlike Babylonia, though, dates could not be grown there, but grapes were cultivated for fruit and wine-making. At Nimrud extensive wine cellars have been discovered, along with lists of their contents. Enjoyment of the grape was actually recorded in a wall relief at Nineveh, Assyria's last capital city: it shows King Ashurbanipal reclining in Greek fashion on a couch, but he does not drink in the company of men, as at a symposium. Only his wife, Queen Ashur-shurrat, shares the occasion with him. She sits on a throne in front of her husband, holding a wine cup to her lips while gazing upon her lord and master. Servants wave fly whisks so that no insect may spoil the royal couple's relaxation. Yet this apparently tranquil scene embodies the bloody nature of Assyrian rule, as the severed head of King Te-umman of Elam is suspended from the branch of a nearby tree. Birds are gathering

King Ashurbanipal in his cups, with the severed head of the Elamite king hanging on the far left

to pluck out the eyes and pick off the flesh. In his cups Ashurbanipal may well have expected the Assyrian empire to last for ever, but within fifteen years of his death in 627 BC, it had disintegrated.

King Ashurbanipal ruled during the last period of Assyrian domination of the ancient Near East. The Amorite invasion of Mesopotamia in around 2000 BC had resulted in the foundation of several states, of which Assyria was one. A dramatic improvement in Assyria's military capacity was stimulated by two invaders, the Mushki and the Aramaeans. After much effort, the Assyrians repulsed the Mushki and pursued them into eastern Anatolia where, as the Phrygians, they set up a kingdom ruled by Mita, known in ancient Greece as Midas.

The Aramaean invasion represented another serious challenge. These Semitic tribespeople had taken up residence in northern Syria, where population pressure obliged them to enter the Euphrates river valley. In defeating the Aramaeans, a royal inscription tells us, the Assyrian army crossed the river twenty-eight times. It even advanced to the Mediterranean where the soldiers washed their weapons in the sea and made offerings to the gods. Despite an impressive run of victories, the Aramaeans remained a thorn in Assyria's side for over a century. The persistence of the Aramaeans can be deduced from the fact that their tongue, Aramaic, became the language of the Persian empire as well as that of Judaism and Christianity. They also chose not to eat pork, a meat esteemed throughout the ancient Near East.

Although the historical record says little about Assyria immediately after this early period, the greatest period of Assyrian power commenced shortly afterwards in the tenth century BC, when its forces finally subjugated the Aramaeans and once again reached the Mediterranean shore. Two kings were responsible for this successful western thrust: Ashurnasirpal II and his son Shalmaneser III. The latter went further west than any of his predecessors, pushing down into Syria as far as Palestine.

From the moment of his accession, King Shalmaneser III believed that he possessed a divine mandate to conquer. Dated to the late 850s BC, an inscription engraved on a large stele found in 1861 near the river Tigris lists his impressive backers: 'God Assur, the great lord, king of all the great gods; god Anu, king of the Igigu and Anunnaku gods, lord of the lands; god Enlil, father of the gods, who decrees destinies; god Ea, wise one, king of Abzu, creator of clever devices; god Sin, light of heaven and the underworld, the noble one; god Shamash, judge of the four quarters, who guides human beings; goddess Ishtar, mistress of war and battle, whose game is fighting; the great gods who cherish my sovereignty, assist my dominion, power and leadership, have established my honourable name and my lofty command over all lands'. The inscription then lists the cities conquered by Shalmaneser, including those in the upper reaches of the Tigris, where at the start of his reign he took the fortified city of Aridu, 'massacred many of its inhabitants, carried off booty, erected a tower of heads before the city, and burned young boys and girls'.

The great Assyrian conquerer, King Shalmaneser III

What might be termed calculated terror at Aridu was enough to cow the entire area: tribute immediately poured in from other cities. For the early foreign policy of Assyria essentially aimed at the acquisition of valuable goods as either booty or tribute. On fifty-two occasions during Shalmaneser's reign from 859 to 824 BC, inscriptions detail the booty taken from captured cities. It comprised palace treasuries, textiles, timber, slaves, weapons, chariots and chariot horses, other animals, foodstuffs and wine. Another feature of Assyrian conquest was the wholesale deportation and resettlement of displaced populations. As many as 20,000 people may have been transferred from Aridu to Assyria. The standard verb for booty-taking was *salalu*, which meant gathering the just rewards of victory.

One of the battles fought by Shalmaneser in Syria is recorded in some detail. By the time this battle happened at Qarqar in 853 BC, the chariot had a rival in the mounted archer, whose ability to control his horse was much improved through the snaffle-bit, as it more readily communicated a rider's intentions to his mount. Yet Shalmaneser still preferred to put the majority of his archers in chariots. Even though the strength of Shalmaneser's forces at Qarqar is unknown, we are fortunate to have a breakdown for his Syrio-Palestinian opponents. Assyrian scribes record the enemy as fielding 3,940 chariots, 1,900 horsemen, 1,000 camel troops and 52,900 foot soldiers.

The prime movers of the coalition opposed to Assyria then were the Syrian king Ben-Hadad II and Ahab, his uneasy Jewish ally. The seriousness of the Assyrian threat obliged these two rulers to put their differences aside, with the result that the drawn battle of Qarqar against the Assyrians gave them a welcome respite. The mention of the contingent of camel troops at Qarqar is the first time that the Arabs appear in any ancient text. The domestication of the camel permitted the Arabs to master the desert lands, from which sudden raids could be launched on settled neighbours. In bas-reliefs, Assyrian soldiers are shown countering such attacks.

To reach Qarqar, the Assyrian army would have crossed the Euphrates on circular rafts made with inflated goatskins. These were quite capable of transporting chariots, horses and men. Such forays eventually converted Syria and Palestine into Assyrian territory, which Tiglath-Pileser III reorganized as provinces, with garrisons and governors, or puppet kings. For the reign of Tiglath-Pileser represented a watershed in the history of the ancient Near East. Before he came to the throne in 745 BC, Assyrian kings raided and plundered neighbouring states, but none of these rulers annexed any territory west of the Euphrates. All this changed in 732 BC with Tiglath-Pileser's conquest of Damascus. How far this belligerent king advanced southwards can be judged from the placement of a gold statue of Tiglath-Pileser in the Philistine city of Gaza 'among the gods of their land'.

A bas-relief discovered at Nimrud by Layard bears witness to the Assyrian advance. It shows Tiglath-Pileser in his royal chariot watching the abandonment of Ashtaroth, a city in present-day Jordan. The accompanying inscription says that he devastated four other cities besides Ashtaroth, and took as spoil 8,650 people, 300 mules, 1,350 cattle and

19,000 sheep. The whole area was then annexed to Assyria, and Mesopotamian people were settled in its rebuilt cities.

At the start of the seventh century BC, the expansion of the Assyrian empire seemed unstoppable, with Esarhaddon and Ashurbanipal invading distant Egypt. These Assyrian kings sacked the holy city of Thebes and carried its immense treasures away. From 663 BC onwards a compliant Egyptian pharaoh was left to rule Lower Egypt on their behalf, but it was not long before he asserted his independence, and his son Psamik founded the last Egyptian dynasty before the arrival of the Persians in 525 BC. That the Assyrians were unable to exercise direct control over Egypt, and had to leave the task to native collaborators, was a sure sign of impending trouble for their empire. Over-reach had already put a severe strain on Assyria, which was compounded by an increasingly rebellious nobility. It took surprisingly little to expose Assyria's vulnerability to determined foes: the fall of Nineveh in 612 BC, to a combined assault by the Babylonians and the Medes, marked the end of a once mighty empire.

PERSIA

When the Assyrians endeavoured to expand eastwards into what is now Iran, the Medes took the lead in forming an anti-Assyrian coalition. The Persians joined this coalition and achieved close relations with the Medes through intermarriage. No Median inscriptions have yet been recovered, but like the Persians they were probably Indo-European speakers. The Persians seem to have left the Central Asian steppe lands later than the Indo-Aryan invasion of India and only settled in Iran around 1000 BC. The longer sojourn on the steppes decisively shaped the Persian outlook, because it was here that the prophet Zoroaster transformed their Indo-European heritage into a singular set of beliefs. He claimed that his inspired utterances were not only divine truths but divine commands, which needed to be accepted by worshippers of Ahura Mazda, a cosmic deity who wore the sky as a garment, if they hoped to be saved. Zoroaster's emphasis on goodness as part of a divine plan was extraordinary, familiar though it now appears to us through Jewish and Christian borrowings.

Friction between the Median and the Persian royal families, however, soon caused a breach that was only resolved by Persian domination.

When Cyrus II, justifiably called the Great, came to the throne in 559 BC, he may have already decided to overthrow the Medes, so that the family dispute offered a golden opportunity for action. Next he attacked Lydia, after lulling the Babylonians into a false sense of security. Following the capture of Sardis, the Lydian capital, Cyrus subdued the Greek cities of Ionia, before turning on Babylon, where the unpopularity of the Babylonian king, Nabonidus, provided the perfect moment to march into Babylon in 539 BC, virtually unopposed. To the delight of the Babylonians and the exiled Jews, Cyrus appeared an ideal king. Whereas the Jewish prophet Isaiah maintained that the rise of Persia was part of a divine plan to rebuild Jerusalem, the Babylonian priesthood claimed that it was the will of Marduk, who 'scanned and looked through every country, searching for a king who would grace his annual procession. Then he pronounced Cyrus to be king of the world.'

Under the Persians there were no more mass deportations, and exiles were allowed to return to their homelands if they wished. Rebellions were not unknown in Babylon or the rest of the Persian empire; but despite periodic usurpation crises, the violent repression of the Assyrians became a thing of the past. Yet trouble lay ahead for the Persians in the form of the Macedonians, who were briefly incorporated in the Persian empire as a result of the conquest of Thrace.

The barrel-shaped clay cylinder describing how Cyrus captured Babylon in 539 BC

In spite of subscribing to such a distinctive religion as Zoroastrianism, Cyrus was a conspicuous restorer of damaged or destroyed Mesopotamian temples, beginning in Babylon with an improvement to Marduk's temple. A tablet recovered from its ruins relates how 'Cyrus, king of all lands, loves Esagila'. He seems to have realized that the cooperation of the Babylonians was vital in establishing his rule on a firm basis. Under his energetic successors, Cambyses and Darius I, Persian power spread right across the ancient Near East, and well beyond. Long before the aid sent by the Athenians and the Eretrians to his rebellious Greek subjects in Asia Minor provoked him to dispatch an expeditionary force to Greece, Darius' imperial ambitions were public knowledge. Darius had already sent ships to reconnoitre the Mediterranean coast as far west as Italy. In one of his inscriptions the Persian king even asserts his entitlement to rule the world as the chosen one of Ahura Mazda, the wise lord of light.

It would indeed appear that Darius and Xerxes, his son and successor, came to see the conquest of Greece as the first stage in Europe of a holy war, part of the final conflict foretold by the prophet Zoroaster which would mark the end of the present world. Xerxes is supposed to have said on the eve of his own invasion that 'the sun should not look down on any territory containing a city or a nation capable of going into battle against us'. For the followers of Ahura Mazda, therefore, the attack on the Greeks was a religious obligation, not unlike a Christian crusade or an Islamic jihad.

Although the Athenian repulse of Darius' expeditionary force in 490 BC was no more than a military pinprick for the Persians, it had represented an affront to their religious beliefs with the result that Xerxes easily raised an army to avenge this defeat. Xerxes' great invasion of Greece in 480–79 BC started a seesawing conflict between Europe and Asia which lasted into the medieval period, when both sides viewed the struggle in religious terms. The unexpected failure of Xerxes was of course the great event for the ancient Greeks, but rivalry between Athens and Sparta gave the Persians a respite from a sustained counter-attack, until war on the old enemy provided a useful battle cry for Alexander the Great when in 334 BC he invaded the Persian empire.

4

ANCIENT RELIGION AND BELIEFS

Exhausted, Ninhursag yearned for a beer.
The great gods languished where she sat weeping.
Like sheep they could only bleat their distress.
Thirsty they were, their lips rimed with hunger.
For seven whole days and seven whole nights
The torrent, the storm, the flood still raged on.
Then Atrahasis put down his great boat
And sacrificed oxen and many goats.
Smelling the fragrance of the offering
Like big flies, the gods kept buzzing about.

From the Babylonian story of the Flood

The sensation caused in 1872 by a translation of the Babylonian account of the Flood was typical of the European attitude to the ancient Near East. Because of the triumph of Christianity in Europe, archaeological discoveries were always evaluated in terms of the Bible. That the Flood story was much older than the Old Testament, indeed much older than the Babylonians themselves, should have brought such an outlook into question, but many years elapsed before it was realized how Judaism, not to say Christianity, arose from a very ancient complex of religious ideas, indeed the earliest to have been recorded anywhere on the planet.

The originators of most of these religious ideas were the Sumerians, whose invention of urban living as well as writing transformed human life once and for all. The extension of thought made possible with written texts was revolutionary, although of course reading and writing were at first the preserve of scribes. That the Assyrian king Ashurbanipal collected an enormous library at Nineveh, and could read the clay tablets in it himself, reveals how knowledge was pursued at the highest levels of society. Hardly surprising then was finding the 1872 text about the Flood in his library.

For the Sumerians, divinity was everywhere. It might be said that they developed their pantheon in order to understand the universe, which they called *an ki*, literally 'heaven earth'. Convinced that creation could not be explained by itself, and needing to give it meaning, the Sumerians envisaged supernatural beings who were responsible for creating the world and ensuring that its processes continued satisfactorily. Totally anthropomorphic though they were in their approach to the gods, they never forgot the original function that each deity performed in the natural order. The great Sumerian goddess Inanna, the prototype for Ishtar, Astarte, Aphrodite and Venus, was still the power behind the rain which

Aphrodite, the chief Greco-Roman import from the Mesopotamian pantheon

each spring brought forth pasture in the desert. It did not matter that Inanna's abundant sensuality also turned her into a love goddess, the protectress and colleague of prostitutes. In Akkadian, the Semitic language of the Babylonians, Inanna is called Ishtar. Essentially the same goddess because of the Babylonian adoption of the Sumerian pantheon, Ishtar does undergo a rather frightening transformation in Assyria, where a preoccupation with warfare turned her into the fierce mistress of the battlefield, armed with a bow and quiver, sometimes even a curly beard.

THE SUMERIAN PANTHEON

Starting out as a nature religion, with worship of natural phenomena such as the sky, the wind, the thundercloud and the underground waters surfacing in rivers and marshes, Sumerian beliefs became more complicated once deities were given a human form. Then the realm of the gods came to be imagined on a model of the earthly world, so that they were seen as a spiritual aristocracy of great landowners, Sumer's all-powerful upper class, dutifully served by human beings.

Eventually, in the second and first millennia BC, the gods became more like territorial or national deities, whose power supported the political aspirations of city-states and empires. So Marduk was believed to assist the Babylonians, and Ashur the Assyrians. But parallel to this, on a personal level, a growing closeness evolved between worshipper and god. Devotees could say 'Marduk is my god', a constant source of advice that anticipates the outlook of the Old Testament. 'Show me thy ways, O Lord,' beseeches Psalm 25, 'teach me thy paths. Lead me in thy truth, and teach me.' Of course a worshipper of Marduk would never have gone on to express a profound sense of personal guilt. 'A broken spirit, a broken and contrite heart' was not 'a suitable sacrifice' for a Babylonian because the general concept of sin had yet to develop in the ancient Near East. Wrongdoing was still primarily a matter for city regulation.

An important aspect of a personal god was believed to be luck. In the Sumerian and Akkadian languages there was only one way to describe good fortune: 'to acquire a god'. An omen informs us that 'the house which acquires a god will endure', whereas 'the house which grows poor

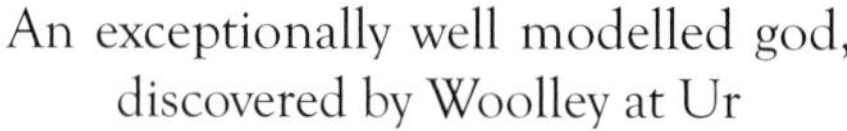

An exceptionally well modelled god, discovered by Woolley at Ur

A Sumerian worshipper, dating from the third millennium BC

will never acquire a god'. Without divine assistance, there was no possibility of success, which explains royal concern about divination. A ruler needed to be certain that his proposed actions had divine approval and support, because even the most respected king was still a slave in relation to the god of his city.

An was ranked as the highest Sumerian deity. He was heaven, and with the earth, his wife Ki, he created trees, reeds and all other vegetation. A text relates how 'an impregnated Ki bore one unafraid of the subterranean demon Azag'. Serpent-like Azag fought a terrible duel with their son Ninurta that was very similar to the contest between Zeus and Typhon, the son of the Greek earth goddess Gaia. The combat between Azag and Ninurta was on a cosmic scale when 'for a club Azag uprooted the sky'. So frightened were the other deities that even the storm god 'Enlil groaned and hid himself'. Yet 'Ninurta, having sufficient self-confidence, stood his ground' and swung 'his mighty mace, the lance of the mountains', driving back Azag and finally killing the monster.

Not only did An produce vegetation, but he was also the progenitor of both gods and demons. As the ultimate source of all authority, An was closely associated with kingship. It was he who proclaimed the king chosen by the assembly of the gods, which met periodically in Ekur, the temple of Enlil at Nippur, the holiest of Sumerian cities. Though subordinate in status to An, the storm god Enlil, whose name means 'lord wind', was more active in human affairs. An ambiguous figure, Enlil could be friend or foe just as the wind varies from a benign zephyr to a destructive tempest.

The Sumerian divine champion, Ninurta

It was Enlil's inability to get a good night's rest that really demonstrated his destructive side. So angry was he with the noise rising from the Sumerian cities that he decided to wipe out their inhabitants. At this stage it seems that the gods had overlooked the timing of death: people were living so long that overcrowded cities became far too noisy. The Flood was the final method Enlil employed for mass destruction, from which Ziudsura escaped in his giant coracle, the predecessor of Noah's Ark. This myth makes no bones about the selfishness of Enlil. Human existence was precarious, for this powerful deity would neither protect nor sustain people if, however inadvertently, they became a nuisance. As long as the Sumerians remained quietly efficient and fulfilled their religious duties, they could expect to survive, but not otherwise.

The third great Sumerian deity was Ninhursag, sometimes called the wife of Enlil, other times of An. She was above all the goddess of animal birth. In myth, Ninhursag is usually pitted against Enki, the guardian of sweet water, the great underground reservoir of Abzu. How ingenious Enki could be is seen in his method of warning Ziudsura. Having sworn not to divulge Enlil's intentions, Enki used a wind to convey the message of warning. The Babylonian version of the Flood actually begins:

Wall, wall! Reed wall, reed wall!
Atrahasis, listen to my advice,
That you may live for ever.
Destroy your house, and build a boat;
Give up your possessions, save your life.

The Babylonians knew Ziudsura, the Sumerian Noah, either as Atrahasis or Utnapishtim. It was to his ancestor Utnapishtim that Gilgamesh journeyed in search of an elixir of life.

Now that cuneiform tablets connected with Mesopotamian beliefs have been translated in such large numbers, it is clear that Judaism by no means developed in isolation, but stood in a close relationship with neighbouring religious faiths as well as cultures. Apart from the Flood, the Jews appropriated the Tower of Babel story, but not the tower itself, which was based on Marduk's ziggurat in Babylon. Rather they borrowed Yahweh's strategy to thwart its completion. For in competition with Enlil, whose universal worship Enki envied, the water god ended the Golden Age by confusing people's speech through the introduction of different languages. Prior to this, everyone spoke the same tongue and perfectly understood each other. Afterwards, 'the change of the speech in their mouths' led to endless strife between human beings.

Despite Enki's crafty reputation, he often astonished the other gods with solutions to apparently impossible problems. Having fashioned from clay the first human servants, the gods held a celebratory banquet, at which, overcome by strong beer, Enki got involved in a creation competition with Ninhursag, who deliberately tried to wreck Enki's creation by declaring that for each person that she made it would be her decision whether 'the fate is good or bad'. Ninhursag's ineffectual creations therefore set a challenge for Enki in finding them suitable employment. But his ingenuity 'found them bread'. The cripple became the servant of a king, the blind man his minstrel, the barren woman entered the royal harem and a sexless person joined the priesthood. What this myth explains are the destinies of individuals who did not take part in Sumerian family life.

This means that the profession followed by a prostitute was divinely decreed, her acceptance of many 'husbands' no more than an impersonation of the goddess Inanna herself. Though 'sixty find relief on her nakedness, and young men are wearied, the goddess is not wearied at all'. Possibly a favourite in taverns as well as temples, the song's meaning cannot be missed. The Greek historian Herodotus claimed that every Babylonian woman had once in her life to sit in the temple and lie with a stranger, because it made her holy in Aphrodite's sight. Incorrect though this is, Herodotus was right about the association of the Greek goddess with Sumerian Inanna and Babylonian Ishtar. A closer link would be the Canaanite goddess Astarte, whose cult was celebrated on Cyprus, the birthplace of Aphrodite. On that island, Herodotus relates, 'a custom like that of Babylon is followed'. In Aphrodite, who was conceived at sea within the severed phallus of the sky god Ouranos, we have the export of Inanna-Ishtar-Astarte to Europe.

Wrong though Herodotus was about the obligation of every Babylonian woman to serve Ishtar once as a temple prostitute, sexual rites were commonplace in Mesopotamian temples from Sumerian times onwards. Clay models of such encounters only date from the era of the Assyrian empire, but the ritual sex which was necessarily involved in the annual rite of sacred marriage in Sumer suggests that the worship of Inanna had always included a sexual element. Inanna herself acknowledges how her father Enki gave her 'the art of lovemaking' as well as the 'cult of the prostitute and the holy tavern'. In a hymn about the sacred marriage rite, an event the Sumerians considered vital for the renewal of each city, the king's penetration of the goddess was followed by the unbounded joy of his subjects, who believed that prosperity lay before them for another year. Their fields would now produce barley in plenty and their flocks increase in number.

Inanna, the original love goddess

An odd parallel of the Eden story of the Fall occurs in the Sumerian paradise myth. Whereas the Jewish version is as much about divine omniscience as the discovery of sexuality, the focus of the encounter between Enki and Ninhursag is the potency of his semen. 'Good and evil' in Genesis means 'everything', the knowledge reserved for a supreme deity. A variant in the Book of Ezekiel tells of a ruler who lived in a mountain paradise, but was cast down from this second Eden when he started to think of himself as a divinity. Having 'walked up and down in the midst of stones of fire', the king became so enchanted with his own 'beauty' that his 'wisdom' was corrupted by the 'brightness'. A reason for the friction between Enki and Ninhursag, on the other hand, was status: both claimed third place in the Sumerian pantheon after An and Enlil.

Ninhursag was beside herself with fury when Enki impregnated her daughter, granddaughter and great-granddaughter, not least because the water god had sired them all. As a result of the last sexual transgression, Enki almost died when his semen overflowed the goddess' loins. In his exhausted state he ate the eight plants that Ninhursag had grown from the spilled semen, falling so ill that the gods expected his end. These forbidden plants seem to have sealed Enki's fate until a fox persuaded the underworld deities to intercede on his behalf with Ninhursag, who relented the curse of death she had laid on him. This myth differs in all respects from the Jewish narrative of the Fall, except for the consequence of eating tabooed food being death.

With the goddess Inanna we meet one of the greatest Mesopotamian deities. Because she combined in her person several originally distinct goddesses, Inanna was unchallenged in the Sumerian pantheon as the source of fertility. In her myths, Inanna appears as a beautiful, wilful young aristocrat who dares to follow her own impulses wherever they may lead. We see her as a sweetheart, a happy bride and a sorrowing young widow; but she was never portrayed as a wife or mother.

In Inanna's impetuous confrontation in the underworld with her implacable enemy Ereshkigal, 'mistress of death', the fertility goddess reveals two aspects of the Sumerian cosmos. The first is the blurred line between immortals and mortals. That Inanna and her husband Dumuzi died, albeit temporarily, as a result of meeting Ereshkigal face to face was unacceptable to most Semites, who preferred to maintain a strict separation between the human and the divine, with the notable exception of the Akkadian king Naramsin who dared to declare himself a god. The second feature of Sumerian religion that Inanna's descent to the land of no return clearly indicates was the anxiety of the gods themselves when it came to the netherworld. Only Enki was prepared to take the risk of helping Inanna escape from its gloom, suggesting that there was a degree of danger for Sumerian deities in getting too close to Ereshkigal's realm.

The Sumerian cosmos

Heaven	An
Middle	Igigi
Sky	Enlil
Earth's surface	Many deities
Abzu	Enki
Underworld	Ereshkigal

In the sacred marriage rite at the New Year the king impersonated Dumuzi and a high priestess Inanna. After their love-making, in which the king was addressed as 'my true Dumuzi', a city's inhabitants showed their satisfaction with offerings of food and drink, and then celebrated a feast 'in plenty'. Even though the earliest cults of Dumuzi are by no means straightforward, since they range from his reverence as an antediluvian king to a powerful warrior whose death provoked ritual lamentation, it was at Uruk that this holy shepherd comes fully into focus. How widespread Dumuzi's cult became is signalled in the anger of the prophet Ezekiel, who bitterly complained that even at 'the door of the gate of the Lord's house in Jerusalem ... sat women weeping for Tammuz'.

The Jews had translated Damu, another name for Dumuzi, into Tammuz, and instituted a cult that may have seen a Jewish king play the role of a god, incompatible though this would have been with strict Yahweh worship. More likely than any sacred marriage, however, is the possibility that the Jewish ruler took part in a nocturnal ritual during which he was supposed to have died and then returned to life in the morning. Psalms suggest such a theme, when the suppliant admits how:

> the cords of death encompassed me,
> the torrents of perdition assailed me,
> the cords of Sheol entangled me,
> the snares of death confronted me.

Whether some kind of humiliation was suffered by the ruler, as a means of warding off ill fortune, followed by his joyful restoration, we have no idea. All that is obvious here is the worry of Jewish prophets about West Semitic cultic practices from the Exodus onwards: worship of the golden calf in Sinai was a harbinger of the religious difficulties that would face the Jews once they settled in a land inhabited by peoples who subscribed to a multitude of ancient Near Eastern deities.

In the southernmost Sumerian cities, situated close to the marshlands, the gods worshipped were connected with fishing and fowling; there Enki, the god of fresh water and of marsh life, ruled over the city of Eridu; upriver, divine influence spread over fields and orchards, with date growers paying special attention to the prodigious powers of Inanna; in the grasslands, worship was given over to Dumuzi, whose wooing of Inanna forms a notable myth. The fertility goddess' preference for a farmer, not a shepherd whose 'clothes are coarse', set Dumuzi a challenge that he overcame with the gift of delicious milk and cream. Invited at last 'to plough' Inanna like a wild bull, Dumuzi satisfied her immense sexual appetite 'fifty times', and was then accepted as her lover.

That Inanna was so enraptured with Dumuzi's boundless affection explains her shock at finding him at a feast in Uruk on her escape from the underworld. In terms of the agricultural cycle, this happened during the dry hot summer months, for Dumuzi's death coincided with the withering of foliage and the scorching of grass, a time when the surface of the ground began to resemble the desolation of Ereshkigal's underground domain.

It was an angry Inanna who allowed the demons to carry off Dumuzi. She had been released only conditionally, and a ghastly detachment from the underworld went along with her to see that she provided a substitute.

The idea of a substitute was deeply rooted in ancient Near Eastern culture. It was used on four occasions by the Assyrian king Esarhaddon, who came to the throne in 681 BC, following the assassination of his father Sennacherib. Relying on the support of Assyrian nobles, who had already sworn an oath of loyalty to the chosen successor, Esarhaddon had marched to Nineveh and executed the assassins. Yet he never felt at ease, and for days at a time he would withdraw into the inner palace, rejecting food, drink and human company.

Because his subjects were more than likely to regard this odd behaviour as a sign of divine disfavour, Esarhaddon's condition had to be kept a state secret. Hence the substitute kings, who wore his clothes, ate his meals and slept in his bed. Four times this ritual was performed, each substitute being executed after one hundred days. The ritual of the substitute king was usually put into motion whenever a lunar eclipse happened, because this omen portended the ruler's death. Even though these victims did not eliminate Esarhaddon's chronic personal anxieties, they removed a number of political adversaries who were carefully selected for the role. And after 672 BC, the king's competent eldest son, the crown prince Ashurbanipal, took on many of the royal duties. One of them was a successful conclusion to the Egyptian campaign.

Mindful of the uncertain circumstances of his own succession after his father's murder, Esarhaddon tried to strengthen the position of the crown prince by the imposition of treaties upon his vassal kingdoms, which required them to ensure Ashurbanipal's accession to the Assyrian throne. The thoroughness of these treaties now seems remarkable as the loyalty oath embraced not just the vassal kings themselves but their descendants too. Here is the introduction to one of them: 'The treaty of Esarhaddon, king of the world, king of Assyria, son of Sennacherib, king of the world, king of Assyria, with Ramataia, ruler of the city of Urakazabanu, with his sons, his grandsons ... and all those over whom Esarhaddon, king of Assyria, exercises kingship and lordship, on behalf of whom he has concluded this treaty with you concerning Ashurbanipal, the crown-prince designate, son of Esarhaddon, king of Assyria'.

This introduction is then followed by a long list naming the gods who have witnessed the treaty. Obviously the treaty's most important clause was the obligation, 'when Esarhaddon, king of Assyria, dies', to 'seat Ashurbanipal, the crown-prince designate, upon the royal throne'. Should this solemn duty be ignored, a curse was laid upon the unfaithful vassal: he would forfeit his good fortune and be squashed like a fly in his enemy's hand.

But treaties like this one failed to prevent a challenge for the throne from Ashurbanipal's younger brother, who refused to swear a loyalty oath and rebelled with the backing of the Elamites and the Chaldeans. Ashurbanipal crushed the uprising, which did not so much weaken Assyria as unsettle its nobility, whose own quarrels ultimately had an adverse impact on the Assyrian empire's stability. Still perplexing is how rapidly Assyria declined and fell, after bringing even Egypt under its sway. But an empire depending on almost continuous conquest to meet the costs of its maintenance could not of course last for ever. Once there were no new sources of booty or tribute readily available after the conquest of Egypt, Assyria's economic and political collapse became almost inevitable.

Unlike Esarhaddon's substitutes, the death of Dumuzi was not permanent, however. Overcoming her annoyance with her shepherd lover, Inanna agreed that Dumuzi could spend half the year with the living and half with the dead. His annual return to Inanna's 'ever youthful bed' almost certainly marked the start of a new seasonal cycle, which the king of Uruk and a high priestess celebrated in a sacred marriage.

Before looking at the Sumerian cosmos, there is one other important god to consider: Ninurta, the son of Enlil. The most pronounced aspect of Ninurta's character was his delight in war. It made him especially attractive to the Assyrians, although the Sumerians regarded him as a divine champion rather than an out-and-out war god. His greatest achievement was the recovery of 'the tablet of destiny', stolen from Enlil by the lion-headed storm bird Zu. Whoever possessed the tablet was supreme ruler of the world. Usually Enlil is described as 'holding the tablet in his hand' or 'clutching it to his chest'.

The Sumerians envisaged the cosmos as multi-layered. From top to bottom, the separate levels were: a heavenly realm above the sky, ruled by An; next the middle heavens belonging to the Igigi, or 'great gods', who were believed to number three hundred; the lower heavens comprised the sky and the stars; then came the surface of the planet, the abode of people who were still alive; the next level down was Abzu, the immense reservoir of fresh water guarded by Enki; the lowest level of all comprised the underworld, 'the land of no return', where Ereshkigal dwelt among the dead along with six hundred Anunnaki, gods who for some unknown reason were obliged to stay there. Possibly the Anunnaki prefigure the gigantic Titans in Greek mythology: after a ten-year struggle, Zeus had imprisoned them in Tartarus, locked behind bronze doors. Ereshkigal's subterranean realm was thought to be a vast circular city with seven surrounding walls, at whose gates Inanna had been obliged to remove an item of clothing or ornament. There are over two thousand Sumerian gods and goddesses mentioned in surviving texts.

THE RISE OF MARDUK

As every Sumerian settlement gave worship to a major deity in a temple which was constantly being restored and improved, it comes as no surprise that the Semites who adopted the Sumerian pantheon did exactly the same. And with the rise of Babylon as a great Mesopotamian power in the second millennium BC, its city god was bound to enjoy a parallel elevation. He was Marduk, the protector of Babylonian kings, once they had clasped the hands of the god's cult statue. This New Year ritual was a means of confirming each king's entitlement to rule, as well as reassuring the Babylonians of the divine protection being afforded to their city. The cult statue of Marduk we know was made from wood and precious metals. That it was the handiwork of craftsmen scandalized the Jewish prophets so much that they launched an impassioned polemic against idols.

Many of the most strident attacks on making an image of a god stem from the Babylonian captivity, which was an immense setback for Judaism because it appeared that Yahweh had either abandoned his people or lacked the strength to protect them. It was the prophet Isaiah who directed the full blast of disapproval against idolatry, when he said 'idols are nothing', no more than 'a block of crafted wood'. Isaiah then pointedly reminded the Jews how Yahweh had 'crafted' them.

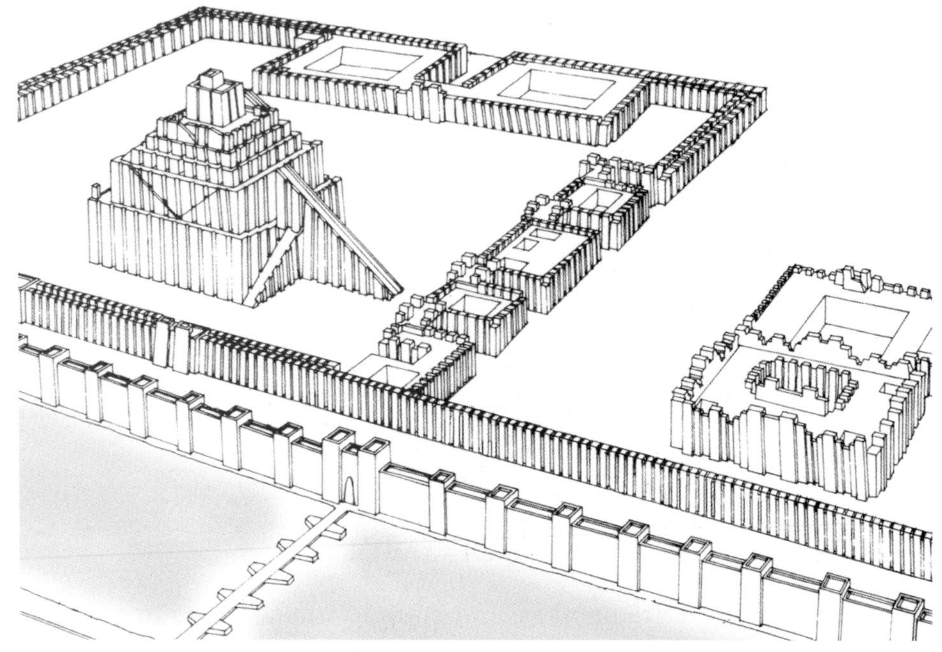

The ziggurat of Marduk opposite the Esagila temple at Babylon

Yet behind this prophetic outburst lay blatant examples of Jewish idolatry. At Tell Dothan, north of Hebron, a bronze bull has been unearthed that once represented Yahweh, who was often called 'the bull of Jacob'. In the northern kingdom of Israel a shrine at Bethel also contained a 'holy calf', while in II Kings we learn how King Hezekiah 'brake the images, and cut down groves, and brake in pieces the brazen serpent that Moses had made: for unto these days the children of Israel did burn incense to it'.

Non-Jewish peoples were also concerned about the authenticity of cult statues. The Assyrian king Esarhaddon expressed grave doubts while refurbishing the temple of Esagila, after his father's sack of Babylon in 689 BC. Whether the Assyrians had forcibly removed Marduk's cult statue and were simply concerned with its repair, or whether another one had to be created from scratch, is unclear. But we know that diviners told Esarhaddon to make good the destruction visited upon Babylon by Assyrian troops. Yet he asked: 'Whose right is it, O great gods, to create gods and goddesses in a place where man dare not trespass? The task of refurbishment which you have given me is difficult ... The making of cult statues is yours, it is in your hands.'

Yet ancient Near Eastern peoples did evolve a method of ensuring that a cult statue was correctly created: that it was 'born in heaven, made on earth'. The special ritual and incantations involved were called in Babylonian *mis pi*, in Sumerian *kaluhuda*, meaning 'mouth-washing'. It was akin to the Egyptian ritual used in workshops where divine statues were carved. Obviously the aim was to credit the gods with the process of manufacture, which is why the craftsmen who actually made the images symbolically cut off their hands with knives of tamarisk wood. They also disclaimed any responsibility for the work they had done. How important it was for Esarhaddon to return the cult statues to Babylon is evident in the festivities which marked their journey from Ashur to Babylon. Every half kilometre, piles of brushwood were lit as the procession passed; while every two kilometres, a bull was sacrificed. On the arrival of the procession in Babylon, the cult statues were taken at once to 'the orchards, where the rituals of mouth-washing and mouth-opening, washing and purification were performed, before the stars of heaven, before the great gods'.

In their view of the cosmos Babylonians were unique, since very few Semites paid much attention to the idea of creation. In the *Enuma Elish* epic there is, however, a detailed description of the origin of the universe as well as Marduk's decisive confrontation with the forces of chaos. Marduk's name more correctly read is Merodakh, as in the Bible; and in its extended form, Bel Merodakh, the connection with the West Semitic storm god Baal is transparent.

Marduk's cosmic opponent was the ocean, in the form of Tiamat, a dreadful sea monster and the prototype of Leviathan, 'the coiled one'. At Marduk's challenge, Tiamat let out a terrible roar and started to tremble with rage as she threw herself into the attack. Like the Sumerian warrior god Ninurta facing Azag, the Babylonian champion did not flinch but instead caught Tiamat up in a great net, so that she opened her mouth in surprise. Then, 'driving in a tempest to stop her closing her lips', Marduk 'let fly an arrow which spilt her belly and penetrated her heart. Finally he held her fast until she died.' From Tiamat's dismembered body Marduk created the world, before returning to Babylon where he was crowned 'king of the gods'. The idea of a serpentine monster passed through Judaism to Christianity, where famously in the story of St George and the Dragon a lone knight battles with a fearsome creature not previously encountered in western Europe.

A Babylonian dragon whose ferocity recalls that of Tiamat

Although the Semites were more interested in dragons than the Sumerians, with snake-dragons and lion-dragons appearing in Babylonian bas-reliefs and statues, encounters with formidable creatures had already happened in Sumer. The divine champion Ninurta dealt with all these troublesome monsters during his heroic adventures. This 'strong son of Enlil' may well be the model for Herakles, 'the doughty son of Zeus', since the twelve labours undertaken by the Greek hero bear a strong resemblance to Ninurta's challenges, from each of which the Sumerian god brought back impressive trophies to his city. So terrified was King Eurystheus of Tiryns by the creatures Herakles captured on his behalf that he kept handy a storage jar in which he could take refuge.

The rise of Marduk to a supreme position in Babylon was the consequence of a synthesis of Sumerian and Semitic beliefs. This process was already underway at the time of Akkad's empire, after which Sumerian gods and goddesses were transformed into Semitic equivalents. With astral deities such as the Sumerian sun god Utu this was comparatively easy, but with complicated goddesses like Inanna the transition was slower: Utu became Shamash, while Inanna was eventually worshipped as Ishtar. Initially Enlil and Marduk were regarded as equals, but later Marduk was raised above all other deities, once Nebuchadrezzar I recovered his cult statue from the Elamites. Before the end of this king's reign in 1104 BC, the *Enuma Elish* epic had ensured Marduk's unstoppable rise to supremacy.

Marduk's overtaking of An and Enlil in the cosmic order was, however, the continuation of a struggle for supremacy which went all the way back to Sumerian times. Then the heirs of the primeval deities Enmesarra and Ninmesarra seized control; they were in fact An and Enlil. This idea of a violent overthrow of the first gods by their offspring ultimately shaped Greek cosmology. According to Hesiod, who composed his *Theogony* soon after 700 BC, the sky god Ouranos feared his children so much that he hid them in a cavern, which pressed tightly inside his wife Gaia, the earth goddess. To alleviate the pain Gaia gave her son Kronos a sharp sickle in order to cut off Ouranos' genitals. Fearing later on that he would also be deposed like his father, Kronos swallowed his own children at birth with the exception of Zeus, for whom his distraught wife Rhea substituted a stone wrapped in swaddling clothes. When he came of age, Zeus obliged Kronos to vomit up all his brothers and sisters, the Olympian gods.

In the subsequent struggle between generations, Kronos and his Titan allies were overcome with the aid of the Cyclopes, one-eyed giants he had earlier imprisoned. The defeated Titans were confined by Zeus in Tartarus, the lowest part of the cosmos. But he allowed his father to live in Elysium, where Kronos held sway over the blessed dead. The stone that Rhea used to fool Kronos remained a holy object at the Delphic Oracle in central Greece.

According to the Mesopotamian priest Berossus, the key event in Marduk's victory over Tiamat was the separation of heaven and earth, which allowed the formation of sun, the moon and the stars. Berossus' account of creation opens at a time when the universe was filled with water, in which creatures resembling human beings with two or four wings dwelt along with fishes and reptiles. In the *Babylonica*, an account of Babylonian cosmology that Berossus wrote for the Macedonian king Antiochus I in the 280s, all these watery life forms were ruled by a woman, who was undoubtedly Tiamat. By 'splitting her in half', Marduk not only separated heaven and earth but even more he 'destroyed the creatures within her'. These denizens of the deep 'all died as they could not stand the force of the light'. That Antiochus, the second king of the

Antiochus I, whose Seleucid kingdom remained true to the multi-ethnic vision of Alexander

Seleucid dynasty, took a great interest in ancient Near Eastern beliefs should not appear as unusual. As a cosmopolitan ruler, this Macedonian king was prepared to be a Greek in the eastern Mediterranean, a Persian in his Asian dominions, and of course a Babylonian in Mesopotamia. Contemporary Macedonian rulers of Egypt, the descendants of Alexander the Great's general Ptolemy, commissioned from an Egyptian priest named Manetho an historical account of the pharaonic period, which stretched from around 3100 BC to the founding of the Ptolemaic dynasty in 305 BC. For both the Seleucids and the Ptolemies there was an urgent need to come to terms with the ancient cultures of their subjects.

WEST SEMITIC DEITIES

At the start of the second millennium BC, the Amorites appeared in the upper valley of the Euphrates and set up a number of kingdoms there, including Mari. These West Semitic tribesmen also took over Syrian cities such as Ebla, or Tell Mardikh, nearly 40 kilometres south of Aleppo. Already a prosperous trading city with 250,000 Semitic inhabitants before the arrival of the Amorites, Ebla was administered by a bureaucracy of 1,100 scribes, whose output accounts for the massive cuneiform archive uncovered there. Some of this archive is written in Eblaite, the name given to this West Semitic language which may slightly pre-date written Akkadian. From Sumerian–Eblaite dictionaries it is clear that Sumerian deities were paired with West Semitic gods and goddesses having the same functions. Thus Namtar, the Sumerian god of pestilence, is paired with Resheph, and the sun god Utu with Shapshu. In the Akkadian language Utu's name was rendered as Shamash. It had been the overwhelming quantity of offerings that the Sumerians dedicated to Namtar which prevented Enlil from reducing the population through plague, and obliged the sleepless storm god to resort finally to the device of the Flood.

Another ethnic change among the West Semites was the arrival of the Aramaeans at the end of the second millennium BC. They came to prominence in Syria, where they stubbornly resisted Assyrian aggression. Before the rise of Damascus, the tiny city-states they founded were preoccupied with their own squabbles, but King Ben-Hadad II of Damascus forced the Jews to combine with the Aramaeans in a defensive alliance against Assyria. Aramaean religious beliefs survived into the Christian era, although infused with Greek elements. Inscriptions written in Aramaic from Palmyra bear witness to this during the reign of Queen Zenobia, who defied Rome

A tablet written in Eblaite, an early West Semitic language

for half a dozen years in the third century. Her attempt to expand Palmyra's influence failed and the emperor Aurelian crushed this impertinence in 273. Palmyra ceased being an independent kingdom but its strategic location on an east–west caravan route soon allowed it to recover economically. There were still impressive ruins to be seen as late as 2015, when the Islamic State blew up its main temples.

The West Semitic pantheon is now fairly well known, thanks to excavations during the twentieth century. A crucial advance in our knowledge resulted from the discovery of religious texts at Tell Ras Shamra, the site of ancient Ugarit in northern Syria. The excavations there from 1926 onwards revealed the city-state's religion at the height of its prosperity in the fourteenth century BC. The supreme Ugaritic deity was El, who had full authority over the gods and humanity. Yet he is described as being 'old' and, not unlike the Sumerian sky god An, he was remote. Even though he is compared with a bull to emphasize his strength, a more active role was usurped by Baal, whose name means 'owner' or 'lord'. This Canaanite god of the storm was not unlike Marduk and Enlil, although his death and resurrection recall the experience of Dumuzi, the earliest known dying-and-rising god in the ancient Near East.

The possibility that Baal was a universal deity is hard to determine because Baal was a title attached to many local gods. Baal-Sidon, Baal-Hazor and Baal-Haran are obvious examples, while Baal-berith, 'lord of the covenant', appears in the Bible. Some biblical scholars look upon Baal as an aspect of El, who seems to have been identified with Yahweh. The Old Testament never disparages El, but rather sees Yahweh as his close associate, on occasion even his subordinate. In Psalms we learn that El 'standeth in the congregation of the mighty; he judgeth among the gods'. Here is the Jewish version of the Mesopotamian divine assembly which met in Enlil's temple at Nippur and Marduk's temple at Babylon. Such a gathering of the gods corresponds exactly with the arrangement described in the Ugarit texts. Even more tantalizing in Genesis is the description of El Elyon as 'the possessor of heaven and earth'. At Ugarit he was also 'the creator of creatures'.

Although the Ark was brought by King David to Jerusalem in the tenth century BC because it represented neutral ground, there already existed a shrine dedicated to El. Its presence seemed less significant than the fact that the site did not belong to any of the twelve Jewish tribes. The Ark was a wooden box symbolizing Yahweh, and it always accompanied Jewish armies on their expeditions in order to secure divine assistance. It was at Jerusalem that El seems finally to have merged with Yahweh, after which El Elyon, 'god most high', became one of the epithets of the Jewish deity.

El, the chief West Semitic deity

For the people of Ugarit, Baal was characterized by the rainstorm. By the provision of water, however heavy the downpour, this deity guaranteed the growth of crops and was therefore worshipped as a fertility god. Baal ruled the sky, and his dwelling place was north of Ugarit at Mount Saphon, which the ancient Greeks regarded as the equivalent of Olympus, the mountain home of their own deities. In spite of the construction of ziggurats in Mesopotamian cities, there was no veneration of mountains there: Leonard Woolley's interpretation of the ziggurat at Ur was therefore misplaced. Only the West Semites revered cosmic peaks as the venue for meetings of the gods, the source of water and fertility, the battlefield of conflicting natural forces, and the place where divine decrees were issued. In the Bible of course the cosmic mountain is Mount Zion, a large hill situated near Jerusalem. Quite different were the Mesopotamian ziggurats, the residences of city-gods. A god or a goddess was believed to dwell at the top of a ziggurat, well above the hubbub of a city, but their cult statues were carried down to a temple at ground level whenever they held court. Even though the city of Nippur was regarded as the cosmic centre of the universe, the Sumerians never compared it with a mountain.

The very different terrain of the biblical lands, a mixture of mountains and hills as well as lowlands and desert, must account for the idea of a cosmic peak, just as the Egyptians envisaged a primeval hill as the place where creation began. Without any high ground at all in Egypt, this could only have happened from watching the sinking of the Nile's annual flood waters and the rise of the first isolated mud banks, refreshed with fertile silt and rich with life. So Amun-Re was said to have started creation on such a hillock arising from Nun, the primeval waters. One Egyptian myth even refers to Nun as 'father of the gods', the source of everything in the cosmos. He appeared in a variety of forms such as the Nile floods, spring water and the ocean surrounding the world. His dwelling place was similar to Abzu, the life-sustaining reservoir which the Sumerian water god Enki protected underground. To Nun's abode the other gods would descend at the end of the annual inundation of the Nile valley in order to request that he maintain a sufficient supply of water in Egypt to ensure good harvests. Nun was visualized as a man standing waist-deep in water, his arms raised to hold aloft the barque of the sun.

Mount Zaphon was the scene of cosmic battles, but Baal's greatest contest happened away from his mountain stronghold when he opposed Mot, death itself. For the name Mot is identical with the Hebrew word *maweth*, which means 'death'. The clay tablets found at Ugarit describing the contest between Baal and Mot are badly damaged, but the storyline is clear enough: it centres upon Mot's attempt to usurp Baal's throne. Mot is represented as the drought and heat of summer which withers vegetation, and confines Baal in the underworld, when the god's death is signalled by the absence of life-giving rain. Baal's escape from Mot's underground kingdom was effected by the goddess Anat, who slew Mot with the aid of the sun goddess Shapshu. Together they reinstated Baal, largely for the reason that another god who had moved to Mount Zaphon in Baal's absence could not properly exercise divine authority.

Their triumph over death is expressed in distinctly agricultural imagery: winnowing, grinding and sowing in the fields. One tablet relates how 'as the days passed, Anat sought Baal like a cow yearning for her calf, like a ewe yearning for her lamb, so the heart of Anat yearned for Baal. Then she seized Mot by the hem of his garment, she constrained him by holding his robe, and demanded Baal's release from death.' When Mot declined to meet her demand, Shapshu glowed hot and Anat 'seized divine Mot and with a sword she split him in two'. Mot's dismembered corpse was then scattered in the open fields for the birds to eat, and thrown into the sea as food for the fish to consume. Anat appears to have been a beautiful but bloodthirsty goddess. At Ugarit she was looked upon as the daughter of El and the sister of Baal, whom she always assisted and with whom she had sexual relations after transforming herself into a cow. Anat was popular in Syria, Palestine and even Egypt, where she was a warrior goddess 'who dresses as a man'.

Prior to his combat with Mot, Baal had already battled with Yam, the sea itself, in an encounter which in some respects can be compared with Marduk's defeat of Tiamat in the Babylonian creation myth. Yet another watery challenger of Baal was Lotan, 'the swift serpent ... the coiled serpent with seven heads', which the storm god also crushed. In biblical tradition, Lotan becomes Leviathan in the Book of Job as well as Psalms. Like Marduk and then Baal, Yahweh is praised for dominating the salt waters: 'Thou didst divide the sea by thy strength: thou brakest the heads of the dragons in the waters. Thou brakest the heads of Leviathan into pieces, and gave him to be the meat of the people inhabiting the wilderness.'

Whereas the Jews adopted the myth of Baal's defeat of Lotan to glorify their own god, placing special emphasis on Yahweh's strength, the Ugarit texts remain primarily concerned with a basic West Semitic idea: the death and resurrection of their most powerful deity.

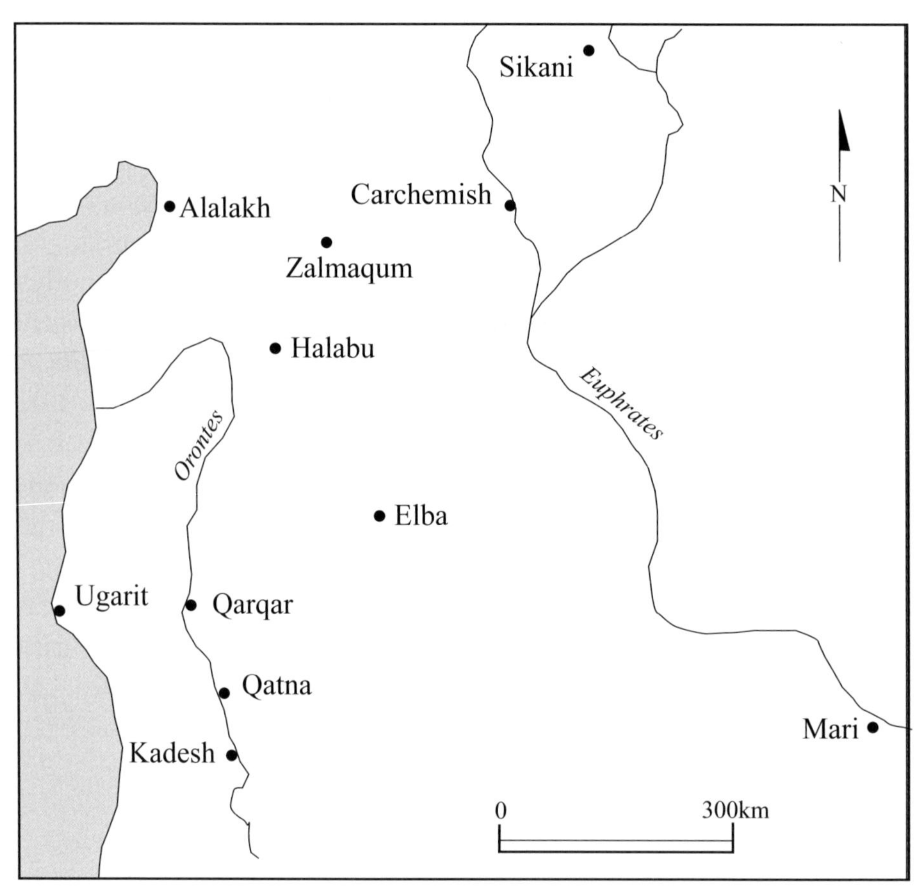

Ancient Syria

5

THE BIBLICAL LANDS

When the Lord thy God shall bring thee into the land whither thou goest to possess it, and hath cast out many nations before thee, the Hittites, and the Girgashites, and the Amorites, and the Canaanites, and the Perizzites, and the Hivites, and the Jebusites, seven nations greater than thou. And the Lord thy God shall deliver them before thee; thou shalt smite them, and utterly destroy them; thou shalt make no covenant with them, nor shew mercy unto them.

Deuteronomy 7: 1–2

That the passage goes on to outlaw marriage between the Jews and the peoples mentioned above only serves to underline the exclusiveness demanded by Yahweh. After conquering the inhabitants of Palestine, the Jews were told 'to destroy their altars, and break down their images, and cut down their groves, and burn their graven images with fire', because they alone were the 'holy people' whom 'the Lord thy God hath chosen unto himself, above all people that are upon the face of the earth'. Despite this assertion in the Bible of an unbridgeable ethnic and cultural divide, historically the West Semites and the Jews lived side by side in what are usually called the biblical lands: Syria, Lebanon and Palestine. Phoenicia was the name given by the Greeks in the first millennium BC to the coastal strip of modern Lebanon.

The Hebrews or Israelites, as the Jews were then called, did not appear in Palestine until late in the second millennium BC. Their most formidable enemy was in fact the Philistines, who may well have been the Peleset, one of the Sea Peoples who remained in Palestine after the failure of their assault on Egypt. The five great Philistine cities were Ashdod, Ashkelon, Ekron, Gath and Gaza, the pillars of whose chief temple a sightless Samson pulled down to crush his captors. At first the Philistines probably formed no more than a ruling warrior-class, but by the reign of King David, who came to the Jewish throne around 1000 BC, they had become indistinguishable from the rest of the population. Prior to David's success against the Philistines, they had come close to wiping out the Jews.

The incredible story of David's slaying of Goliath, the giant Philistine champion, clearly has a legendary source. Heroic feat though it certainly was, the contest is reminiscent of the Egyptian hero Sinuhe's killing of another fearful challenger who 'fell on his nose with an arrow sticking in his neck'. What the defeat of Goliath reflected was David's growing popularity as well as the power 'of the Lord of hosts, the God of the armies of Israel', who let David triumph with one of the 'five smooth stones' he had gathered from a brook. A single stone was enough to sink into Goliath's forehead, so that 'he fell upon his face to the earth'. When the Philistines saw David cut off the head of their prone champion, they fled.

The savage eruption of the Sea Peoples was halted by Ramesses III when these invaders tried to conquer Egypt. In 1182 BC one group was stopped by the pharaoh in Palestine, another in a sea battle off the Nile delta. On the walls of his memorial temple at Medinet Habu, Ramesses records how the Sea Peoples moved south from Syria. They had: 'made a conspiracy in their islands. All at once the lands were on the move, scattered in war. No country could stand before their arms from Hatti ... to Alasiya ... They were advancing on Egypt ... The Peleset, Tjeker, Shekelesh, Denyen and Weshesh, united lands ... Against them I readied my troops and made the mouth of the Nile into a strong wall of ships ... manned with picked men. The chariotry comprised the best runners and every accomplished charioteer warrior'.

Most of these attackers were new enemies. The Tjeker seem to have come from western Asia Minor and wore their hair in the distinctive upright fashion favoured by the Peleset. The Shekelesh were most probably the Sicels who gave their name to the island of Sicily. The Denyen

An Egyptian ship battles against the Sea Peoples

were no strangers to Egypt, since letters in the Amarna archive refer to the 'land of Danuna', situated to the north of Ugarit. But the homeland of the Weshesh remains a mystery. Even though we can dismiss any notion of coordination amongst these peoples, the evidence suggests that Asia Minor was the epicentre of the storm of destruction which then swept across Syria and Palestine, before coming to a halt on the Egyptian frontier. A variety of peoples were attracted by the opportunities for plunder and land that this great disturbance offered.

In the Medinet Habu account of Egypt's successful resistance to the Sea Peoples, attention is drawn to 'the best runners and every accomplished chariot warrior'. On the battlefield these two had to work closely together, because the runners protected the chariots from being attacked by enemy infantry. 'The swarms' of Sea Peoples which had overwhelmed other chariotries could not repeat this tactic against the Egyptians, because their runners, the Shardana, remained loyal to the pharaoh.

These tough mercenaries hailed from Libya, from where another group of Shardana migrated to Sardinia, to which island they gave the name.

SYRIA

Ignoring perhaps Hittite advice to 'fortify your towns, bring troops and chariots into them, and wait for the enemy with firm feet', King Ammurapi of Ugarit was unable to offer much resistance to the Sea Peoples. The city's destruction around 1190 BC seems to have coincided with a rundown of its armed forces. Shortly before this event, the Hittites complained to Ammurapi that 'the charioteers you sent are of inferior quality and their horses half-starved', making this contingent impossible to deploy in their army. With growing instability in Syria, Ugarit may have been reluctant to dispatch its best troops to Hatti.

This hesitation made little difference in the event; Ugarit was still seized by the Sea Peoples and set ablaze. We are fortunate in the survival of Ugarit's extensive archive of clay tablets, which were written in an alphabetic cuneiform script. These texts provide a rare insight into the

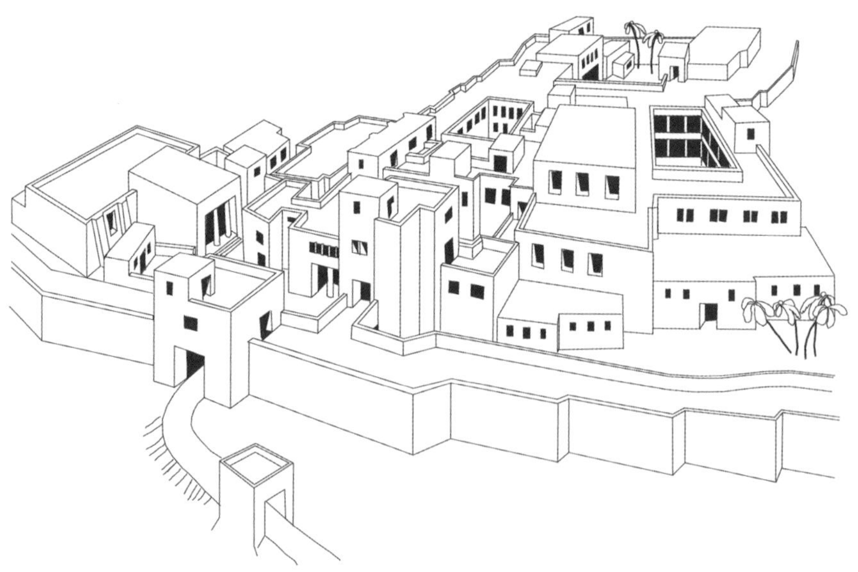

The royal palace at Ugarit

nature of West Semitic worship. Great stress is laid on the sacrificial role of the king: he provided animals for the major public ceremonies and presided over these events. One list, which included a bull and a ram for El, mentions five bulls, one cow, ten rams and a bird that were 'burnt offerings' for other deities. Clearly the royal palace safeguarded the kingdom by pleasing every god and goddess, while also asserting its primacy in religious observances. It would appear that the king of Ugarit was active in one form of ritual or another throughout the hours of daylight, so that only with the departure of the sun goddess Shapshu westwards did these sacred duties come to an end.

In Ugarit, the queen mother was the high priestess of Athirat, an astral deity. In Egypt the queen and the queen mother were both high priestesses of Hathor, a cow goddess with solar associations. In her capacity as the bearer of the solar disc, Hathor sustained the sun as well as the pharaoh. Queens in Egypt and Syria were therefore high priestesses of the sun goddess, if indeed Athirat was a sun goddess too. In Ugarit, though, no text refers to the Flood, a myth with obvious Mesopotamian connections. But in Egypt, however, the goddess Hathor does feature in a flood story, when the sun god Ra became convinced that human beings were plotting against him and sent Hathor to drown them. Luckily for the Egyptians, the cow goddess was so entranced by her own reflection in the water that she forgot her grisly task, and they were therefore saved from drowning.

A prince from the city of Ugarit

Unlike Ugarit, the inland city of Mari's nemesis was not the Sea Peoples, but the Babylonian king Hammurabi. Situated on the Euphrates, Mari rose to prominence during the 1800s BC, when it expanded slowly in order to provoke neither Assyria nor Babylon. Subsequent rulers followed this foreign policy down to the reign of Zimri-Lim, who threw caution to the winds and triggered in 1761 BC the Babylonian sack. The archive found in Zimri-Lim's palace is another rich source of information about ancient Syria, even though Mari was inevitably more concerned with Mesopotamian affairs. It is indeed from the letters of Zimri-Lim that we learn about the Amorite kingdoms of Yamkhad, with its capital at Halabu, modern Aleppo; Qatna, located north-east of Homs; Zalmaqum and Alalakh, both of whose ruins are situated just across the border in modern Turkey.

Without any success, Zimri-Lim asked the king of Qatna for horses, which he offered to exchange for a quantity of tin, a crucial ingredient for the manufacture of bronze. He may well have received wine instead, for on one occasion Zimri-Lim sent to Hammurabi 'ten jars of the wine of the sort I drink myself'. Beer was still the main alcoholic drink at Mari, where a sweet beer was brewed with barley and pomegranates: it always featured in royal banquets, with as much as 1,000 litres being drunk at a single meal. Here, as elsewhere in the ancient Near East, beer was imbibed through a straw, as this protected the drinker from bits and pieces floating in the beer itself, plus any insects which may have landed on its surface.

Hammurabi's destruction of Mari was carried out systematically. An inscription relates how the Babylonian king 'pulled down the walls and left the place as no more than mounds and ruins'. That is why Zimri-Lim's palace was discovered by archaeologists in a relatively good condition. When the upper storey was smashed, it tumbled down onto the rooms below on the ground floor, where some of them when excavated still had walls 4 metres high.

The political vacuum left by the fall of Mari was briefly filled by the kingdom of Alalakh, one of whose rulers acknowledged Parattarna, the first king of Mitanni, as his overlord. No power in the ancient Near East could claim supremacy without undisputed control of the kingdoms and cities that lay between the Euphrates and the Mediterranean, a feat first achieved by the Mitannians. At Tell Atchana, the site of ancient Alalakh, Leonard Woolley unearthed in the 1930s a statue of King Idrimi. The cuneiform inscription on the statue, written in Akkadian, throws light on

Mitanni's supremacy, an otherwise unrecorded period of power. After suffering a long exile, Idrimi persuaded King Parattarna to install him as the ruler of Alalakh. Idrimi had set his sights on the kingdom of Yamkhad, where he had a claim to the throne, but in the end he contented himself with Alalakh. Other Syrian kings objected to this arrangement, but Mitanni put down their armed opposition with brute force. Alalakh fell in 1370 BC to the Hittites, a bitter enemy of Mitanni.

Idrimi, the Mitannian-backed king of Alalakh

South of Aleppo the most important Syrian city was Ebla, which phoenix-like recovered from two destructions before finally disappearing as a major trading centre. King Sargon of Akkad is said to have destroyed Ebla first of all in the late third millennium BC on his drive to the Mediterranean, but it was his grandson Naramsin who claimed responsibility. The arrival of the Amorites proved a shot in the arm for Ebla, although it has been plausibly argued that these Semites always lived in Syria and later migration merely increased their numbers. Whatever the truth, Ebla's trading network was re-established and the city prospered until it provoked the wrath of Mitanni, whose storm god Teshub is credited with its second destruction in the middle of the second millennium BC. During the third and final phase of its prosperity, Ebla was noted for the fine quality of the textiles which were widely exported. The territory over which the Eblaites held sway was a substantial one, but low rainfall meant that it could only be used effectively for grazing flocks that produced an abundant supply of wool. Apart from this valuable commodity, Ebla's wealth derived from its central position in east–west trade.

The Hittites finally destroyed Ebla as they pushed south into Syria, most likely as a punishment for the city's friendliness with the Egyptians.

Rivalry between Hatti and Egypt over Syria led in 1274 BC to the climactic chariot engagement at Kadesh. Thousands of these fast-moving war machines clashed beneath the walls of this Syrian city, whose switch from being an Egyptian vassal to a Hittite one had caused the conflict. An impetuous advance by Ramesses II almost cost the young pharaoh his life when he ventured into a cleverly laid Hittite trap. What Ramesses did not realize as the few Egyptian chariots with him in the vanguard approached Kadesh was that behind the city thousands of chariots awaited the moment to attack. Without his entire army at his disposal, the pharaoh had to fight off the Hittites as best he could until reinforcements arrived. Ramesses just managed to do so and claim the victory, but a military stalemate forced the Egyptians to accept a degree of coexistence with several ancient Near Eastern states, despite a deep uneasiness in Egypt about the pharaoh's parity with their rulers. That was the reason for a prohibition on the marriage of Egyptian princesses to foreign kings. Pharaohs could take foreign wives, but non-Egyptians were regarded as socially inferior to members of the Egyptian royal family, no matter how exulted their status was at home. Princesses were simply not available for marriage outside Egypt.

With such a national outlook, the request of Tutankhamun's widow, Queen Ankhesenamun, for a Hittite prince as a husband was unprecedented. Pharaoh Tutankhamun had died after a short reign in 1346 BC, probably from injuries sustained in a chariot accident. Early examination of the nineteen-year-old pharaoh's mummy revealed a wound on the left cheek, over the jawbone near the ear, suggesting that he may have suffered a cerebral haemorrhage. This discovery encouraged the notion of assassination until an x-ray found considerable additional damage, since the mummy lacked a breastbone as well as the frontal ribcage. Most likely he died hunting, if Tutankhamun was rash enough to drive alone, as he is shown doing so on the handle of an ostrich feather fan recovered from his tomb. A scene shows him firing a composite bow from a speeding chariot, with the reins tied around his body. Should the wheels of the vehicle have struck a stone, or one of the chariot horses stumbled, the pharaoh would have been shot through the air head first like a missile fired from a catapult. Only the most experienced charioteers were capable of steering a spending chariot without using their hands.

Tutankhamun hunting with the reins of his chariot around his waist

The only surviving son of Pharaoh Akhenaten, whose religious reforms had thrown Egypt into turmoil, Tutankhamun allowed worship in the country to return to normal. Within three years of his succession, the temples of the ram-headed god Amun were functioning once again, and the young pharaoh changed his own name from Tutankhaten, 'the living image of the solar disc Aten', to Tutankhamun, 'the living image of Amun'. Unfinished funerary monuments attest to the unexpectedness of Tutankhamun's death, which left a vacuum at the Egyptian court that Queen Ankhesenamun endeavoured to fill herself. A patriarchal society though it was, Egypt appears more liberal as regards female leaders than ancient Near Eastern states. Possibly continuing military reverses in Syria at the hands of the Hittites prompted Queen Ankhesenamun's request for a princely husband. In the letter that the widowed queen sent to the Hittite King Suppiluliuma I, she said: 'I do not want to take a servant of mine and make him my husband ... Give me one of your sons; to me he will be husband, but in the land of Egypt he will be king!' The Hittite king Suppiluliuma was at Carchemish when this letter arrived. His initial reaction was incredulity. Surely the request hid bad intentions, because a Hittite prince would be a useful hostage to threaten during an international crisis. But finally Suppiluliuma came round to the view that the queen offered a way for 'the land of Hatti and the land of Egypt to enjoy eternal friendship with each other'.

So King Suppiluliuma dispatched one of his sons by the name of Zannanza to Egypt. How far Queen Ankhesenamun had the backing of the courtiers in her bid to stay in power is now impossible to tell, but opponents of handing over the throne to a foreigner could have easily ambushed the Hittite prince as he travelled through Palestine, because Zannanza never reached Egypt. A considerable delay in Tutankhamun's burial was undoubtedly intended to give Zannanza time to arrive and be proclaimed pharaoh. With the non-arrival of the Hittite prince, and little likelihood that Suppiluliuma would risk sending another son, an Egyptian candidate came forward to play the essential role in Tutankhamun's internment, and belatedly become the pharaoh. This happened to be Ay, the seventy-year-old commander of Egypt's chariotry.

Whatever the cause of Zannanza's disappearance, Suppiluliuma held the Egyptians responsible and his fury knew no bounds. The new pharaoh wrote to him, denying any involvement in the tragedy, and seeking to renew the former ties of friendship between the two kingdoms. Brushing aside Ay's paltry excuses, the Hittite king attacked the vassal states of Egypt in Syria and Palestine, carrying off many thousands of Egypt's subjects to Hatti. It is not a little ironic that they took with them a plague which ravaged the Hittites for a generation: among its victims were Suppiluliuma and his eldest son. Plague had been rampant in Syria, Palestine and Cyprus for a number of years, and it spread to Egypt during a durbar arranged by Akhenaten, when 'all the countries came together, and the lands in the midst of the sea, bringing gifts to Aten'. A letter in the Amarna archive from a Cypriot king blames the tiny gift of copper that he had sent upon the plague which decimated his copper workers.

PHOENICIA

After the upheavals of the twelfth century BC that witnessed the sudden incursion of the Sea Peoples as well as the arrival of the Aramaeans and the Jews, the only area in which local cultural and political traditions survived relatively undisturbed was the narrow coastal plain now known as Lebanon. Here the Phoenicians responded to pressure inland by turning to the Mediterranean as a means of dealing with a surplus population in their port-cities. Like the Greeks later on, they sailed in search of places to colonize, and built up a trading network second to none: its hub was the great city of Carthage in present-day Tunisia. By the end of the sixth century BC, Phoenician merchants had begun employing sailing vessels capable of transporting anything from 70 to 500 tonnes of cargo, depending on the size of the ship. Although these sailing ships did not replace the merchant galley, they existed alongside it and from this time onwards competed with it for cargo on runs where the prevailing winds were favourable.

The Greek historian Herodotus' account of the conflict between Persia and Greece during the early part of the fifth century BC is full of praise for the Phoenicians. He tells us how they were excellent sailors and great explorers, circumnavigating the African continent before anyone else.

A Phoenician merchant ship

The strength of the Phoenicians at sea made their navy vital to the Persians, once they became a subject people in 538 BC. Herodotus is also scrupulous in drawing attention to the positive contribution that Phoenicia made to Greek civilization. According to him, the Phoenicians introduced the alphabet, without which the Greeks could not have written down their language. Much earlier a linear script had been used in mainland Greece at palaces such as Mycenae and Pylos, but after they were sacked by the Sea Peoples it disappeared as there were no longer any palace records to keep.

Phoenician cities were not unlike Greek settlements in their interest in self-government and commerce. Evidence of international trade comes from the Egyptian story of the priest Wenamun, who was sent to Byblos on an official mission. By an almost miraculous stroke of good fortune a copy of Wenamun's own account of the trip was found on a tattered roll of papyrus in an Egyptian field. Sent from Amun's great temple at Thebes, Wenamun's objective was the purchase of cedar wood needed for the construction of a ceremonial barge. The absence of forests in Mesopotamia as well as Egypt made Syria and Phoenicia an indispensable source of supply. Wenamun's journey around 1130 BC occurred at a time when Egypt was no longer the power it had been in the eastern Mediterranean. As a result, Wenamun was robbed, ignored and overcharged. As the ruler of Byblos pointed out, the city-ports of Phoenicia were now independent states. What he did not mention, though, was the steady depletion of the cedar forests, a concern expressed as early as the composition of the *Gilgamesh* epic. A newly discovered section of the poem records the sadness felt by Gilgamesh and his companion Enkidu after they slew Humbaba and his seven sons, the guardians of the great cedar trees. They seem to be saying that there should be some limit to the damage inflicted on a foreign land.

No such idea ever entered the heads of the Assyrians, for whom almost continuous military campaigns were a sure method of gathering vast quantities of loot. But it was only in Esarhaddon's reign that the Phoenician port-cities were brought under Assyrian control. In 676 BC Sidon was sacked, its ruler executed and its inhabitants deported, for siding with rebellious Syrian states. Some of Sidon's possessions were given to Tyre, then still loyal to Assyria, while the rest was reorganized under an Assyrian governor. When the Tyrians defaulted on their tribute in 635 BC, however, those who lived onshore as opposed to the island city itself were massacred.

Within the Assyrian empire, vassal rulers were bound to Assyria through treaties which were solemnized by religious sanctions, witnessed by the god Ashur and local deities. Breaking such agreements allowed the Assyrians to react without any kind of restraint. Yet Assyria tended to leave the internal affairs of a vassal kingdom alone, provided tribute was regularly paid. Defeated rulers, on the other hand, were regarded as the Assyrian king's slaves: their fate depended entirely upon individual circumstances. One ex-ruler was obliged to run alongside the wheel of Tiglath-Pileser III's chariot. This form of public humiliation remained popular in the ancient Near East until the Sasanian period. After his surrender in 260, the Roman emperor Valerian acted as Shapur I's footstool whenever the Sasanian king mounted his horse.

Whenever it was considered expedient, the Assyrians converted vassal states into administered provinces. This happened in Phoenicia where Assyrian officials attached to local courts took over responsibility for internal affairs. This might turn the existing ruler into a 'governor' responsible to Assyria, or it could lead to his replacement. At Tell Fekheriye, ancient Sikani in northern Syria, a 2-metre-high basalt statue of Adad-iti, probably a contemporary of Shalmaneser III, throws a sharp light on these arrangements. Along the skirt of this figure's tunic are two inscriptions, one at the front written in Akkadian, the other at the back in Aramaic. Whereas the front inscription says Adad-iti was an Assyrian 'governor', the back inscription describes him as a 'king'. Obviously the latter was cut in order to reassure his Aramaean subjects about their situation by giving the impression that it was business as usual.

An outstanding feature of Phoenician culture was its close relationship with Cyprus, where colonization was not in all probability the result of conquest, but rather the arrival of Phoenicians seeking commercial opportunities. Kition, modern Larnaca, provides the clearest evidence for Phoenician occupation; by 850 BC, this settlement possessed a great temple dedicated to the goddess Astarte. That it was an adaptation of an existing Greek building indicates Cyprus' earlier links with mainland Greece.

Perhaps it should be recalled that Elissa, the sister of the Tyrian king, fled first to Cyprus after her husband, the high priest of Melqart, failed to secure the throne for one of their sons. Tyrian nobles and their families resident on the island joined Elissa as she voyaged onwards and formed the nucleus of the population of Carthage, which she founded in 814 BC. The name Carthage derives, through Latin, from the Phoenician Kart-hadasht, meaning 'new city'. It shows that the Phoenician settlers intended that this city should be more than a convenient stopping point on the route to Spain, where the Straits of Gibraltar had already been named the Straits of Melqart. Identified with Herakles by the Greeks, the Phoenician Melqart was in fact a solar deity with marine attributes, and not a semi-divine hero.

Before setting out for Carthage, Elissa's expedition recruited eighty young girls in Cyprus who were destined for sacred prostitution so as to ensure the continuation of traditional Phoenician worship in the west. These young women would have served the goddess Astarte in the same manner as their equivalents in Mesopotamia participated in the worship of Inanna and Ishtar. For the Greeks and the Romans these fertility goddesses were reincarnated as Aphrodite and Venus respectively. Never quite comfortable with the erotic side of Venus' cult, Rome may have had good reason for its concern, because we know how sacred prostitution was practised in Carthaginian-dominated western Sicily. The Roman people always had a puritanical streak.

Another religious trait that disturbed Rome was *molk*, the sacrifice of Phoenician children in the *tophet*, a sacred enclosure set aside for this bloody rite. At Carthage, there are an estimated 20,000 urns filled with the burned bones of infants. *Tophet* seems to have come from the name of a place which the Bible locates in the valley of Ben Hinnom, near Jerusalem, where Jewish children were also sacrificed. Against this evil the prophet Jeremiah railed, saying that Yahweh had never requested the Jews 'to burn their sons and their daughters in the fire'. Although Jeremiah's prophetic career spanned the reigns of four Judean kings, his absolute devotion to Yahweh made him unpopular with royal officials, priests and other prophets, so that he suffered an attempted assassination and a term of imprisonment. Jeremiah's prophecies seem to have happened during the most turbulent period in the history of the southern kingdom of Judah. King Zedekiah was particularly deaf to Jeremiah's warnings about the threat posed by Babylon: he was weak and vacillating, sometimes attentive to them and sometimes not, with the result that an association of Judah with Egypt led to the fall of Jerusalem and the Babylonian exile in 586 BC. Jeremiah ended his days in Egypt among a group of Jewish refugees who to the prophet's dismay continued to worship other deities instead of Yahweh.

An earlier Jewish version of *molk* may have been Yahweh's temptation of Abraham, when he was told to make 'a burnt offering' of his son Isaac. But when Abraham was about to cut his son's throat, an angel appeared and ordered him to put the knife aside. This strange episode reveals how deeply rooted child sacrifice was among the Western Semites. *Molk* had passed from Phoenicia to both the Syrians and the Jews, who practised it in honour of Baal and Yahweh respectively from the twelfth century BC

The hand of Yahweh stopping Abraham's sacrifice of Isaac

onwards. Not for another five hundred years would the *tophet* be dismantled in Jerusalem, the valley of Ben Hinnom declared impure, and child sacrifice finally forbidden.

Arguably the 'ram caught in the thorns' which Abraham substituted for his son established animal sacrifice as an integral part of Jewish worship. Sheep, goats and cattle as well as birds such as the dove, turtledove and pigeon were regularly used to petition or thank Yahweh. Sacrifices and offerings brought to sanctuaries were usually handled by priests, who slaughtered the animals, flayed their skins and poured the blood on the ground. Meat was either burned for Yahweh, cooked and reserved for priests, or apportioned among the worshippers. Yahweh's evident pleasure in the smell of cooking meat and burning grain is a parallel of the Sumerian practice of feeding their deities. After the Flood, the first thing Noah did was build an altar for 'burnt offerings' which Yahweh smelled and consequently said, 'I will not curse the ground any more for man's sake.'

PALESTINE

The Bible informs us that the history of the Jews began when Abraham was called by Yahweh to leave the Sumerian city of Ur and move to Palestine. Notwithstanding the Egyptian interlude, the Jews always knew that this was where they were intended to live.

The origin of Yahweh worship is obscure, but it was the bond which kept the Jewish people united during their wanderings in the desert under Moses. Once they arrived in 'the promised land', though, they split into twelve tribes, two of which settled in Phoenicia. However attractive their non-Jewish neighbours' beliefs, the tribes could never entirely forget Yahweh's insistence on being the exclusive god of his people. This was not yet monotheism, since the existence of other deities was still not denied. Among these deities was Asherat, the consort of Baal, a favourite of King Solomon as well as Jezebel, the wife of King Ahab. It is likely that this West Semitic fertility goddess was once associated with Yahweh as his consort.

Stories about Samson's exploits undoubtedly derive from tribal accounts of early Jewish victories over the peoples already in occupation of 'the

The fertility goddess Asherat, a favourite of King Solomon and the possible consort of Yahweh

promised land'. One of these were the Philistines, whose sturdy independence lasted until the Greco-Roman era; from them derived the name Palestine. The fullest story of a Jewish tribal leader is that of Samson, a legendary hero endowed by Yahweh with superhuman physical strength. His birth was foretold to his mother by an angel, who also told her how Samson should be brought up. Several incidents illustrate his extraordinary powers: killing a lion with his bare hands; setting fire to the crops of the Philistines by putting flaming torches on the tails of three hundred foxes; slaying a thousand Philistines with a donkey's jawbone; and carrying off the gates of Gaza one night. But his inordinate sexual passion finally made Samson a victim of the Philistines, who through the voluptuous Delilah discovered that his long hair was the source of his strength. Shorn of his locks and blinded, the Jewish strongman became an abject Philistine slave until Yahweh restored his power long enough for Samson to take his revenge on his tormentors. In Gaza, Samson pulled down the city's main temple, sacrificing his own life in the disaster.

One of Samson's exploits may have been, however, a garbled version of a spring ritual designed to promote the growth of corn, since we know that in Rome it was the practice to tie burning brands to the tails of foxes and let them loose in the Circus Maximus. Possibly the fox with its red colour and burning tail symbolised the warmth and vitality that the Romans hoped the corn goddess Ceres would confer upon their crops. A similar agricultural rite seems to have taken place in Babylon, where a 'Dumuzi of Grain' was connected with the grinding of cereals and with beer making. Here the divine shepherd has been transformed, through his annual death and resurrection, into the protector of harvests.

Yahweh's encouragement of Samson's belligerence prefigures jihad, the duty of Muslims to defend their religion. The current debasement of jihad by suicide bombers, however, should not be allowed to blur its twofold meaning. 'Lesser jihad' was concerned with the spread of Islam at the expense of other faiths, while 'greater jihad' was the obligation of each believer to control evil inclinations. So among the Jews the trumpet was sounded to call men to a holy war, which could only succeed if the soldiers involved were sanctified, literally 'made holy', a state of ritual purity maintained through sexual abstinence.

But the Jewish holy war was unlike any other war in the ancient Near East through its requirement not to keep any booty. After Yahweh had brought confusion and panic upon the enemy, the victorious Jews were expected to destroy the spoils, presumably as a consecration or dedication to Yahweh. On one occasion the Bible actually says that captured silver and gold vessels were consecrated. Totally different was the attitude of the Assyrians to warfare, who looked upon aggression as not only acceptable but also praiseworthy, since a triumphant king was extending the territory of the national god Ashur. And the spilling of blood was equally gratifying to Ninurta, a warrior god renowned for his delight in the most terrible conflicts. The Hittites, on the other hand, always invoked a quasi-judicial ritual to convict their enemies and their deities before starting a war, a much less certain justification than that of the Assyrians, who came to regard their annual campaigns as nothing less than holding back the forces of chaos. On a pair of bronze doors King Sennacherib had himself depicted with the inscription 'A picture of Ashur on his way to do battle with Tiamat', a myth borrowed from the Babylonian champion Marduk.

What Sennacherib meant was that war against peoples who refused to acknowledge the divinely willed Assyrian leadership of the world was fully justified and should be pursued with the utmost vigour. In this cosmic crisis there was no room for mercy. Coming under Assyrian control, either as an ally or an imperial province, was the only guarantee of protection. Restoring order out of chaos was at least a positive and constructive Assyrian idea, however strange it may seem to us now. Yet the demand for absolute obedience to Assyrian authority did qualify this concern for human welfare when we recall the cruel punishment of rebels and an enthusiasm for booty. Yet hard-pressed rulers still invited Assyrian intervention, even though they knew it meant becoming vassals. The arrival of tribute with such a request was always enough to spur Assyrian kings to action.

It was indeed a similar pressure exerted by the Philistines that led to the Jewish adoption of a monarchy. Saul was in 1020 BC the first Jew to be chosen king; he defeated the Amorites and then fought the Philistines with varying results. Twenty years later David had replaced Saul and, as 'the anointed one', he was regarded as the son of Yahweh. King David modelled his rule on the pattern of other ancient Near Eastern kingdoms, but selected for his capital a neutral site, not belonging to any of the twelve tribes. This was Jerusalem. What the new king did not expect to happen there was a syncretism between Yahweh and El Elyon, 'the most high god' of the West Semitic pantheon.

Samuel anointing David as the Jewish king. A mural in the synagogue at Dura-Europos

David was succeeded in 960 BC by his son Solomon, whose political astuteness inaugurated a welcome period of peace. He concluded peace treaties with Tyre and Egypt. Although these treaties were an attempt to counterbalance the power of the Philistines, Solomon also built up his armed forces with some 4,000 chariots. Because they never went to war, there is a degree of scepticism about their number, but we know that the Jewish king was prepared to pay high prices for both horses and chariots. Solomon financed his chariotry through trade, and acted as a middleman in the export of Egyptian chariots to Syria. With Egypt unsuited for horse-breeding, and without a single god associated with horses despite the reverence shown to other animal deities, Solomon also clearly profited from the passage of horses southwards through his kingdom from the northern borders of the ancient Near East. The profits would have helped to pay for the temple he erected in Jerusalem.

Solomon's wisdom was proverbial. Nearly everyone is aware of the visit of the queen of Sheba, who came to test him 'with hard questions'. Her gifts were magnificent because the wealth of her land, present-day Yemen, derived from a near-monopoly of frankincense and myrrh. Quite remarkable embellishments to the famous meeting occur in Jewish as well as Muslim myths. The latter have Solomon visit Sheba, where he expects the queen to have 'legs like a donkey as her mother was a *jinn*', a female demon. To his relief, the queen's legs proved attractively human, though they were hairy. So Solomon married Sheba, after she had used depilatories.

On the death of Solomon around 922 BC, tension between the northern and the southern tribes led to the establishment of two separate kingdoms: Judah in the south under Solomon's son Rehoboam, and Israel in the north under Jeroboam, one of Solomon's former officials. The history of these kingdoms was quite different: Judah had a relatively stable dynastic experience, while Israel was fundamentally unstable.

One ruler of Israel stands out: the seventh king Ahab. Along with Ben-Hadad II of Damascus, Ahab was a prime mover of the coalition which thwarted the Assyrian king Shalmaneser III at the battle of Qarqar. But Ben-Hadad soon made demands on Israel that exceeded those considered acceptable in a relationship between a dominant and a subordinate state. War ensued and, in 841 BC, at the battle of Ramoth-Gilead on the eastern bank of the Jordan, the armies of Damascus and Israel clashed. Fearful of Ahab's skill as a tactician, Ben-Hadad ordered his best squadron of chariots to seek out the Israelite king and 'fight him only'. The wily Ahab avoided its attention, fighting throughout the day in spite of a severe arrow wound. He feared that his soldiers might mistake his absence from the battlefield to receive medical treatment as a sign of impending defeat and break ranks. 'So the king of Israel stayed himself in his chariot until the evening; and about the time of the sun going down he died.'

It was Ahab's widow, the Phoenician princess Jezebel, who roused the prophet Elijah to action by her support for the worship of Baal. When the queen learned of the slaughter of her own prophets, she sought Elijah's head; but he struck first by encouraging an army coup against the royal family. Jezebel herself was thrown out of a palace window and then trampled by horses. Afterwards, only her skull and the bones of her hands and feet were found, which were insufficient for a proper burial. Even her bitterest enemies deemed this a shameful event. Prophet Elijah seems to have fully supported the coup which destroyed the royal family, a bloodbath unequalled in Jewish history.

The prophets believed that their entitlement to speak out came directly from Yahweh. Whereas Hosea thundered against Israel's idolatry and apostasy, Jeremiah tried to get Judah to appreciate its weakness when faced by Babylonian power. Aware of Jeremiah's warnings about the foolishness of defying Babylon, King Nebuchadrezzar II allowed the prophet to go wherever he wished, unlike the deposed Jewish king who, after being forced to watch the slaughter of his children, was blinded and led away in bronze chains as an exile.

The weakness of Jeremiah's position as a prophet was demonstrated by the angry reaction of the Jews not included in the Babylonian exile. Prominent among his detractors were women, who declared: 'We are not going to listen to you. We will do everything we like, making offerings to the Queen of Heaven and pour out libations to her, just as we and our forefathers, our kings and officials used to do in the cities of Judah and the streets of Jerusalem. We had plenty of food, lived well, and did not encounter misfortune. But from the time we stopped making offerings to the Queen of Heaven and pouring out libations to her, we have lacked everything and have perished by the sword and famine'.

Pointedly they asked where Yahweh was when the disaster of the Babylonian attack took place. It was a point also made by Nebuzaradan, the captain of the Babylonian guard who released Jeremiah, when he said of Jerusalem that 'the lord thy God hath pronounced this evil upon this place'.

The identity of the mysterious Queen of Heaven remains obscure, but she was probably Astarte. There can be no doubt that Yahweh used Nebuchadrezzer II's army to punish the Jews for their worship of other deities like her. That is why, Jeremiah tells the Jewish remnant, 'the promised land' had been allowed to become 'a wasteland and a desolation'. The Jewish people had brought the catastrophe upon themselves.

But the prophet associated most with the Babylonian exile, which lasted for the Jews from 597 to 539 BC, was of course Daniel. In the Book of Daniel there are two significant episodes related to Yahweh worship. The first is the refusal of three Jewish servants to bow down before 'the golden image' that Nebuchadrezzar II had set up. When the Babylonian king learned of this insolence, he had Shadrach, Meshach and Abednego 'cast into a fiery furnace' without ill effect; Nebuchadrezzar was convinced that an angel had been sent by their god to save them. The second ordeal was suffered by Daniel himself under the new Persian administration for refusing to do homage to King Darius. When this ruler learned that Daniel's overnight stay in the lions' den had done him no harm, Darius admitted the power of the god that Daniel worshipped.

It is already transparent that we encounter from this time onwards a unique outlook when the Jews contemplate the supernatural. 'The gods of the peoples are idols, but God made the heavens': the psalmist means that other West Asian deities were nothing but a human invention. This is obvious in the apocryphal book, 'Daniel, Bel and the Snake'. With the aid of ashes sprinkled on a temple floor, Daniel demonstrates to the Persian King Cyrus, the ruler to whom he had refused homage rather than Darius, that the footprints of those who came secretly to eat the food set out for the god Bel belonged to 'the priests, with their wives and children'. He also disposed of the sacred serpent by feeding it with cakes of boiled 'pitch and fat and hair': these ingredients burst its belly asunder.

Daniel in the lions' den, a Byzantine view of his miraculous escape

Here then is fully-fledged monotheism, an attitude to divinity that would greatly appeal to Muhammad over a millennium later. In addition, the Babylonian exile threw up another idea of interest to the Prophet, which the Jews acquired from the Persians. It was resurrection and a final reckoning of accounts, the so-called *frashkart*, or 'final rehabilitation'. Considering the undeveloped notion of an afterlife in the ancient Near East, this Zoroastrian idea came as an absolute revelation. Derived from the Akkadian word for 'desolation', Sheol was the Jewish equivalent of the Sumerian underworld: a place, the Book of Job informs us, where the worm is addressed as father, mother and sister, for in corruption all 'rest together in the dust'. After the Persians let the Jews rebuild Jerusalem, the possibility of physical resurrection no longer seemed in doubt. Daniel could proclaim: 'And many of those who sleep in the dust of the earth shall wake, some to everlasting life, and some to everlasting contempt.'

At first the number of exiles returning to Palestine was small. When other Jews followed in greater numbers the work of reconstruction at

A reconstruction of Solomon's temple

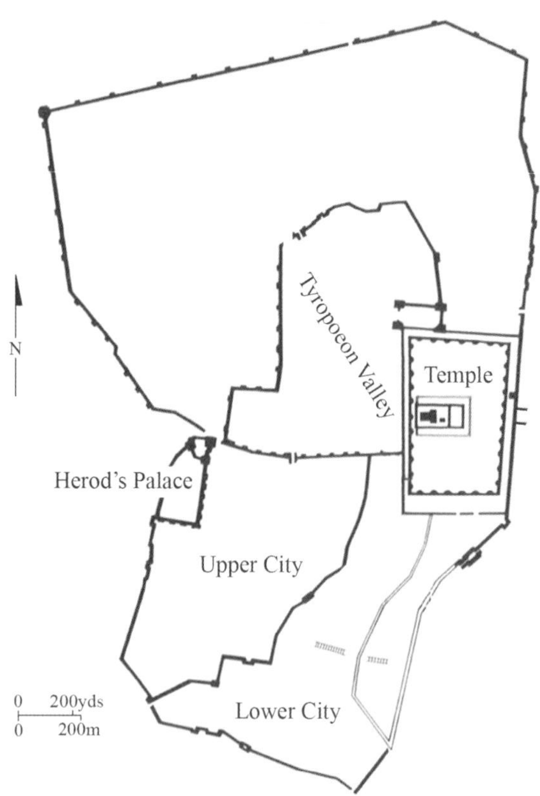

The location of the Second Temple in Jerusalem

Jerusalem gathered pace, and in 515 BC another temple was dedicated to Yahweh. As large as the First Temple, though much less ornate, the Second Temple seemed more impressive to the inhabitants of the city, when so much still lay in ruins. Solomon's temple had risen amid a formidable complex of royal buildings, the king's palace, the barracks, the arsenal, all enclosed within a single large compound. None had been rebuilt. The Second Temple thus stood alone upon high ground, set in its own courtyards and surrounded by its own wall. It was a potent symbol of the revival of Judaism and appeared to inaugurate a splendid new era for the Jewish people. Future problems with later conquerors could not then be foreseen, nor the ultimate loss of Jerusalem under the Romans, after a bitterly fought uprising devastated Palestine. Under the Persians, the Jews lived in tranquillity, but they were to experience cultural trauma first under the Greeks, and then the Romans. Providing they met the annual payment of tribute which the Persians imposed upon them, the Jews were left to their own devices. Persian rulers had little interest in the internal affairs of subject peoples. What drove their ambition was the establishment of a universal monarchy, since they intended to be 'kings of the four quarters' and much more besides. Their empire stretched as far east as India and might well have reached Italy in the west had not a failure to subdue the Greek mainland in 480–79 BC halted their expansion into the central Mediterranean.

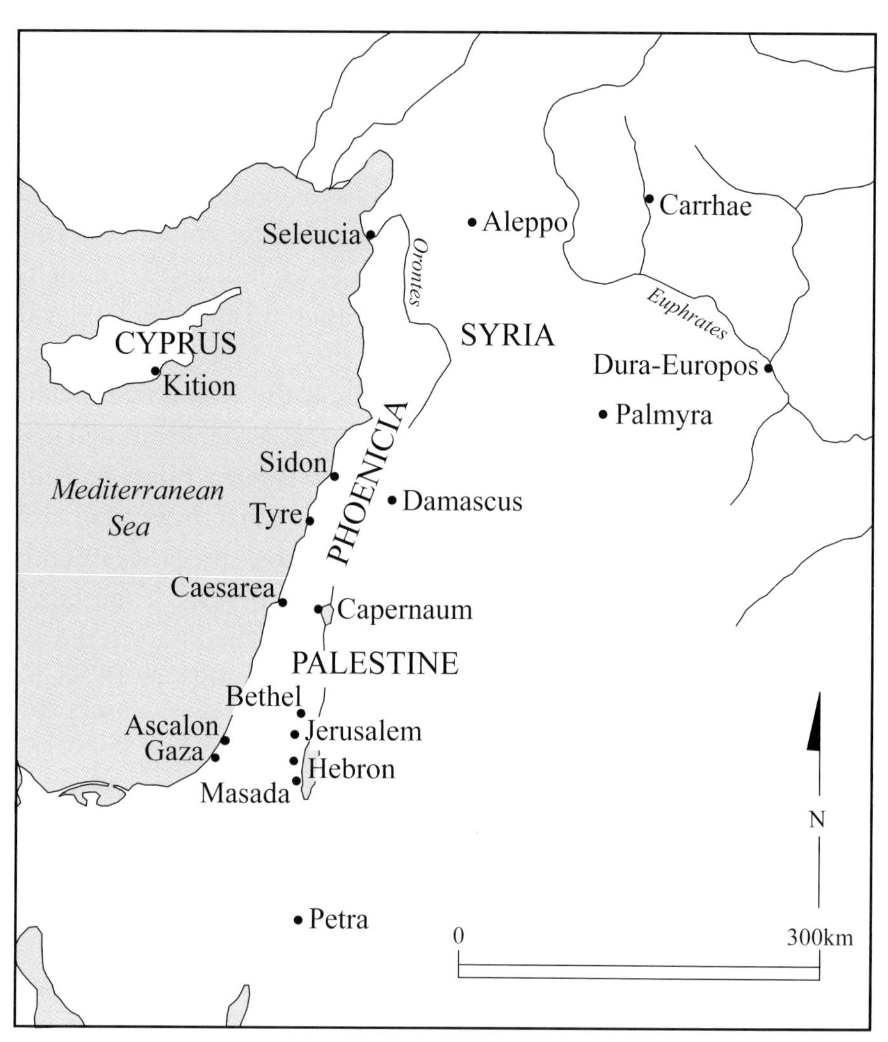

The Greco-Roman Near East

6

GRECO-ROMAN DOMINATION

At Jerusalem the emperor Hadrian founded a city in place of the one which had been razed to the ground, naming it Colonia Aelia Capitolina, and on the site of the Temple he raised a new temple to Jupiter.

The Roman History of Cassius Dio

Direct Greek involvement in ancient Near Eastern affairs dates from the Trojan War, an event that preceded the onslaught of the Sea Peoples in the twelfth century BC. Five hundred years later, Homer described a short but vital period in the tenth year of the siege of Troy by a Greek expeditionary force under the command of Agamemnon, the king of Mycenae. Greece in Homer's lifetime was a collection of petty city-states, still barely above a subsistence level of existence, unlike the network of well-organized kingdoms which had sent a thousand ships against Troy. The rulers who accompanied Agamemnon in this armada lived in luxurious stone-built palaces, filled with furniture decorated in silver, gold and ivory.

Because this lost world only reappeared through the efforts of modern archaeologists, following in the pioneering footsteps of Heinrich Schliemann, the Trojan War was for a long time regarded as no more than a legend, a half-remembered Greek assault on a trading rival in Asia Minor. It is now recognized that Homer recorded, however poetically, an actual expedition in the *Iliad*.

Although archaeology reveals how Troy suffered a number of attacks, the Greek sack around 1250 BC would seem to have been the decisive one, since the city never fully regained its previous prosperity. So certain were the ancient Greeks about their capture of the city that Alexander the Great made a special pilgrimage to its ruins, before he set off in 334 BC to vanquish Persia. The place he visited, ironically, was not the true site of Homer's Troy, but a later foundation; this did not stop him from offering sacrifice at the tombs of Patroclus and Achilles, after which he and his close friend Hephaestion raced around them naked and anointed with oil in traditional fashion.

After Greece and Asia Minor had fallen under Roman rule, the supposed site of Troy was built over and the Roman city of Ilium arose. The Romans were intent on celebrating the Trojans, since they believed that an important element in their own ancestry had escaped from a burning Troy with Aeneas. The son of Anchises and the goddess Aphrodite, Aeneas gave his name to the *Aeneid*, Virgil's celebration of Rome's greatness under the first Roman emperor, Augustus. After sailing to Crete, where he learned in a dream that Dardanus, an ancestor of the Trojan royal family, hailed from Italy, Aeneas continued to Epirus on the eastern Adriatic coast, and then on to Sicily and Carthage, where he resisted Queen Dido's charms. Arriving at the mouth of the Tiber, Aeneas received a cordial welcome from the river god, which meant that the Trojan refugees had reached their final destination.

The earliest mention of Rome's belief in its Trojan origins occurs in the third century BC. At the beginning of the first war that it fought against Carthage, the Sicilian city of Segesta, which had charge of Aphrodite's chief temple in Sicily, chose to side with the Romans because of their common descent from Aeneas. Here the legend served Rome well, just as it did in the eastern Mediterranean whenever Roman intervention needed justification. That was the reason why Ilium always received preferential treatment from the Romans. The first temple dedicated to Venus, the Roman version of the goddess Aphrodite, was built in 181 BC. So widespread did the idea of the Trojan ancestry of the Romans become that the claim of Julius Caesar's family to be descended from the goddess surprised few citizens. On his return from Gaul in 49

BC and his refusal to relinquish his military command, Caesar was called by his soldiers as well as his opponents 'the descendant of Venus'. Just before the decisive battle of the civil war at Pharsalus, in central Greece, he vowed on the battlefield to build a temple in honour of the goddess if he won.

Aware of this cultural heritage, the Ottoman sultan Mehmed II was baffled by Italian hostility over his seizure of Constantinople in 1453. In a letter that the sultan addressed to the pope he expressed his astonishment at the lack of gratitude shown by the descendants of the Romans for his avenging the Greek treatment of their ancestors, the Trojans. It was an idea picked up by the contemporary Byzantine historian Laonicus Chalcondyles, who wrote that the Greeks living in Constantinople were being punished by the Ottoman Turks for the atrocities they had committed during the Trojan War. Shocked though western Europe was by the Muslim acquisition of Constantinople and the Bosphorus, the only route joining the Black and Mediterranean seas, there was no response to a papal call for another crusade.

MACEDON

When the Persians advanced through northern Greece in 480 BC, the Macedonians submitted to King Xerxes, but they were secretly in league with Greek city-states farther south, whose refusal to accept Persian suzerainty had provoked the great invasion. The subsequent defeat of the Persians freed Macedon from any political restraint.

Under the Temenid kings, whose ancestors included the hero Herakles, the Macedonian kingdom gradually increased in size and influence. Alexander's father, King Philip II, not only strengthened Macedon's hold on the Balkans, but he subjugated any Greek cities that opposed him and sometimes transplanted their inhabitants, if they were north of Greece proper. In Greece itself Philip II's policy was different. He sought alliances where he could, and resorted to arms only when necessary. He did so at the battle of Chaeronea in 338 BC, when the Macedonians defeated the Thebans and the Athenians, Philip's superbly drilled pikemen opening a gap in the Greek line into which Alexander charged with

A coin showing Alexander with horns, a sign of divinity in the ancient Near East

the Companion cavalry. Down to the reign of Alexander's father, Macedonian horsemen were like other cavalry forces, but during this period they became the battle-winning arm, reaching perfection in the well-timed charges which Alexander employed to shatter enemy formations in Asia. The Companions formed an elite group of horsemen, personally commanded by Alexander himself.

After Chaeronea, King Philip was elected as the head of a league of Greek city-states, whose purpose was to wage war against Persia. Sparta alone refused to participate. Philip's assassination in 336 BC left Alexander in charge of the expedition. The young Macedonian king was so much under the spell of Homer that he associated the crossing of his army from Europe to Asia with the Trojan War. On the European shore Alexander sacrificed to Protesilaus and prayed for a happier landing than this hero. The *Iliad* narrates that 'He was the first of the Greeks to leap ashore, but fell victim to a Trojan foe, leaving his wife Phylae with lacerated cheeks and a house half-built.' Again the first of his own expedition to reach the Asian shore, Alexander drove his spear into the ground marking it as a spear-won gift of the gods. It was a prophetic claim, for Alexander's later policy showed that he intended to make his Asian subjects neither part of the Macedonian empire nor slaves of the Greeks. It was a policy of Alexander's which won many Asian hearts. Also unnoticed, at the time of the landing, was his intention of conquering more than just the Persian empire. Yet Alexander's dislike of slavery was not exceptional. The Macedonians left most of the people they subdued in the Balkans on the land where they lived: occasionally a town might be destroyed or a native tribe expelled, but no one was ever reduced to slavery or serfdom. Even in the palace, women of the Macedonian royal family undertook domestic tasks.

After the pilgrimage to Troy, Alexander rejoined the main army. Keen to secure an early victory in order to obtain supplies, the young king marched inland and met the Persians at the river Granicus, where they had adopted a strong defensive position, along with some 20,000 Greek mercenaries. Alexander acted with characteristic speed and confidence, attacking without waiting for all his men to arrive. His commanders urged caution but Alexander said: 'I am ashamed if, after crossing the Hellespont, this little stream will stop us from crossing as we are.' Once again the longer spears of the Macedonian infantry gave Alexander the edge, while he, at a critical juncture in the battle, charged at the head of the cavalry. In ferocious, hand-to-hand fighting, the Macedonians gradually pushed the Persians back until they gave way and fled, leaving the phalanx of Greek mercenaries exposed on the battlefield. Alexander refused to let them surrender, for he knew that they would fight again in Persian service. So they were slaughtered, with the exception of 2,000 captives who went to Macedon to labour in chains for life. The punishment was justified by their treachery: he said, 'being Greek they had fought against Greece in violation of the decisions of the Greeks'.

The morale of the Persian governors in Asia Minor was broken, allowing Alexander enough time to consolidate his position before moving eastwards into the heart of the Persian empire. Starting with the victory at the river Granicus, Alexander overthrew Persia in three pitched battles. In the first he used only his Macedonian troops and some Greek horse-

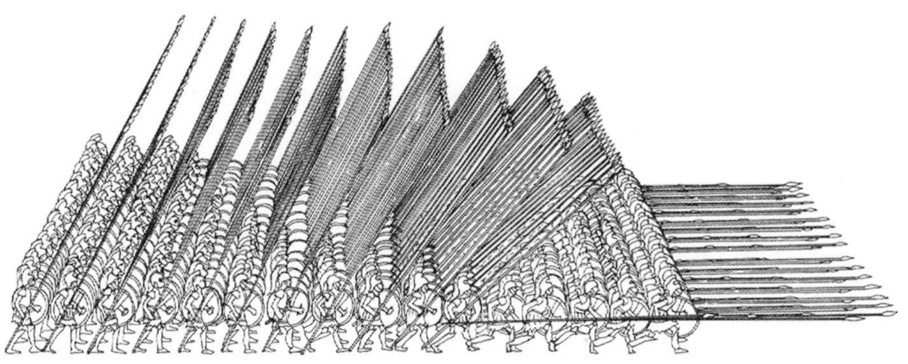

The irresistible Macedonian phalanx

men. In the second and third his army consisted of Greek, Balkan and Macedonian soldiers. Alexander was the spearpoint and the Macedonians the spearhead in battle, but the other contingents were indispensable on the battlefield. Once the Persian king was dead, Alexander began to recruit Asians as soldiers, who with his Balkan forces comprised nearly half of the army of 120,000 men whom he led in an invasion of India. His ambitions seemed to know no bounds.

It was the Macedonians, however, who ultimately determined the limits of Alexander's conquests. They constituted the Macedonian assembly, the final arbiter of the king's wishes, and worn out by the effects of monsoon rain they felt they had been misled because the promised end of Asia was nowhere in sight. Alexander himself was baffled by India's size and, even though he wished to advance against Magadha, a state centred in the populous Ganges river valley, he realized that this was now impossible. When omens confirmed the correctness of going no farther east, Alexander agreed to turn back. But his army knew that it still had to conquer the southern part of the Indus river valley before striking westwards. Still a young man, Alexander must have thought it was possible to campaign later in India.

For Alexander felt that he had a mission to fulfil, which worried some of his Macedonian and Greek followers. As the Greek historian Plutarch put it: 'Alexander considered that he had come from the gods to be a governor and reconciler to the world. Using force of arms when he could not bring men together by reason, he employed everything to the same end, mixing lives, manners, marriages and customs, as it were, in a loving cup'.

Possibly the innovation his followers disliked most was the court ceremonial that Alexander decided to adopt, since it involved the Persian custom of prostration, which to both Macedonians and Greeks smacked of an acknowledgement of divinity. Though Alexander could have practised one form of ceremonial for Europeans and another for Asians, his insistence on the new custom shows the extent to which his mind was set on treating all his subjects alike.

Alexander actually believed that he was not only descended from Herakles, but also from the chief Greek deity Zeus, a belief that seemed to be confirmed on his visit to the oracle at Siwah in Egypt. On the journey across the desert to the Siwah oasis, after he became hopelessly lost in a dust-storm, he received divine aid in the form of rain and two crows as guides. At Siwah, he was addressed by the priests as a son of the god, the usual greeting of a reigning pharaoh, since only in Egypt were rulers automatically attributed divine honours. Despite the oracle's private revelation of future greatness, however, Alexander's feet were firmly on the ground when it came to matters of administration. The children of his soldiers by Asian wives were made legitimate and educated at his expense. Many of these veterans and their families were settled in the seventy new cities he founded in Asia; strategically sited, these fortified settlements were self-governing but subject to the edicts of the king. Their political, social and religious life developed on Greek lines, so that they spread a new culture across Alexander's empire.

Representative of his foundations was Ai Khanoum in present-day Afghanistan. Located at the confluence of the river Oxus with one of its major tributaries, the city was perfectly sited to manage the resources of the surrounding plain and the mountains to the south. It incorporated a raised acropolis which sloped down to a lower residential area. Excavations have revealed Greek temples, a theatre and a gymnasium next to a large temple dedicated to a local deity. The ancient name of the city is not known, yet from its buildings and inscriptions we can appreciate how it was a thriving urban centre for well over a century. Alexander was the standard-bearer of Greek civilization in Asia.

AFTER ALEXANDER

The most innovative decision that Alexander made was obliging his senior commanders to marry the daughters of the Persian aristocracy. During the wars that followed Alexander's premature death in 323 BC, these men fought for the lion's share of his conquests. Only one of the new kingdoms which emerged, founded by Seleucus at Babylon in 305 BC, stayed close to the ideal of a multicultural society. At his eastern capital, Seleucia upon Tigris, in present-day Iraq, a suburb was named Apamea after Seleucus' Asian wife, whom he had married at Alexander's behest. This marriage lasted, unlike the others contracted by Alexander's

A fragment of a Babylonian astronomical diary recording in 323BC Alexander's death

commanders, and Apamea was the mother of Seleucus' eldest son, the capable Antiochus I.

Except for the Jews, the Seleucid dynasty was a godsend for the ancient Near East, because Seleucus appreciated the need to respect its age-old traditions. Well before his death in 281 BC, Seleucus also recognized the talents of his eldest son Antiochus by appointing him co-regent, an unusual move that ensured the dynasty's survival. Although Antiochus was sent to take charge of the eastern territories, it would be wrong to see anything formal in this division of responsibility: father and son were both monarchs with complete authority wherever they happened to be operating. The man on the spot needed to have the power of decision belonging to a ruler. From the start, Seleucus understood the difficulties of running a far-flung empire.

That was the reason for reaching an early agreement over the Indian border with the first Mauryan emperor, Chandragupta. In return for ceding several outlying areas, Seleucus received five hundred war-elephants for use in the ancient Near East. These great creatures were to prove decisive when Antiochus I had to cope with a Celtic invasion. After ravaging Greece, the Celts poured into Asia Minor, destroying towns and cities in their search for plunder. In response to calls for aid, Antiochus quickly raised a sizeable army and engaged the invaders in battle, when fear of the unfamiliar war-elephants dented the usual ferocity of the Celts. Hard fighting was still necessary before the Celts were driven into the interior, the old heartland of the Hittites near the river Halys, where they were henceforth called the Galatians. Both Greek and non-Greek peoples expressed their relief at Antiochus' swift campaign by calling him *soter*, or 'saviour'. Hemmed in though they were by Seleucid arms, the Galatians remained troublesome neighbours until the Romans conquered Galatia in 253 BC. Despite 8,000 Celts falling in battle then, the Roman senators denied the two victorious generals a triumph on their return to the capital. Deployment of slingers to soften up the enemy before the legionaries charged was considered unmanly. Greco-Roman disdain for missile-weapons died hard.

In Asia Minor, the Seleucids had to tolerate the creation of an independent state based on the natural fortress of Pergamum, less than 20 kilometres from the Aegean. Its first king, Attalus I, assumed power after dealing with the Celts locally. Although Pergamum developed into a power of almost equal status with Seleucid Asia, its reliance on Roman support came at a price. For Rome's defeat of the Seleucid king, Antiochus III, at Magnesia in 189 BC turned Pergamum into nothing more than a pawn in Roman foreign policy. And this victory did not please every Roman either. Marcus Porcius Cato deplored the luxury items brought back as loot, such as ornate couches and expensive fabrics. The moral outrage of Cato touched a Roman nerve by reminding his fellow citizens how simplicity had been the source of their ancestors' strength. But the mood did not last and subsequent generations looked eastwards for personal gain. Realizing the weakness of his kingdom, the last Attalid king bequeathed Pergamum to Rome in 133 BC: it became the province of Asia, a happy hunting ground for Roman speculators.

The Roman defeat of this king, Antiochus III, was a major setback for the Seleucid dynasty

Conflict with the Romans was the result of Antiochus III's revival of Seleucid claims to Thrace. Possibly his successful campaigns on the eastern frontier had blinded the Seleucid king to the growing power of Rome in the eastern Mediterranean. Yet the heavy defeat did not stop the Seleucid dynasty from ruling a large part of the ancient Near East for another century. Quite typical was the conduct of Antiochus immediately after Magnesia. He went to Babylon, a cuneiform inscription relates, and with his wife and sons sacrificed at the great temple of Marduk. A local priest was pleased to note, 'That day, King Antiochus entered Esagila and prostrated himself.' Following sacrifices to other deities worshipped in Babylon, 'He went, in the afternoon, to Seleucia upon Tigris, the royal city.'

Public satisfaction with these elaborate ceremonies indicates that Seleucid authority remained popular, and it was not until the Parthians invaded Mesopotamia half a century later that the Seleucids suffered a body blow from which they never recovered. By 126 BC they had been driven west of the Euphrates, leaving them with a restricted economic base and no chance of mustering enough troops to fight back with any hope of success. The extinction of the dynasty was therefore unavoidable, when in 64 BC the Roman general Pompey annexed Syria, observing how he found Asia a frontier but left it at the heart of Rome's empire.

It was during the closing years of Seleucid rule that the first great cultural clash occurred with the Jews. Perhaps in reaction to the growing Parthian threat, Antiochus IV agreed with a pro-Greek delegation of Jews that the time had come to stamp out outmoded Jewish customs. The persecution of his Jewish subjects by the Seleucid king, and the proscription of ritual practices, resulted in circumcision becoming a hallmark and a test of faith. After the parting of ways between Christianity and Judaism, it was inevitable for early Christians that the rite of circumcision would become optional, despite heated argument on the subject among the apostles. Today, only the Christians of Ethiopia continue the practice, circumcising their children between the third and eighth day after birth. Although to traditional Jews Antiochus IV was an outright monster, his contemporaries regarded him more as an eccentric. He liked to stroll through his capital, Seleucia-in-Pieria, located close to the mouth of the Orontes river in Syria, alone or with one or two attendants, distributing largesse as the fancy took him. He also enjoyed drinking parties and, like the Roman emperor Nero, fancied himself to be a great actor.

GRECO-ROMAN DOMINATION

Antiochus IV died on a campaign against the Parthians; among his final acts the dying king rescinded his decree of persecution against Judaism. But this volte-face came too late to head off a Jewish uprising led by Judas Maccabeus and his brothers Jonathan and Simon. They could never forgive Seleucid persecution, which included throwing mothers of circumcised male children from city walls with their babies strung round their necks, and the enforced eating of pork and ritually unclean cattle. By 141 BC the rebels had frustrated four Seleucid attempts to subdue Palestine but, with both Judas and Jonathan dead, the Jews elected Simon as their leader on the condition that he would bring the bloodshed to an end, which he did by negotiating with the Seleucids their independence. He also founded a dynasty that produced King Herod, the notorious client of the Romans.

EARLY CHRISTIANITY

During these troubled times, the Qumran community near the Dead Sea studied the scrolls that startled the world when they were discovered in nearby caves between 1946 and 1956. Known as the Dead Sea Scrolls, these religious texts were written on parchment and papyrus in Hebrew, Aramaic and Greek. The scrolls may have belonged to an ancient Jewish sect called the Essenes. According to the Roman-Jewish scholar Josephus, the Essenes 'apply themselves with extraordinary zeal to the study of the works of the ancients choosing, above all, those which tend to be useful to body and soul. In them they study the healing of diseases, the roots offering protection and the properties of stones.' Even though the Qumran community is no longer seen as connected with Jesus' ministry, its deliberations remain important to Judaism as well as Christianity. For the Dead Sea Scrolls contain very old biblical material which offers an insight into the composition of the Old Testament, demonstrating how fluid the text actually was before being canonized in its present form.

It is worth remembering that initially Christianity was a Jewish sect: one of many competing sects in which Judaism was then divided in Palestine. Among their fellow Jews, the adherents of Christ were only distinguished by their belief that the Messiah had already appeared in the

One of the caves in which the Dead Sea Scrolls were found

person of Jesus. In addition to his renown as a man of miracles, Jesus was also admired as an inspiring teacher who spoke to worshippers in synagogues as well as large gatherings around the Sea of Galilee. Excavations at ancient Capernaum, a town on the seashore, have revealed that Jesus lived there during a period of great prosperity. There the teaching of Jesus first challenged privileged social status based either on ethnicity or wealth. The healing of a Roman centurion at Capernaum was a turning point in his mission, for Jesus said he had 'not found so great faith, no, not in Israel' than this Roman soldier showed towards him. So he added how 'many shall come from the east and west and shall sit with Abraham, Isaac and Jacob in the kingdom of heaven', while those who claimed to be 'the children of the kingdom shall be cast into outer darkness where there shall be weeping and gnashing of teeth'. In the centuries that followed the crucifixion, Capernaum became even richer as a centre of Christian pilgrimage. An early conundrum was how far Jewish traditions such as circumcision should be binding on Christian converts. Christian

The synagogue at Capernaum where Jesus preached

Jews living in Jerusalem worried that St Paul's ready acceptance of Gentiles would in the end erode their distinctive character as the chosen people. They even denied him the status of an apostle like St Peter.

Another uncertainty which exercised all early Christians was Christ's return, a second stage in the judgement and redemption of the world. The earliest book in the New Testament, St Paul's letter to the Thessalonians, dealt with anxiety about the second coming. Because the death of Christians in that community had cast doubt on the timing of Jesus' reappearance on Earth, St Paul gave an answer that has remained the standard Christian position ever since. He boldly asserted the certainty of physical resurrection: 'the dead in Christ will rise first'.

By the reign of the first Roman emperor to embrace Christianity, the Church possessed a coherent and homogeneous structure and a body of agreed beliefs. But the newly converted Emperor Constantine discovered that there were still unresolved issues concerning the nature of Christ. Intending to establish at Constantinople a Christian Rome, the emperor was in no mood for unnecessary disputes; and so he decided that the feuding bishops would settle their differences in 325 at the Council of Nicaea, present-day Iznik in Asia Minor. The emperor himself presided over the crucial debates, guiding discussion towards a satisfactory conclusion. 'Internal strife in the Church of God', he declared, 'is far more evil and dangerous than any kind of war or conflict.' Just how aware Constantine was of the profound theological shift in Christ's position that he oversaw we have no way of knowing now. But in casting aside the view that the eternal Father was in some way superior to the begotten Son, the Council of Nicaea awarded Jesus the same status as Yahweh himself. After this any suggestion of inequality between Father and Son amounted to heresy.

There were, however, groups of Christians who resisted the identification of their faith with the Roman empire. They could not accept that it was an image of the heavenly kingdom, despite Constantine taking to calling himself the thirteenth apostle. But the ascetic and monastic movement was not essentially a movement of protest against a Church too closely associated with Roman government. Its origin lay in the Egyptian desert, where in 270 St Anthony began his solitary vigil. Utterly different was this personal quest for salvation from the behaviour of bishops and clergy whose status was approaching that of public officials. In spreading a self-denying message in society at large, monks came frequently into conflict with the episcopal order. A kind of resolution happened when the first monk-bishops linked their flocks to a spiritual life with an ascetic tinge, but it was not long before they also faced the problems of administering a growing property portfolio and, even worse, having to handle the divi-

A colossal head of Emperor Constantine, who dominated the Council of Nicaea in 325

sions thrown up by heresy. At the root of all the self-searching, all the desire to remain faithful to the Gospels, was an acute sense of having lost the purity of the first-century Church.

Only a pangloss such as Eusebius of Caesarea, a favourite bishop of the emperor Constantine, could declare that 'it was not just a result of human effort that the greater part of the world should have been under Roman rule at the precise moment Jesus was born. The coincidence that saw our Saviour begin his mission against such a background was undeniably part of a divine plan.'

THE LOSS OF THE PROMISED LAND

The Jews took a quite different view to Bishop Eusebius. Prior to official Roman endorsement of Christianity, this faith had to endure persecution like Judaism. Yet the level of animosity directed against Christians never matched that suffered by the Jews, who were crushed and ultimately dispersed by the Romans. Impatient with Jewish unrest following Pompey's settlement of the eastern Mediterranean, Rome handed over to Herod a kingdom that included all of Palestine and territories beyond the Jordan river valley. This kingdom was not at all what proponents of Jewish independence wanted, because as a client king Herod took his orders from the Romans.

The first Roman emperor, Augustus, recognized that Herod's Judaism was superficial through a personal attachment to Greek culture. Besides building a Greek-style city on the coast at Caesarea, Herod also introduced both a theatre and an amphitheatre to Jerusalem. The nude athletes who competed in the games held there shocked traditional Jews. Essentially Herod's position depended on non-Jewish mercenaries and a string of fortresses such as Masada, constructed on an isolated rock near the Judean desert. Because family quarrels forced Herod to alter his will many times, the king's death, in 4 or 5, caused further disputes which Augustus settled by dividing Palestine between three of his sons, none of whom was allowed a royal title.

Roman administration in Palestine was established in stages. As vassal kingdoms were considered already a part of the Roman empire, there was no need to rush annexation. It was not indeed until the reign of the emperor Claudius that, in 44, Palestine was formally annexed by Rome. The presence of Pontius Pilate in Jerusalem during the arrest of Jesus is explained by the supervisory role he discharged as prefect. He strove to avoid entanglement with Judaism, only reluctantly bowing to the demand of 'the chief priests' that Jesus should be crucified. But Pilate was prepared to act when Rome's interests were threatened, and in 37 he was replaced after harshly suppressing a Samaritan revolt.

Throughout the period of Roman domination, popular Jewish uprisings alternated with provocations by the authorities. In 41, the emperor Caligula decided to erect his statue in the Temple. Convinced of his own divinity, the emperor took offence when a Jewish mission tried to explain that their religious principles made it impossible to sacrifice to him, although they could sacrifice for him. Agitation by the Jews over Caligula's statue obliged the Roman governor of Syria to delay its installation in the temple, before ignoring the imperial order altogether after the emperor was assassinated in Rome.

Even those upper-class Jews who had gained most from collaboration with the Romans were now disturbed by the authorities' growing indifference to Jewish law. The inevitable revolt that broke out in 66 is probably the most famous of all the rebellions because of its consequences: the destruction of the Temple and the abolition of the high priesthood. The ensuing settlement did not immediately provoke another uprising, possibly because the scope of the disaster of 66–70 deeply shocked the Jews. But the subsequent confiscation of land and its redistribution to soldiers and other foreigners meant that the new owners hired Jewish labourers, an affront in a traditional society of landowning peasants, whose discontent provided most of the recruits in Simon bar Kokhba's great revolt. Between 132 and 136, the rebels set up a separate state which many Jews viewed as the start of a messianic age. Bar Kokhba was prepared to use strong-arm measures to compel wavering Jews to fight, but the vast majority were fully behind him, for at first the Romans fared badly. Once the Roman army mastered the rebels, though, the province was reduced to a wilderness. Jerusalem became a Roman colony for veteran soldiers, and Jews were forbidden from entering the city on pain of death, except for one day each year during the fast that commemorated the Temple's destruction. This prohibition remained in force for centuries, thereby depriving the Jews of 'the promised land'.

THE EASTERN FRONTIER

The Jews were not the only problem which confronted Rome on the eastern frontier, since the annexation of Syria brought the Romans face to face with the Parthians. Remarkable as the Persian revival was under the Parthian kings, they were hardly the heirs of the great empire conquered by Alexander. Nor were the Parthians as powerful as their Sasanian successors, for the good reason that Parthia comprised a loose collection of provinces over which its kings exercised little authority. Yet this did not prevent the Parthians from being formidable enemies, as the Romans learned to their cost at Carrhae in 53 BC.

An ill-fated Roman expedition resulted then from Marcus Licinius Crassus' desire to emulate the eastern conquests of Alexander the Great. Though part of the so-called First Triumvirate, a political group devoted to the exercise of power in Rome, Crassus felt himself to be militarily inferior to Pompey and Julius Caesar, its other members. Ignoring his weakness in cavalry, a vital component of any army crossing the open plains of eastern Syria, the sixty-year-old Crassus was entirely surrounded by Parthian horsemen at Carrhae, now located just inside the border of modern Turkey. The Parthians fought from horseback, firing arrows beyond the range of the Roman infantrymen, who were baffled by the Parthian willingness to break off action when it offered no advantage. The readiness of the Parthians to retreat suggests a nomadic ancestry, which the record seems to confirm when it says that they 'still wore their long hair bunched over their heads in the Scythian fashion in order to make themselves look more dreadful'. But at Carrhae it was their arrows that made them terrifying, not their hairstyles.

Nearly 10,000 Romans were taken prisoner, some of whom were settled on Parthia's eastern border. Near the Central Asian city of Turfan they may have eventually met Chinese opponents. A Chinese text tells of the surrender in 36 BC of a Hunnish chieftain, whose followers included a group of mercenaries suspiciously like ex-Roman legionaries, from a description of their drill.

Only disunity in Parthia saved Rome from an immediate counter-attack, but a defensive posture was thereafter the usual Roman strategy along its eastern frontier, a part of which was the border city of Dura-Europos, first noticed by British soldiers in 1920 when a company bivouacked in a ruined fortress on the western bank of the Euphrates. In a letter sent to his commanding officer, Captain M. C. Murphy wrote that they had chanced upon 'some ancient wall paintings in a wonderful state of presentation ... three men, one woman, and three other figures partly obliterated'. Careful excavation by American archaeologists was to uncover many other murals in excellent condition, whose subjects drew upon Judaism, Christianity and Zoroastrianism, besides the worship given to local deities.

Founded by the first Seleucid king, Dura-Europos has an interesting history. Already prosperous before its conquest by the Parthians, the city became a frontier outpost of Parthia without severing its cultural contacts with the Greek communities in Syria. Given the extent to which the Parthians themselves were influenced by Greece, this enduring link is readily explained. When Crassus' head was taken to Ctesiphon, the Parthian capital situated on the eastern bank of the Tigris opposite Seleucia, King Orodes II was watching a tragedy by the Athenian dramatist Euripides.

Although the Roman emperor Trajan captured Ctesiphon in 114, the first of several forays into Mesopotamia, the rationalization of the frontier under his successor, Hadrian, turned Dura-Europos into a Roman stronghold. Its garrison probably consisted of archers from Palmyra, a trading city keen to protect east–west trade. Various legionary detachments were stationed at Dura-Europos from time to time, and thanks to the dry conditions and the eventual abandonment of the site, a large number of Roman documents have survived intact. These include guard rosters, quartermasters' records, and even a military calendar. But the easterly location of Dura-Europos meant that it could never easily be reinforced, and in 256 the city fell to the Sasanians, whose king Shapur I also captured Antioch, the provincial capital of Roman Syria. When Emperor

Valerian arrived to restore the eastern frontier, he was taken prisoner in 260 by the Sasanians. At Naqsh-i-Rustam, Shapur celebrated his triumphs over the Romans in a gigantic rock carving. A submissive Philip is shown pleading for peace, while on his knees a second Roman emperor, Valerian, watches as a prisoner of war.

Sympathetic though the Parthians were to the Seleucid heritage they inherited, their attitude to ancient Mesopotamian culture was marked by indifference. At Babylon, the cult of Marduk disappeared from sight, while at Nippur the temple of the storm god Enlil and its ziggurat were converted into a fortification. The great Sumerian–Babylonian cities gradually gave way to rural settlements and, where the irrigation system fell into disrepair, the desert spread across the land. Parthian buildings exhibited a strange mixture of styles: to the ancient Near Eastern tradition of a central courtyard were added Greek architectural ornamentation and the Parthian preference for open galleries. These vaulted galleries, known as *liwan*, were to become the characteristic architectural feature in Sasanian and, more particularly, Islamic times.

Persia triumphant. The famous celebration of Rome's defeat at Naqsh-i-Rustam

The conflict between the Romans and the Parthians had little impact on Roman holdings south of Syria. In 106, Trajan added a province called Arabia Felix as a means of protecting Palestine; its most celebrated city was rose-red Petra, the capital of the Nabataean Arabs, who had successfully held their own against the Greeks. Prior to his death, Alexander the Great planned the conquest of the whole of Arabia, but his successors never bothered to follow this up. In spite of the tomb of a Roman officer at Petra, there is no evidence of a permanent military presence there; rather Bostra, modern Bursa, acted as the provincial Roman capital and legionary headquarters. The location of the fortress has now been identified in the north of the town near a spring.

Away from the eastern frontier, however, Rome had a determined opponent in Mithridates VI of Pontus, a state in northern Asia Minor. Mountainous yet fertile, the kingdom of Pontus derived most of its wealth from the iron it exported to the Greco-Roman world. Deeply influenced by the example of Alexander the Great, Mithridates launched three wars against Rome, whose interests in Asia Minor clashed with those of Pontus. Disagreements with Rome's puppet rulers led to a Roman ultimatum in 88 BC, which Mithridates chose to ignore. Mithridates put his trust in a well-trained army and a powerful fleet, knowing that anti-Roman sentiment would provide him with a number of valuable allies, including Greek cities such as Athens, which contributed to his initial successes on land and sea. The attraction of the Pontic king for the Greeks and Macedonians lay in the possibility of throwing off the Roman yoke. In the province of Asia, Mithridates symbolically signalled Roman greed by forcing a captured official to drink molten gold.

A Roman counter-attack had by 86 BC recovered Athens, where Lucius Sulla only agreed to stop a massacre of its citizens because of his admiration of Greek culture, remarking that he spared the few for the sake of the many, the living for the sake of the dead. Then this ruthless Roman general concluded a generous peace with Mithridates so that he could hurry back to Italy and settle accounts with his political opponents in Rome. Punishment for the war therefore fell on the rebellious cities in the form of pillage and reparations. This abandonment was never forgotten: no one joined Mithridates when he twice renewed the conflict with

Rome. In 67 BC the totally defeated Pontic king fled to the Crimea, where he took poison. Even though most of Mithridates' defeats predated Pompey's arrival in Asia Minor, they did not stop this ambitious general from claiming all the credit for himself; in his triumph in Rome he wore the cloak of Alexander the Great, an item of loot once belonging to Mithridates.

In the Anatolian interior two formally powerful peoples, the Lydians and the Phrygians, were also incorporated into the Roman empire, like the inhabitants of Pontus. According to ancient Greek tradition, the Phrygians emigrated to Asia Minor from the Balkans before the Trojan War, but it is more likely that they were later arrivals and part of the great movement of the Sea Peoples. The Assyrians had been harassed by the Mushki people, who may well have been the Phrygians. Their first kingdom in Asia Minor was ruled by their leader Mita, whom the Greeks called Midas.

King Midas' famous reputation for riches was surpassed by the Lydians, one of whose kings has given us the phrase 'as rich as Croesus'. In the

A Christian funerary monument from Roman Phrygia

cultural interaction with the Greeks, who were settled along the Aegean coast of Asia Minor and in many of its river valleys, the Phrygians gained the most. In addition to the alphabet, they adopted the names of Greek deities and modified them with appropriate epithets. They also used Greek names for deities who had no equivalent in the Greek pantheon, like the gods of justice, Hosios and Dikaios, the protectors of Phrygian settlements. Quite distinct, however, was the indigenous goddess Cybele, the mother of the gods. Her original name in Phrygian was Matar Kubileya, or 'mother of the mountain'. The triumphant progress of her cult statue westwards ended in Rome during the darkest days of the struggle against the Carthaginian general Hannibal. Despite a marked aversion to her bloody worship, which often ended in self-castration, the Romans prized the value of Magna Mater's supernatural support.

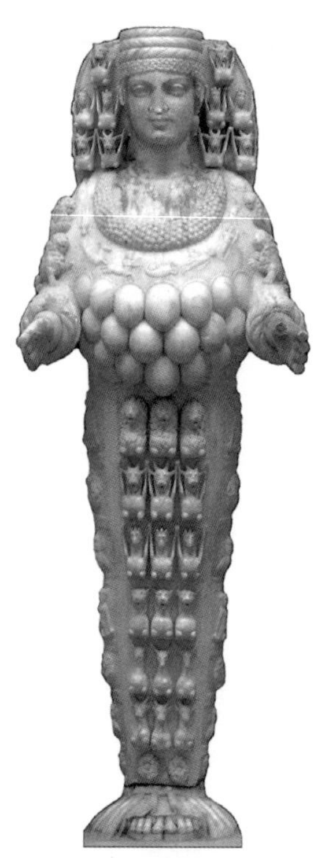

Artemis of Ephesus, the Greek version of the indigenous mother goddess Cybele

It is now clear that Cybele had a profound influence on the cult of Artemis at Ephesus, a Greek goddess who really worried the early Christians. Competition between Artemis and the Virgin Mary led to the erection of Christian shrines on sanctuaries previously dedicated to the goddess. And it is significant that in 431 the Council of Ephesus, which met in a church supposed to contain Mary's mortal remains, confirmed her title of Theotokos, 'God-bearer', which translated into Latin as Mater Dei, meaning 'the Mother of God'. Today the cult of the Virgin Mary continues to flourish locally, because in 1892 it was announced that she had lived in a house on a hillside near Ephesus, the supposed location of which was apparently pinpointed in the visions of a bedridden German nun. A new chapel now standing there was confirmed as a place of pilgrimage by both Pope Paul VI and Pope John Paul II. The Phrygians became Christians during the second century, but they were soon accused of heresy. Called Montanism after its founder Montanus, their approach to Christianity relied upon prophecy inspired by the Holy Spirit, which was condemned as unseemly worship.

Montanism spread far beyond Asia Minor. It had its followers in Italy and France, but the idea of divinely inspired utterance took firm root in north Africa, when Tertullian of Carthage, a prolific Christian writer, became a Montanist. Concerned about the growing pretensions of the papacy, Tertullian challenged Callistus, then the bishop of Rome, to justify his entitlement of absolution. 'Now then, apostolic man,' wrote Tertullian, 'show me samples of your prophetic works so I may recognize your divine authorization; after this, claim for yourself the power to forgive sins.' In the eastern Mediterranean, Greek Orthodox priests were content to say 'May God forgive your sins.' This did not stop them from excommunicating Montanists, since they called their beliefs 'the pure', a way of worship quite separate from organized Christianity.

After the decline of Phrygian power, Asia Minor came under the sway of Lydia. Rich enough to sustain almost continuous warfare, Lydia pursued an aggressive foreign policy. Its prosperity rested upon excellent agricultural land as well as plentiful mineral resources including deposits of silver and gold, while an additional source of royal income was the taxation levied on trade, once the Lydian kings invented the first coinage of the ancient Near East. Lydian interest in commerce definitely pleased the ancient Greek settlers. They were much less restive under the Lydians than under the Persians, who defeated the Lydian king Croesus at Sardis in 456 BC. The Greek historian Herodotus tells us that an oracle encouraged Croesus to give battle. When the king asked at Delphi whether or not he should oppose the Persian king Cyrus, he was informed that such an undertaking 'would destroy a great empire'. It was unfortunately his own.

PART 3

THE MEDIEVAL NEAR EAST

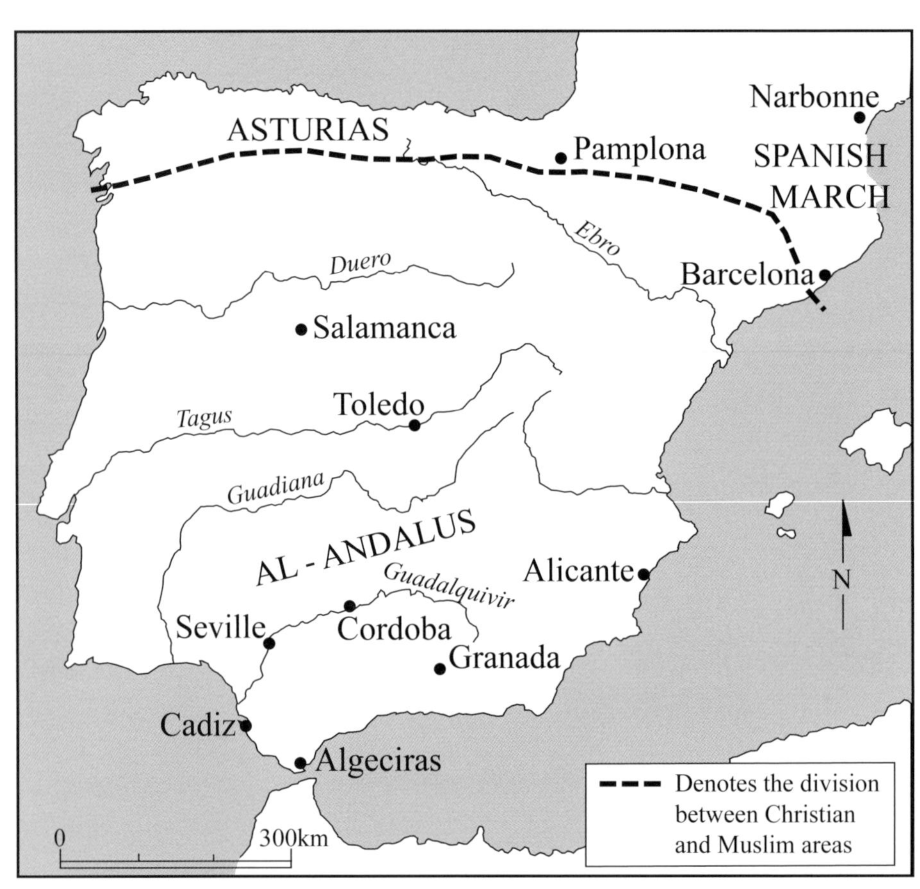

The Iberian Peninsula around 800

7

A WORLD CRISIS

THE RISE OF ISLAM

It should be known that in Muhammad's opinion, all of this world is a vehicle for transport to the next, the world of eternity. He who loses the vehicle can go nowhere.

The Muqaddimah *of Ibn Khaldun*

The year 622 witnessed the start of a profound change in Near Eastern culture. That year a middle-aged merchant by the name of Muhammad moved from Mecca to Medina, where he lived for the rest of his life. A decade earlier, Muhammad had begun to receive the revelation of the Qur'an, the Muslim scripture. In the bleak hills north of Mecca the archangel Gabriel had revealed this divine truth: it was meant 'to make everything clear'. Once Muhammad was satisfied with the authenticity of the message, he realized that he had been chosen as the Prophet, whose duty was to call upon the Arabs to acknowledge the glory of Allah and pray to him. Yet he was acutely aware of the lateness of his prophecy, when he told converts that their 'appointed time compared with those who had gone before is as from the afternoon prayer to the setting of the sun'.

Muhammad's first convert was his wife, followed by his close relatives. What galvanized his listeners was his utter certainty that those who failed to recognize Allah would be consigned to hell, where 'a flaming fire' awaited them. Although the deity upon whose behalf Muhammad spoke was addressed as 'the Merciful, the Compassionate', someone to whom people could look for help and guidance, Allah's wrath was terrible for anyone who had the temerity to deny his existence. Idolatry in particular roused Allah to fury.

At first the reception of Muhammad's message had been mixed in Mecca, and after persecution Muhammad took up residence in Medina. Trouble began for the Prophet when he disparaged local deities, which offended most Meccans who thought that Muhammad was actually suffering from a mental illness. They tried to obtain medical treatment for him, but his absolute espousal of monotheism meant that there was no choice but removal elsewhere. The move to Medina was a major turning point in the growth of Islam because, away from the restricting atmosphere of Mecca, Muhammad could preach without any interference and his followers could evolve the rituals of worship which distinguish the faith from other Near Eastern beliefs.

The stages by which Muhammad established his authority in Medina are now unclear. But he seems to have begun the struggle against the Meccans on his arrival at the city: since he appreciated the Arab delight in fighting, attacks on Mecca were bound to attract many new recruits. Muhammad participated himself in raids on caravans passing through Mecca, winning a notable victory in 624. From the spoils and the ransoms paid afterwards, there was enough money to put the new religion on its feet.

In Medina, the large Jewish community resident there was initially sympathetic to Muhammad's message. But just as Christians could never understand how the Jews persisted in their refusal to accept Jesus as the Messiah, so Muhammad was in the end frustrated by a Jewish unwillingness to regard him as the Prophet. The rejection caused Muhammad to accuse the Jews of falsifying revelation and then secure their expulsion from the city. Jews posed a real theological challenge to Muhammad, because he could not allow them to live alongside Muslims, lest they confuse his revelation in the minds of converts. After civil disturbances, male Jews were executed while women and children were sold into slavery. With the elimination of the Jewish community, Muhammad was in complete control of Medina, an essential condition for the success of the new religion, because it gave access to trade routes that facilitated the spread of his message.

In 628 Muhammad went to Mecca. He did not lead a military expedition but a group of pilgrims who came to worship in peace. Originally Muhammad's converts had prayed in the direction of Jerusalem, but during the break with the Jews the direction was changed to Mecca, where the Ka'ba acted as a focus for worship. What Muhammad sought to do by undertaking this first *hajj*, or pilgrimage, was to persuade the Arabs that they should adhere to the pure monotheism established by their ancestor, Abraham. Believed to have been set up by Abraham and his eldest son Ismail, the Ka'ba and its black stone could be a survival of ancient veneration for prominent rocks among the Arabs. A similar reverence was given to the Mount in Jerusalem, close to the site of the old Jewish temple: Muslims held that this was the place of Abraham's attempted sacrifice of his son Isaac, the point from which Muhammad ascended for his tour of heaven, and the location of the Last Judgement.

ISLAM: THE FINAL REVELATION

The Qur'an is supposed to embody the third and final revelation of the deity and complement the Bible, because from the beginning of Islam both the Jews and the Christians were acknowledged as 'the people of the book'. Even though their scriptures incorporated the divine will up to the time of Muhammad's revelation, the Prophet considered that they gave a seriously distorted account of events, which explained the many differences from the Qur'an. Adam, Noah, Abraham, Moses and Jesus came to be regarded in Islamic tradition as Muslim; they were all prophets who anticipated the prophecy of Muhammad, in spite of their messages so often being entirely misunderstood.

The mission of Noah, for instance, was to warn his contemporaries against the iniquity of worshipping a multitude of deities, when Allah was the only god. We are a long way from the sinfulness of the Old Testament, and even further from the Sumerian reason for the original Flood, the inability of the sky god Enlil to get a good night's sleep because of the excessive noise people were making in overcrowded cities. For Muslims, the Flood was no more than a just punishment for polytheism. This was the reason for the revelation of the Qur'an 'wherein is no doubt, a guidance to the godfearing'. Such guidance could even rescue those who had gone astray, since 'truly Allah was gracious to the believers when He raised up among them a Messenger from themselves, to recite to them His signs and to purify them, and to teach them the Book and the Wisdom, though before they were in manifest error'. A prime instance of the correction of error involved the Ka'ba itself. Having finally taken control of Mecca, Muhammad purged the site of idols, confirming the Ka'ba as the chief object of Muslim pilgrimage.

Possibly through enjoying a more sustained period of divine contact than Moses, when the Jewish leader received the Ten Commandments during the wanderings of the Jews in Sinai, Muhammad worshipped a

A Turkish tile of the Ka'ba, Islam's holiest site

very different kind of deity to the Jews and the Christians. The directness of the Qur'an must have also owed something to his early upbringing in a desert encampment, ringed at night by nothing but stars, as Allah's cosmic role is never in doubt. The Qur'an announces that there 'is no god but He, the Living, the Everlasting ... To him belongs all that is in the heavens and the earth ... for He is the All-high, the All-glorious.' Yet nothing at all was beneath Allah's notice, which explains how Muhammad could present the Muslim deity as being seated on a throne comprising the heavens and the earth, while reminding the Arabs of divine interest in the most mundane matters. An individual's soul was said to be 'closer to Allah than the jugular vein'.

Another early influence on Muhammad was his nurse Baraka, better known as Umm Ayman. That she was an Ethiopian is a reminder of how far Africans had integrated with Arab society. During much of the sixth century, southern Arabia was actually occupied by the Ethiopians, who sent traders and priests to live in cities, such as Mecca, that were not under their direct control. Although Ethiopia converted to Christianity during the fourth century, its version of the Christian faith had diverged significantly from the official Byzantine model. Whereas Constantinople remained wedded to the dual nature of Christ as agreed in 325 at Nicaea, the Ethiopians preferred the strict Monophysite view of a single divine nature; hardly a surprising difference, perhaps, when the Monophysites were so strong in Egypt, the nearest Byzantine province to Ethiopia.

Like the Arabs before Muhammad, the Ethiopians had worshipped a great many gods and goddesses until their rulers in Axum, the Ethiopian capital, proclaimed the worship of the Christian deity and, through a still little understood legend, claimed descent from Solomon and Sheba. Their son Menelik was anointed by Solomon as the king of Ethiopia, founding a royal house which ended with the overthrow of Haile Selassie in 1974. It was the same Menelik who is supposed to have stolen the Ark from the Temple in Jerusalem and brought it to Axum. Whatever the historical circumstances behind this tenacious dynastic claim, Ethiopian rulers came to see themselves as the champions of Christianity around the shores of the Red Sea.

A coin struck by the Christian king of Axum, with Ethiopic script

It explains their swift reaction to the Himyarites of present-day Yemen after these Arabs adopted Judaism as their state religion. This sudden spread of monotheism into the Arabian peninsula took everyone by surprise. In 523 a Himyarite king by the name of Yusuf Asar Yathar started to persecute Christians living in his kingdom. A massacre of Christians unwilling to convert to Judaism at Najran was enough for King Kaleb in Axum to dispatch a huge seaborne expedition of 120,000 men against the Himyarites. Already Yusuf had closed churches by destroying them or converting them into synagogues. He even burned Christians alive in their own places of worship. Kaleb's offensive probably had motives other than religious concern, for Ethiopia had a past history of involvement with the Arabian peninsula. Having removed any threat to Christianity there, the king set about rebuilding churches, especially for the Ethiopians whom he left behind as permanent settlers.

The success of the Ethiopian invasion was celebrated by the Byzantines as a victory for Christianity. The link between religious and political power had progressively strengthened in the eastern Mediterranean with the concentration of what was left of imperial Roman government at Constantinople. Sasanian Persia was partly responsible for this outlook through its persecution of its non-Zoroastrian subjects. Under King

Shapur I, the name of Kartir was synonymous with religious intolerance. This influential Zoroastrian cleric attacked Jews, Buddhists, Hindus, Manichees and Christians alike. Within his own faith he was responsible for replacing cult images with sacred fires, an iconoclastic tendency that would later be given full reign by Muhammad. As Kartir said with some satisfaction: 'Images were destroyed, the lurking places of demons demolished and the abodes of angels set up.'

One reason for Byzantium's pleasure at the discomfort of the Himyarite kingdom was a suspicion that Judaism was pro-Persian. Incorrect though this view was, it did not help that the Sasanian Persians started to meddle in Arabian affairs. Having expelled the Ethiopians, they claimed authority over the whole peninsula in the 580s, although Persian control was in all probability restricted to the eastern coast. This is hardly a surprising situation, given how much of Persia's military resources were then tied up in its war against the Byzantines.

Without reliable local sources for this period of intense competition between two closely related monotheisms, Judaism and Christianity, and between the two belligerent superpowers of Byzantium and Persia, it is impossible to describe in any detail the background to the emergence of Islam, the key event in south-western Arabia. And because Muhammad was of little consequence to the outside world during his lifetime, there are no external sources to elucidate his actions either. Although later Muslim historians assume that the Prophet was bent on world dominion from the beginning, no evidence exists to justify such a view. If anything, Muhammad may have encouraged the advance of Arab arms beyond the Arabian peninsula as a convenient way of reducing internecine tribal warfare.

Having been a merchant before the revelation of the Qur'an commenced in 610, Muhammad may well have travelled to Ethiopia himself. His sympathy for Ethiopians can be judged from his sending some of his closest followers as missionaries: he must have thought that his message would receive a welcome there. We know that the Bible was read aloud in Mecca by Ethiopian clerics. Without this public recital of both the Old and New Testaments, Muslims could not have understood the biblical references in the Qur'an. In particular, those who embraced Muhammad's message realized why it denied the divinity, the crucifixion and the resurrection of Christ. A prophet such as Jesus could never have raised Lazarus from the dead, nor reappeared himself after his burial. Only Allah was powerful enough to return the dead to life. Whereas non-believers reduced the dead person to bones, true believers envisioned the deceased as a complex entity of soul and bones, which Allah would reconstitute at the end of the world.

Before his death in 632 at the age of sixty, Muhammad had outlined the duties of the faithful—ritual washing, daily prayers, regular almsgiving, prescribed fasting and at least one pilgrimage. Except for the inferior status of women and slaves, there were to be no inequalities among Muslims other than religious merit, which alone Allah could determine. Muhammad's aversion for alcohol, an Arabic word in origin, seems at first to be no more than nomadic disdain for city life. The Qur'an does not expressly forbid the consumption of alcohol, although it strongly advises against it. Muhammad appears to have tried to block the making of wine by limiting the kinds of vessels in which fruit juice could be stored, but tending vines was very much part of Arab culture as the Nabateans had a long tradition of wine production.

Why then did Muhammad so dislike wine? The answer is by no means straightforward, although there are a number of possibilities. An obvious influence was Christian asceticism. Among Christian communities situated on the edge of the Syrian desert, groups of austere monks simply wandered from place to place. They were called 'the shepherds as they had no houses, ate neither bread nor meat, and drank no wine', their extreme diet consisting of uncooked vegetables and seeds, soaked in olive oil. Apart from attempting to liberate the spirit through such physical hardship, these Syrian ascetics were putting a safe distance between themselves and non-Christian cults, in which wine was offered alongside meat in sacrifice. They saw this kind of worship as impure and corrupted by evil spirits.

A yet more compelling reason for Muhammad's concern about alcohol was the role that wine had come to play in the central Christian ritual of the Eucharist. He seemed determined to separate Islam completely from every aspect of Christianity. Once wine became a spiritual drink at the Last Supper and was incorporated into Christian worship, there was

A fourteenth-century miniature of Muhammad preaching

every reason for Muhammad to warn his followers against its consumption. Allah was so removed from earthly things that he could never be commemorated as Christ was in the ritual of communion: the eating of bread and the drinking of wine. And it is not entirely irrelevant that St Paul had earlier shared Muhammad's worry about the closeness of the Last Supper to pagan feasts.

Just how different Muhammad's monotheism was from Christianity is apparent in the famous conversation in 781 between the third Abbasid caliph al-Mahdi and the Nestorian bishop Timothy the Great. When the caliph asked about veneration for the cross, Timothy explained how the death of the Son of God had redeemed sinners. Al-Mahdi then asked whether this meant that God could die, and after listening to the bishop's careful distinction between Christ's divinity and humanity, he said 'they did not kill him, nor did they crucify him, but he made a likeness for them'.

Living under Muslim rule, Christians like Timothy met monotheists of an entirely different order to themselves. Allah was simply too powerful, too unlike anything else in the universe, ever to be incarnated in human form. Above all, Muhammad could never accept in the Christian service of communion that the bread was actually divine flesh and the wine was divine blood, an idea which is expressed in St John's gospel. 'Then Jesus said unto them, verily, verily, I say unto you, except ye eat the flesh of the Son of Man, and drink his blood, you have no life in you.' Such an antidote against everlasting death had no place at all in Muhammad's thinking; nor did Christian controversies about the nature of Christ, which the Roman emperor Constantine tried to contain at the Council of Nicaea, feature within Allah's absolute divinity. Such complex theological disputes could never trouble Islam, for the good reason that the Arabs would have no truck with Mesopotamian dying-and-rising gods.

THE ARAB ONSLAUGHT

After he had delivered his message, the death of Muhammad brought Islam to a standstill. Ali ibn Abi Talib, Muhammad's son-in-law, was a possibility for leadership, although he was probably too young to be generally acceptable. Anyway, Ali was more concerned with making funeral arrangements for the Prophet than the politics of the mosque. So Muhammad's father-in-law Abu Bakr became *khalifat Allah*, 'the deputy of God'. Even though a compromise choice as 'caliph' (the usual rendering in English of this title), Abu Bakr was able to hold the volatile Arabs together for several reasons. First of all, he was related to Muhammad, whose revelation he had early endorsed, through the Prophet's marriage to his daughter; secondly, he possessed a vast knowledge of the Arab tribes as well as the causes of their apparently endless feuds; thirdly, he was skilfully diplomatic in his dealings with chieftains, but never forgot the essentials of Islam; and last but not least, he was an old man, which meant that there would be scope in the near future for the ambitious to succeed him.

Of the four caliphs who were appointed after Muhammad's death, Abu Bakr alone escaped the dagger of an assassin. Umar ibn al-Kattab, Uthman ibn Affran and Ali himself were all struck down before the Umayyad clan in newly conquered Syria founded a dynasty that lasted almost a century. Despite the Umayyads' bloody overthrow in 750—in a kind of delayed reaction to Ali's murder—this first caliphate effectively established Islam as a universal religion and made Arabic the key language in the medieval Near East.

At one moment, a handful of followers listened to the Prophet. A mere fifty years later, his successor as the leader of the Muslim community was one of the most powerful rulers in the medieval world. As Muhammad expected, the Arabs exported Islam by force of arms. Victories over the Byzantines and the Sasanian Persians seemed to confirm the power of Allah, encouraging yet more Arab conquests. Once the concept of holy war took root, there was no point in any dialogue with non-Muslim states. For the world was divided into two starkly different zones: the Dar al-Islam, the 'house of Islam'; and the Dar al-Harb, the 'house of war'. The result was that peace was not seen to be interrupted by war, but rather continuous warfare against the infidels only came to a halt whenever outright victory or an enforced truce occurred.

The Arab onslaught could not have been launched at a better time for the attackers. Perhaps as much as one-third of the medieval Near Eastern population outside Arabia had been carried off by plague, even before the bitter struggle between the Sasanian Persians and the Byzantines added widespread destruction. Yet the unexpected Arab advance in the last decade of Emperor Heraclius' reign so worried Byzantium that some of his subjects wondered if the military reverses indicated the loss of divine approval for the Christian empire. Sophronius, the patriarch of Jerusalem, was sure that Muslims would not have triumphed so readily had Christians remained truly devout.

So impressive was the surge of Muslim power that not only was the city of Constantinople itself threatened, but even more Arab arms pushed along the north African coast and on into Spain and France. In 732 an Arab army crossed the Pyrenees, burned churches in Bordeaux and Poitiers, and was thrown back near Tours by the Franks under the command of Charles Martel. This victory halted the Arab advance in western Europe; but Berber resentment, rather than Christian courage, may have tipped the balance in favour of the Franks on the battlefield. As native north Africans, the Berbers had fought within the ranks of Arab armies

The Byzantine emperor Heraclius with his son Constantine III

without receiving proper recognition for their services. Too much was being demanded of them for the benefit of the Arabs: without Berber manpower there could have been no invasion of the Iberian peninsula. The exasperated Berbers rose in 740 against their Arab overlords and, though they remained Muslims, the unity of the faith was lost.

But the Umayyads had cause to pause before this uprising, since in 678 an earthquake devastated northern Syria. An ageing Muawiyah, the first Umayyad caliph, wondered whether Allah was withdrawing his favour from the Arabs. He also had to deal with a daring Byzantine counter-attack in the form of an extended commando raid, which stirred up local insurgency.

Muawiyah's elevation as caliph had been confirmed in Jerusalem, a city recognized by Jews, Christians and Muslims as a sacred city. We are told that Muawiyah went to Golgotha, the hill on which Jesus was crucified, and prayed there; then he went to the tomb of Mary and did the same. These actions indicate how early Islam was open to all 'the people of the book'. The caliph showed due reverence to the Christian holy places, but he made it absolutely clear that both Jesus and his mother were located on the human plane. The conquest of Palestine, following a decisive victory at Gaza in 633, was therefore seen by the Arabs as a divine gift. Muslim conquests were *futuh*, a term derived from *fath*, which means 'to open' and by extension to 'open for judgement'. It appears to have been first used for Muhammad's conquest of Mecca. The implication was that Muslim soldiers were Allah's earthly agents, the means of opening up the world to the teachings of Islam. As far as the Byzantines were concerned, their eastern provinces were largely lost as a result of Yarmuk, a battle fought in broken country below the Golan Heights. The month-long contest in the summer of 636 culminated in a Byzantine rout. The Muslims took few prisoners and they consolidated their victory by a rapid advance across Syria. As Emperor Heraclius had no further troops to spare, he stopped trying to hold Syria. The Byzantine army fought doggedly and capably through crisis after crisis, but it faced long years of warfare against a fresh and enthusiastic enemy.

THE UMAYYAD CALIPHATE

After the assassination in 661of Ali ibn Abi Talib at Kufa in central Iraq, while he prayed in a mosque, the Muslim governor of Damascus, Muawiyah, made his bid for personal power. Despite being secure in Syria, Muawiyah faced immense problems in the rest of the Muslim world, and especially among the Arab tribes settled in Iraq. So badly damaged was Islam by the conflicts of the preceding years that the would-be caliph had to convince many of the faithful about the value of a central government. Numerous revolts against Muawiyah and his successors started in Iraq, where in 680 the leaders of one uprising asked Hussein, the son of Ali and the grandson of Muhammad, to come from Medina and take charge of their opposition to Umayyad rule. When Hussein's small caravan was surprised by Umayyad soldiers and everyone was killed, the incident seemed no more than a skirmish, but the religious consequences were immense. For the supporters of Hussein glorified his death and suggested that he had deliberately embraced martyrdom to atone for the sins of Allah's worshippers. From this notion arose Shia, and the view that all political authority outside the family of the Prophet and his kin was illegitimate. It is still accepted by the majority of today's Shiites.

Perhaps the crucial Shia dogma was that Muslims require priestly guidance to achieve eternal salvation. Most of all, this guidance was expected to come from a succession of imans, the last of whom was to be the Mahdi, or 'messiah'. When the Mahdi appears, he will found a kingdom of peace and justice that will last a thousand years. Only after that era is over will the Day of Judgement occur. The Shiites presently living in Iraq have congregated around imams' tombs, although their clerics have never equalled the power of the mullahs in Iran, who were able to secure their dominant position by drawing upon a long tradition of pre-Islamic clerical authority.

Muawiyah's method of establishing the Umayyad caliphate was more subtle than outright conquest. Realizing that most tribal leaders wished to secure the position of their own families, Muawiyah came to terms with those who controlled the provinces, thereby gaining their support without conflict. Such a decentralized form of control actually suited the Arab temperament. Later Umayyad caliphs followed the lead of Muawiyah, so that Damascus never exercised anything approaching control over those who ran the provinces; rather it tolerated a confederation of local leaders who acknowledged its overall authority.

Against the Byzantines, though, Muawiyah used his armed forces which were enhanced by the development of a navy. Two attacks on Cyprus displayed Islam's new-found naval power. Warned in 668 of a major seaborne expedition heading for Constantinople, Emperor Constantine IV had large warships constructed and ordered them to

The Byzantine architectural input to this Umayyad mosque is obvious

guard the city's harbours. Neither the Umayyads nor the Byzantines gained the upper hand despite the Muslim capture of the ancient city of Cyzicus, just across the Sea of Marmara from Constantinople. From this anchorage, the Umayyad fleet was able to challenge the Byzantines at sea; but without a decisive victory, the attackers were obliged to abandon the siege, apparently driven away by 'the pain of hunger and pestilence'.

Two other factors might have thwarted the Umayyad assault. The first is that the emperor Constantine reinforced his naval forces by bringing back squadrons from the central Mediterranean. The second is that the Byzantines invented a new weapon, aptly called Greek fire: it consisted of naphthalene, a flaming substance which could be directed against enemy vessels by means of a long metal siphon. This weapon the Byzantines put to good effect time and time again.

During the last seven years of Muawiyah's reign, the caliph's son Yazid led raids on Byzantine territory and other islands were captured, but they provided tribute rather than space for colonization. One particular prob-

Caliph Abd al-Malik's Dome of the Rock in Jerusalem

lem disturbed Muawiyah's later years: how to secure the succession of his son Yazid. When the caliph died in 680, Yazid tried to hold on to power; but his own early death, apparently from natural causes, left his young son briefly in charge, but he also died quite soon. His passing ignited a civil war that eventually ended in 685 with the succession of Abd al-Malik ibn Marwan. Despite continued opposition, Abd al-Malik proved to be a really effective ruler. Besides holding the Byzantines at bay in Asia Minor, the new caliph reformed the administration and introduced a coinage that could be used throughout the Muslim world. Abd al-Malik's success derived in part from a ten-year truce to which, in 686, he got the Byzantine emperor Justinian II's agreement. The terms amounted to a massive payment to Constantinople in the form of slaves, horses and gold currency. Abd al-Malik also agreed to share the revenues of Cyprus with Justinian, provided the Byzantines withdrew the commandos who were still stirring up so much trouble in Syria and Palestine. Having removed the threat of foreign attack, the caliph was able gradually to impose his will on the more restive provincial governors.

Yet a seven-month siege was required to recover Mecca from a rival 'caliph'. Abd al-Malik even sanctioned a bombardment with catapults to break the deadlock, which lasted well into the month of pilgrimage, the *hajj*. Elsewhere his forces quelled rebellions as far apart as Iraq and Afghanistan. Abd al-Malik also increased the extent of the Muslim empire, since in 695 the city of Carthage fell to a combined force of Arabs and Berbers. The rise of Tunis as the premier settlement in this region dates from this period. Fighting against the Byzantines had resumed in Asia Minor, but without any lasting success. The initial onrush of Muslim arms was over.

Remembered for his reforms and the soundness of his administration, Abd al-Malik is today celebrated above all for the Dome of the Rock in Jerusalem. One of the world's architectural masterpieces, the Dome drew upon Byzantine building techniques in its unequivocal statement of Islam's position in the holy city. During the rivalry with the 'caliph' in Mecca, this new building provided a useful alternative destination for pilgrims, but a stronger motive behind its construction would have been the Umayyad assertion that political and religious

'Greek fire', a weapon the Byzantines deployed effectively at sea

authority was no longer centred upon Arabia. When the Dome's two architects informed Abd al-Malik that: 'a hundred thousand gold coins were left unspent at the end of the project, the caliph offered them the money as a reward. But they declined, indicating that they had already been generously rewarded. So Abd al-Malik ordered the coins to be melted and cast on the Dome's exterior, which at the time had such a glitter that no eye could gaze upon it'.

Inured to living as a minority people under foreign rule, the Jews kept well away from Islam, but not so the Christians who began to convert in large numbers during Abd al-Malik's enlightened reign. Bishop Jacob of Edessa, who died three years after the caliph in 708, told his flock that penitent apostates on the edge of death could receive the Eucharist; Christians who became Muslims and then returned to Christianity did not need rebaptism, but they should observe a period of penance; and Christian wives of Muslims could also receive the Eucharist, but only after an appropriate penalty. That they had married Muslims was in itself a sin because they knew that their children were bound to be raised as Muslims. An apocryphal exchange between Abd al-Malik and a distinguished scholar concerns Islamic leadership. When the caliph learned that non-Arab converts acted as the religious authorities in many cities, Abd al-Malik exclaimed that they 'are going to predominate over the Arabs to such an extent that they will preach to them from pulpits, with the Arabs down below listening'. To which the scholar is supposed to have replied: 'But Commander of the Faithful, it is a matter of belief; whoever fully embraces Islam will rise and whoever neglects it will decline.'

After Abd al-Malik's death, his close relations succeeded him one after another. The reign of his eldest son, al-Walid, from 705 to 715 saw the furthest extension of the geographical frontiers of the Umayyad dominion. In 711, the year that the Arabs invaded Spain, an expeditionary force of 6,000 cavalry and 6,000 infantry marched through southern Iran to the Indus delta, while supplies and siege equipment were sent by sea. The target was Daybul, a port on the site of modern Karachi. The specific cause of the attack was piracy, because an Arab ship carrying precious gifts from the ruler of the Maldives to al-Walid had been intercepted by marauders from Daybul. There were Muslim women on board as well. Once the port-city's walls were demolished by huge catapults, a large number of people living there were shipped off as slaves. Though conversion does not seem to have been a priority for the Arabs, many Indians became Muslims as a result of Daybul's capture, and especially those with a low-caste status, who were hardly integrated into Hindu society. Here, and elsewhere in the subcontinent, Muslim invaders were to find that Islam's marked egalitarian outlook would prove attractive to people whom fellow Hindus regarded as social inferiors.

Al-Walid's younger brothers were all short-lived, but his cousin Umar II lived long enough for his political initiatives to offend traditionalists. His effort to break down barriers between Arab rulers and their non-Arab subjects, and between different Arab tribes, badly backfired. These policies threatened too many vested interests, and in 720 Umar II was poisoned. Opposition to the Umayyads steadily grew, as usual in Iraq but also in north Africa, where the Berbers were treated as unworthy auxiliaries in Arab armies. The problem was that, despite Umar II's belated attempt to broaden the base of the regime, Umayyad government essentially meant Syrian domination, and the dynasty collapsed in 750 before a movement in favour of rule by the Prophet's descendants. It was the killing of Hussein ibn Ali which ultimately ruined the Umayyads, because the Arabs could never forget that Muhammad had once bounced this grandson on his knee. After the murder, the Umayyad caliphate was regarded as bloodthirsty and impious.

THE ABBASID CALIPHATE

Opposition to the rule of Damascus was never anti-Muslim, since rebellions were driven by the ambitions of provincial leaders and the discontent of their followers; or, in the case of the Berbers, by an acute sense of injustice. But the widespread agitation was enough to bring down the Umayyads, who were slaughtered with the sole exception of Abd al-Rahman. Fleeing westwards, he seized power in Spain where he ruled at Cordoba as another 'caliph' until 788. Four years before the end of his reign, Abd al-Rahman started to build that city's great mosque, which remains one of the finest buildings in Europe today. Even Emperor Charles V, who had given his consent to the building of a cathedral chapter in the centre of the mosque, later repented the decision and reproached himself for destroying 'what was unique in the world'.

Quite remarkable was the development of Cordoba as the foremost centre of artistic and literary culture in medieval Europe. Two twelfth-century philosophers made the city famous: an Arab named Ibn Rushd, but known to the Christians as Averroes; and the Jew Maimonides. Ibn Rushd's admiration of Aristotle, whose works he summarized in 1168 at the request of the caliph Abu Yakub, led to this ancient Greek philosopher's ideas spreading to Christendom. Ibn Rushd also knew the work of Plato, but he did not have the same degree of admiration for him as he had for Aristotle, whose thought he regarded as the summation of the human intellect. Rejecting Aristotle's conception of an eternal universe, Maimonides endeavoured to reconcile philosophy and religion, but some of his interpretations of sacred texts were attacked by fellow Jews as blasphemous, in part because he was so frank about his debt to Muslim ideas as well as Greek science. Whilst acknowledging divine providence, Maimonides believed that the good and evil visited on individuals were 'consequent upon their deserts'. He also wrote how the deity was an infinite distance from creation.

Interior of the great Cordoba mosque

The claim of the Abbasid family to be descended from Muhammad, however contrived, satisfied enough Arabs to permit the establishment of a second caliphate. Because the revenues of Iraq, the home province of the Abbasids, were critical to the new government, the second caliph al-Mansur shifted the capital in the 760s to Baghdad, which soon became the largest city in the world outside China. Within little more than a century, the Arabs had transformed themselves from desert dwellers into the owners of a metropolis.

In spite of the Abbasids placing emphasis on their descent from the Prophet, some of their most prominent supporters were of Arab origin but spoke Persian, having intermarried with local people. Certainly the Abbasid caliphate was not exclusively run by Arabs, as had been the case under the Umayyads. If anything, al-Mansur and his successors emphasized the equality of all Muslims regardless of their ethnicity. Notice was being given that the Muslim empire was no longer the preserve of its founders, the Arabs. Welcome though this enlightened policy was for the different peoples who lived within its borders, the Abbasids discovered in

Coins showing two Abbasid caliphs: al-Muqtadir drinking on the left and al-Radi strumming a lute on the right

the end that they could prevent neither territorial fragmentation nor sectarian conflict.

Yet Baghdad still functioned as a great cultural centre, a gathering place for leading scholars whose intellectual interests were then in advance of the rest of the world. Philosophers, inventors, doctors, mathematicians, astronomers, chemists and geographers were all attracted to the Abbasid capital. A Central Asian by the name of Muhammad ibn Musa al-Khwarizmi stands head and shoulders above all the rest. He pioneered trigonometry and was the advocate of a decimal system of numbers and its concept of zero. Among his many achievements, al-Khwarizmi collected information on the precise latitudes and longitudes of over two thousand locations during his geographical researches. Adelard of Bath travelled as far as Antioch in search of al-Khwarizmi's writings, and returned home with his books on algebra and astronomy, both of which he translated into Latin.

What triggered the intellectual revolution in Baghdad as well as Cordoba was the recovery of ancient Greek authors such as Aristotle, Ptolemy, Euclid and Archimedes. Translations of their works into Arabic were available well before al-Khwarizmi arrived in Baghdad at the start of the ninth century. Another important source was neglected Indian works on astronomy and geometry.

But Baghdad did not suit everybody and Avicenna, as Ibn Sina was known in Europe, had nothing good to say about the city and soon left. Regarded by many as the greatest of all Muslim philosophers, Ibn Sina was a Persian who was educated in Arabic and wrote most of his works in that language. As his medical skills were in such great demand, he travelled from one sultan's court to another: his *Canon of Medicine* summarized the classical heritage, to which he added acute observations of his own. It was consulted by European doctors until the seventeenth century. Ibn Sina was never universally popular during his lifetime, because modesty was not one of his character traits. He died at the age of fifty-seven in 1037, most probably from colon cancer, which a follower rather unkindly blamed on Ibn Sina's strenuous sex life.

Despite Abbasid Baghdad witnessing a cultural flowering in the arts as well as the sciences, the city steadily became irrelevant to Muslim politics. The reign of Harun al-Rashid, from 786 to 809, is usually regarded as a glorious moment in Abbasid history, but there is little to support such a conclusion in contemporary records. If anything, this caliph was a rather nondescript character: he seems to have taken little interest in the day-to-day business of government, nor was he unduly worried by rebellions which government forces had ever greater difficulty in suppressing. One explanation for Harun's favourable reputation is his association with the *Arabian Nights*. Another must be the disastrous series of events which followed his reign: the civil war between his sons, and the later domination of the caliphate by Turkish slave-soldiers. In 812 the city of Baghdad endured a year-long siege, from which the dynasty never fully recovered. Even though the caliphate was still seen as an ideal, the political tide flowed towards provincial autonomy and the independence of rulers outside northern Iraq, the only area under effective Abbasid control.

In 814, the future caliph al-Mu'tasim began to strengthen his position by recruiting a personal bodyguard of slaves, the nucleus of a formidable fighting force that he was to build up over the next few years. It was this military power base, coupled with al-Mu'tasim's own forceful personality, that induced his brother, the reigning caliph, to nominate him as successor. When he became caliph in 833 there were murmurings of dissent, but nothing could be done to block his elevation. Because the Turkish rank and file of his army were so profoundly disliked in Baghdad,

Part of the great mosque at Samarra

al-Mu'tasim moved his court to a new city at Samarra, about 100 kilometres to the north.

A poorly chosen site virtually condemned this city from the start, and Samarra only functioned as a capital when caliphs were doggedly determined to stay there. Today its mud-brick ruins are still impressive but the massive investment in the city's construction represented a gross waste of money, a commodity which the Abbasids progressively struggled to raise from their empire, since a decade of anarchy at Samarra allowed provincial discontent to come into the open. Taxes no longer arrived regularly from the provinces, where local dynasties established themselves and often acted independently of Baghdad. Central government was also undermined by the blatant manipulation of several caliphs, whose Turkish troops had an agenda of their own. The eventual return to Baghdad in 892 hardly altered the situation and mounting difficulties culminated in the eventual replacement of the Abbasids by the Seljuks, a nomadic people who flooded into the medieval Near East from the Central Asian steppe. By the 1060s these Turkish tribesmen dominated the whole area.

With the passing of the Abbasids any notion of a unified Muslim empire disappeared, as rival caliphates had already sprung up in Egypt, Tunisia and Spain. But the collapse of Abbasid rule also signalled the end of Mesopotamia as the heartland of an empire. Since the third millennium BC a succession of great powers, Sumerian, Babylonian, Assyrian and Persian, had exploited the fertility of 'the land between the two rivers' to sustain their civilizations. Now all that was left in an impoverished landscape were transitory principalities, which neither the Seljuk Turks nor the Mongols could hold together. The reunification of the Near East had to await the establishment of the Ottoman empire.

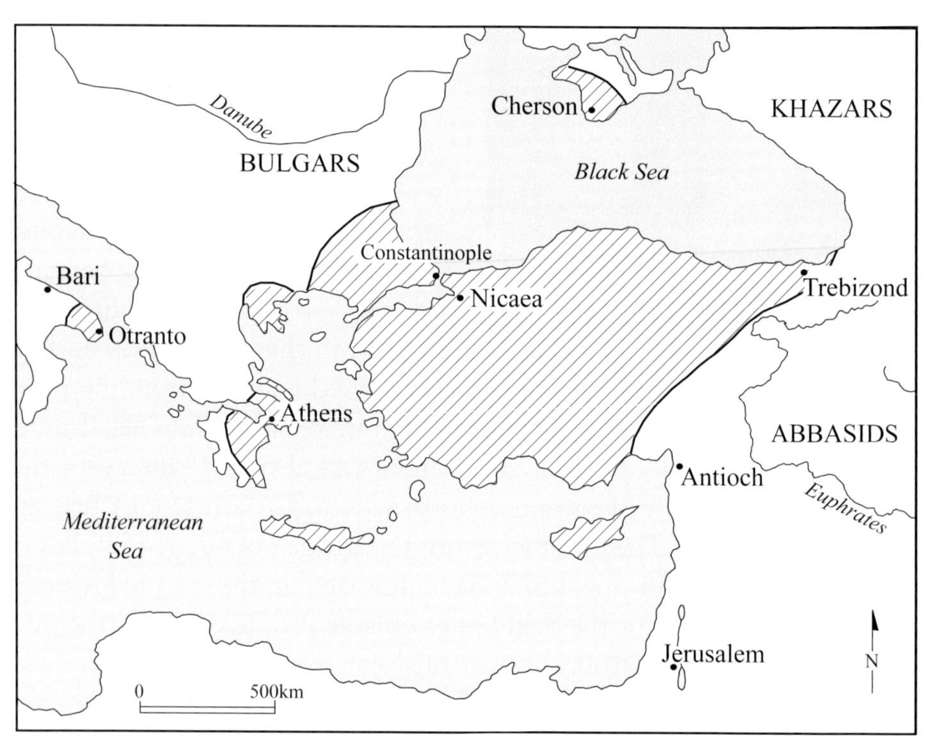

The Byzantine empire in 780

8

BASTION BYZANTIUM

Then we went to Constantinople and the Greeks showed us the buildings where they worship their God, and we knew not whether we were in heaven or on earth. For on earth there is no such splendour or such beauty, and we know not how to describe it. We only know that God dwells there among men, and their worship is more splendid than all the ceremonies of other nations.

The report of a Russian delegation in 986

The Byzantines, the name given to the Greek-speaking inhabitants of the medieval eastern Mediterranean, inherited from Rome a long-standing quarrel with the Sasanians. The successors of the Parthians, these determined Persians sought control of the entire Near East, and they got very close to achieving this aim in 626, when together with the Avars, the Sasanians reached Constantinople. The only remedy was the boldest possible counter-attack, which Emperor Heraclius launched once it was clear that the Sasanian king Khusrau II was uninterested in negotiations.

One of the ironies of history is that the duel between Heraclius and Khusrau arose from Byzantine political strife. In 590 the Sasanian ruler had been driven into exile by a rebellious nobility, but he discovered in the Byzantine emperor Maurice someone who was prepared to restore him to the throne. In return for ceding a large part of Armenia to the Byzantines, Maurice dispatched an army that reinstated Khusrau as king. For Maurice himself peaceful relations with Persia were priceless. So short of money was the imperial treasury that he had cut the rations of his troops, whose inevitable mutiny led to Maurice's overthrow in 602. Even though Heraclius had restored order at Constantinople by 610, Khusrau remained unconvinced that this second coup was anything more than continued Byzantine intrigue, and so he remained intent on avenging the murder of Maurice.

By 619 King Khusrau had overrun Syria, Palestine and Egypt. Not even the True Cross was spared as booty. Once the Sasanians moved into Asia Minor, Heraclius realized that a critical moment had arrived for what was left of the Roman empire. The loss of so much territory made meeting the army payroll impossible, but the emperor got the Church to furnish a massive loan. He also appreciated how his armed forces needed a programme of intensive training. We are told that: 'Heraclius gathered his soldiers together and added new contingents. He then began to train them and instruct them in military tactics. He divided his army into two and bade them draw up in lines of battle and attack each other, without shedding blood. He taught them a battle cry, battle songs and shouts, and how to be on their guard, so that in a real battle the soldiers would not be frightened, but bravely advance on the enemy as if it were a game'. What the beleaguered emperor clearly understood was how the survival of Byzantium depended upon military versatility. With a limited pool of manpower, the Byzantine army could not afford to waste the lives of its soldiers. Only by carefully husbanding such a precious military resource would it have any chance of recovering from reverses on land and sea. Like their modern counterparts, and unlike most medieval warriors, Byzantine soldiers were trained to fight in different ways, according to specific tactics adapted to the terrain and the enemy at hand. This was how Byzantium managed to last for so long against all the odds.

The Avar nomads had already broken a truce when they tried to capture Heraclius during peace talks. 'The barbarians, transgressing the agreements and oaths, suddenly attacked the emperor in a treacherous manner. But he took flight and returned to the city', according to George of Pisidia, a churchman who moved in high circles and knew the emperor personally. An Avar vanguard of 30,000 men arrived at Constantinople during 626. He says that the total number of Avars committed to the investment topped

80,000. The Byzantines thought they were much like the Huns, who had earlier arrived from the Central Asian steppe. The Avars wore armour and fought with the lance as well as the bow. One Byzantine general remarked that 'the Avars are scoundrels, devious and very experienced in military matters'. What set them apart from the Huns, he added, was 'their concern with military organization, which makes them stronger than other nomads when it comes to pitched battles'.

The Avars could handle the lance effectively through the use of the stirrup, which was immediately adopted by the Byzantines and the Franks, since it gave improved stability to the rider. When added to a built-up saddle, the stirrup gave the Franks with their wing spears and protective armour the shock of heavy cavalry, and laid the basis for knighthood in Europe. The Frankish charge was renowned and feared throughout the medieval Near East during the Crusades.

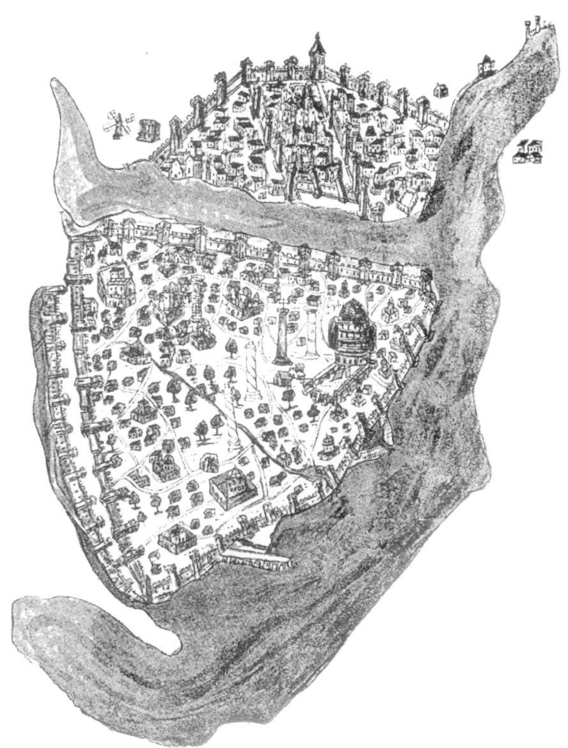

Medieval Constantinople with its powerful land defences shown on the left

Initially the allies of Byzantium, the Avars turned into enemies once they were denied permission to settle within the imperial borders. Patriarch Sergius carried an icon of the Virgin around Constantinople's defences as a supernatural supplement to its great walls, the last resort in time of siege. Despite active encouragement from the Sasanians, the assault was abandoned by the Avars who left behind their wooden siege towers, which the Byzantines promptly set on fire. The frustration of the Avars was a great relief for Byzantium, still confronted by the Sasanians in the east.

BEATING THE SASANIANS

The Avars simply lacked the technology and the patience to take Constantinople, but the assault on the city and Heraclius' campaigns in Asia Minor against the Sasanians prompted the Visigoths to roll up the remnants of Byzantine Spain.

There was nothing Heraclius could do to save the territories recaptured by his predecessor Justinian I in 554. More important to him was carrying the counter-attack into the Sasanian heartland, which seemed possible now he was pushing King Khusrau's forces steadily eastwards. Heraclius' sense of timing and his willingness to combine battle with diplomacy had put the Sasanians on the defensive. King Khusrau foolishly dismissed Shahrbaraz, his best general. Even worse, the Byzantines intercepted a letter from the Sasanian king ordering Shahrbaraz's execution. When the general was shown the correspondence, he ceased fighting the Byzantines altogether in Asia Minor, leaving Heraclius free to retake Syria and Palestine.

Although he did not receive any Sasanian military assistance, Heraclius profited from the intelligence that Shahrbaraz willingly supplied. It was indeed the passivity of the disaffected general and his men which permitted the Byzantine emperor to invade Mesopotamia and capture Ctesiphon, the Sasanian capital. A fifth column also helped the Byzantines, either inspired by Christian sentiment or hatred of King Khusrau's rule; just as critical was an alliance with the Kok Turks, who provided 40,000 men for the final push against the Sasanians. Their set-

The Sasanian King Khusrau II, the determined opponent of the Byzantines

tled animosity towards the Sasanian king made them invaluable allies of the Byzantines. The decisive battle took place near the ruins of ancient Nineveh in late 627, and ended with a severe Sasanian defeat.

In a panic, King Khusrau endeavoured to flee Mesopotamia; but his son, Kawadh-Siroy, imprisoned him instead. 'So they made a prisoner of the king in one of the royal palaces', we are told. 'They gave him no food, but set before him a heap of gold and silver and jewels, telling him to enjoy those things which he had loved insanely and amassed.' In this way the deposed ruler was starved to death and his son Kawadh-Siroy became king. That the sons of Shahrbaraz participated in the coup suggests that the general had come to some agreement with Heraclius. Such an arrangement would explain the Byzantine emperor's immediate acceptance of Kawadh-Siroy's elevation, although Heraclius remained deeply concerned about the fate of the True Cross. It was eventually returned intact to Jerusalem in 630.

Having restored the authority of Byzantium in the medieval Near East, Heraclius must have imagined his work done. But he was about to face another enemy, because the Arabs had begun their raids on southern Palestine. An engagement at Mu'tah, in present-day Jordan, was the first occasion on which Arab forces clashed with Byzantine troops. Three Arab commanders fell there, along with many of their men. This happened in 629, while Heraclius was still withdrawing from Mesopotamia.

Prior to the wars with the Arabs, Palestine had become a favourite destination for non-Greek pilgrims. Taken aback by the level of its prosperity, these visitors from the western Mediterranean and farther afield marvelled at this Byzantine province's riches, large population and crowded churches. The most vivid description was written about 570 by an unnamed pilgrim from Piacenza. He enthused about 'the city of

Nazareth, where many miracles take place. In the synagogue there is kept the book in which the Lord wrote his ABC, and in this synagogue there is the bench on which he sat with the other children. Christians can lift the bench and move it about but the Jews are unable to move it, and cannot drag it outside.' That the 'Jewesses in the city are better-looking than any Jewesses in the whole country' was not missed by the Piacenza pilgrim, nor the mutual disdain of Jews and Christians. He adds that the Jewesses declare that their good looks are 'Saint Mary's gift to them, for they say that she was a relation of theirs'.

On the bank of the Jordan, a minor miracle happened when the river 'turns back on itself with a roar and the water remains calm till the priests finish the baptism'. The Piacenza pilgrim was just as surprised by the interest of Alexandrian ship-owners in the river's holy water which 'they use for sprinkling their ships when they are about to set sail'. After the ceremony was over, 'the water returned to its place'. But Jerusalem was of course the goal of every pilgrimage, where the places associated with the Gospels were visited in turn. Here the pilgrim saw from the Mount of Olives 'the vast numbers of men and women in cloisters' in surrounding valleys; then he went to the valley of Gethsemane where Jesus was betrayed and saw 'the fig-tree from which Judas hanged himself'. Its trunk still stands 'protected by stones'; afterwards he moved on to Golgotha, the place of the crucifixion, and 'the Lord's tomb, where from iron rods hang bracelets, necklaces, rings, tiaras, belts, emperors' crowns of gold and precious stones, and the insignia of an empress'; and finally he prayed in the city's churches, including Saint Sophia built on the site of Pilate's palace. This church housed the stone upon which an accused person had to stand while being judged by a Roman official. Jesus' footprints were still to be seen on it, 'a well-shaped foot, small and delicate'.

So thorough was the Piacenza pilgrim's tour that, besides the holy places in Palestine, he visited Sinai, the Nile delta and Syria. At the ancient Egyptian city of Memphis a converted temple possessed a door that no one could open since it was slammed in Jesus' face. Another miraculous exhibit was 'a piece of linen on which there is a portrait of the Saviour. People say that he once wiped his face with it, and that the outline remained.' Much less impressed was this energetic pilgrim by

Pilgrims at the Holy Sepulchre in Jerusalem

Alexandria, whose 'people are worthless, though they welcome travellers'. Sadly he noted how the city 'is full of sects'.

The ease with which such an Italian visitor could travel through Egypt, Palestine and Syria is a testimony to the Byzantine peace. Though it was not to last, this did not stop the flow of Christians completely. On the very cusp of this change from Christian to Muslim control stood the patriarch of Jerusalem, Sophronius. Brought up and educated in Damascus, Sophronius started his working life as a teacher of rhetoric, but in 580 he became a monk at St Theodosius' near Jerusalem. Following a stay in Sinai as well as Alexandria, he became patriarch of Jerusalem in 633. The recovery of the True Cross from the Sasanians seemed to augur well for Christianity, but eight years later Sophronius had no choice but to surrender Jerusalem to the Arabs.

HOLDING OFF THE ARABS

The sweeping Arab advance in the last decade of Emperor Heraclius' reign so shattered Byzantine confidence that many of his subjects thought that it indicated the loss of divine approval for a Christian empire. Sophronius said that the Muslims would not have triumphed had the Christians remained truly devout: they had instead 'injured the gift-giving Christ and impelled his wrath against us'. So in 638 this senior churchman handed over the keys of Jerusalem to the second caliph, Umar ibn al-Khattab.

The Arab general who was conducting the siege of the city offered either conversion to Islam or the payment of a fine for the safety of the inhabitants; otherwise, he informed Sophronius, they faced death. The patriarch knew that the cities of Damascus and Aleppo had already come to terms, their places of worship spared any damage or confiscation. As a violent assault could only mean the destruction of Christian shrines in Jerusalem, Sophronius agreed to surrender to the caliph in person, without realizing how much Muslims esteemed the city themselves. Umar received news of Sophronius' offer while in Syria, arriving post-haste on a camel. The two met on the Mount of Olives. Surprised by Umar's shabby appearance, Sophronius lent the caliph a cloak until his own camel-hair clothes could be washed. A Muslim version of the story, how-

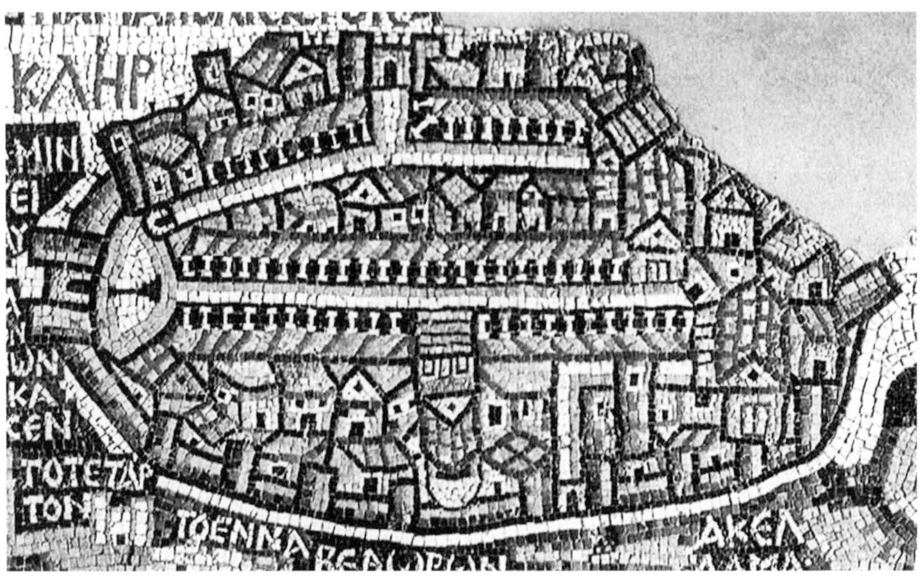

The mosaic map of Jerusalem from a church at Madaba in Jordan

ever, puts an entirely different slant on the historic encounter. It relates how Umar changed his dirty clothes and rode into the city, whereupon the Arabs refused to acknowledge him as their leader until he changed back into them.

Whatever the truth, the caliph and the patriarch got on well together. The seventy-year-old Christian recognized Umar's humility and, as a monk who followed a regime of daily prayer himself, Sophronius appreciated the caliph's need to pray. He even provided a mat for this purpose. In return, Umar gave the patriarch a document that exempted the steps of the church on which he prayed from congregational Muslim worship. Otherwise, he told Sophronius that his use of the church would lead to its inevitable seizure by the Muslims because the caliph had worshipped there.

All Umar did before leaving Jerusalem was erect a small shrine on the Temple Mount. The agreement that Sophronius reached with Umar extended toleration to Christians and Jews, allowing the followers of both faiths to worship freely in the city. This arrangement lasted until 969, when control of Jerusalem passed to the Fatimids of Egypt. Their less tolerant Shia outlook led to the demolition of synagogues and churches, a policy that prompted the Crusades and culminated in the Christian capture of Jerusalem in 1099.

When Jacinthus the Presbyter travelled to Palestine shortly before the First Crusade, he found that 'the city of Bethlehem is destroyed' except for the church of the Nativity which escaped Fatimid attention because the local Muslims used it for worship as well. It was the sixth Fatimid caliph, al-Hakim bi-Amrallah, who took the first steps in 1009 against Christians and Jews. In Jerusalem, every effort was made to destroy the Holy Sepulchre: the structure was physically broken and dug up. Jacinthus' description of Christ's tomb suggests that some restoration work had taken place since then: he says 'at the entry to the Tomb are three wooden gates'. Even though the caliph was looked upon as unhinged by some of his contemporaries, the religious views of al-Hakim bi-Amrallah chimed nonetheless with the growing intolerance of the Shia Muslims. He simply could not stop himself from introducing ever more restrictive measures, ordering the destruction of everything that was not difficult to demolish, and confiscating the property of Jews as well as Christians.

Caliph al-Hakim, the destroyer of Christian places in Jerusalem

Towards the end of his reign, though, al-Hakim was less interested in persecution, even allowing reluctant Jewish and Christian converts to Islam to resume their previous beliefs and rebuild their places of worship. The emergence of the Druze, a sect which actually considered the caliph to be divine, captured his imagination. The Druze faith incorporated a wide spectrum of ideas drawn from Islam, Judaism, Christianity, Hinduism and Greek philosophy. It still has a couple of million adherents in the modern Near East. The increasingly bizarre behaviour of al-Hakim, who made a point of eating in a mosque, scandalized his family. The public burning of a Muslim cleric for denying the caliph's divinity may well have been the last straw. One day in 1021 al-Hakim failed to return from the solitary walks he enjoyed in the hills on the outskirts of the city, rather like Muhammad's own rambles outside Mecca. The body of the caliph was never found and, in the opinion of the Druze, he had simply withdrawn from the world until the end of time.

Before al-Hakim mysteriously disappeared, the bulk of Byzantium's Near Eastern provinces were lost for ever. Whereas four hundred years earlier the two great empires of Byzantine Rome and Sasanid Persia had dominated the eastern Mediterranean, there was no vestige of Sasanian power to be seen and little more than a diminished Christian state was still visible, engaged as it was in a grim struggle to survive. That it managed to endure and act as a bastion for the rest of Christian Europe is one of the wonders of the medieval world; it is still not properly acknowledged by some historians today. For the impact of the Arab onslaught hit Byzantium at the very moment that continued theological argument over the nature of Christ was undermining its unity. Emperor Heraclius had tried to unify his subjects by means of a compromise, which held that the two natures of Christ, human and divine, were united in a single will. This formulation by the patriarch Sergius was at first well-received, and willingly accepted by the pope, but not by the Monophysites who held that Jesus was entirely divine. Less committed therefore to Byzantium, these Christians almost rejoiced at the Muslim conquest of Egypt. A Monophysite bishop could actually say that 'the expulsion of the Romans and the victory of the Muslims was due to the wickedness of Emperor Heraclius and his persecution of Cyrus, the patriarch of Alexandria'.

THE ICONOCLASTIC CONTROVERSY

Religious anxieties must also account for the outburst of iconoclasm in the Byzantine empire during the eighth century. The cause of the iconoclasm was a mixture of religion and politics, for in Constantinople the two were inseparable. In the seventy years after the death of Heraclius in 641, twelve emperors presided over a steady decline in Byzantium's military position. This was halted by Emperor Leo III, who was raised to the purple by troops guarding the eastern frontier. Of Syrian origin, Leo deposed Theodosius III and was immediately obliged to attend to a second Arab siege of Constantinople.

Born in Asia Minor, Leo and his family were among those who had been resettled by imperial edict in Thrace. As a young man Leo had come to Justinian II's notice in 705: as the emperor was leading his troops

A gold coin, minted in Rome, of the usurper Leo III, the original iconoclast

towards Constantinople in order to deal with a usurper, Leo presented him with a flock of five hundred sheep. Leo then rose swiftly through the ranks of the Byzantine army, and in 717 was in a position to lead a military coup and install himself as emperor. A usurper he may have been, but once on the throne Leo proved an able ruler, because he appreciated the pressing need for an effective defence against the Arabs.

The first seaborne assault on Constantinople happened in 670–71, when the Arab fleet launched a bold attack on the city before the Byzantines could recall their own naval forces from the central Mediterranean, where they had been drawn by an Arab invasion of the province of Africa. When the Arab fleet withdrew and based itself on the coast of Asia Minor, the Byzantines gave chase and caught the Arabs off guard in Lycia. There in 674 they heavily defeated the Arab expeditionary force and completely destroyed the Arab fleet. It was a decisive victory, which the Byzantines followed up by landing commandos on the Syrian coast, where these soldiers soon raised such a Christian rebellion that it threatened Arab rule in Syria as well as Palestine.

Soon after his occupation of the throne, Leo had to defend Constantinople from another Arab attack. He used fire-ships against Arab convoys supplying the besiegers who surrounded the city for over a year. Cutting the Arab supply line proved the turning point of the siege and resulted in a total failure for the Arabs. The Umayyads glossed over the event by praising the accession of a new caliph, Umar II, the son of Abd al-Malik's brother. Several factors had assisted the Byzantines. First of all, Constantinople was well prepared with plentiful stocks of food to withstand a long siege. Secondly, the severe winter of 717–18 had little impact on the defenders, but it undermined Arab morale once supplies ran low. And a third factor was harassment on the European shore by the Bulgars, with whom Leo had evidently struck a deal. Even on the Asian shore, however, the Arabs discovered that they were just as vulnerable to sudden attacks by Byzantine commandos. The emperor conducted the defence of Constantinople with great skill and, after the departure of the Arabs, he had the additional satisfaction of learning how the Arab fleet suffered considerable damage through storms on its way home.

Provided the Byzantines controlled the waters around Constantinople, and in particular the Sea of Marmara, the city was safe. The land defences were so strong that it was only when the Ottomans obtained an exceptionally powerful cannon in 1453 that they would be breached. This so-called Theodosian wall ran in an unbroken line almost from the Golden Horn to the Sea of Marmara. It had been built on the orders of Emperor Theodosius II, whose long reign from 408 to 450 witnessed the enhancement of city defences in the eastern Mediterranean. The wall offered

The restored Theodosian wall

three lines of defence: on the outside edge was a deep ditch some 80 metres wide, sections of which could be flooded if required; inside the ditch was a low breastwork, protecting an open space in front of the outer wall, which was some 30 metres in height and strengthened with square towers; behind this wall was the final line of defence, a formidable inner wall which was studded with towers rising to twice the height of the outer wall. The Theodosian wall was pierced by a number of gates, some used by the general public, others reserved for the military.

Having secured what remained of the Byzantine empire, Leo restored the army to efficiency, reformed the administration, and allowed Slavic settlers into depopulated districts. Perhaps his most successful measure was recruiting the peasantry to defend Byzantium. In return for military service, the serfs became free peasants. His code, the *Ecloga* or 'selection', was an attempt to put Byzantium back on its feet, although it paid most attention to military matters. Because arms were so expensive, stern penalties were introduced for those who stole soldiers' equipment and horses, and the arms and horse that a cavalryman inherited from his father were exempted from tax.

But most controversial of all was Leo's attitude to religious images. Believing that Muslim successes on the battlefield had a connection with the prohibition on representations of the deity, Leo issued edicts against the worship of icons. In 730 he ordered the removal of an image of Christ from over the entrance to the imperial palace in Constantinople, an action that provoked condemnation from the pope. The figure's replacement by a cross was considered blasphemous in Rome. Although Jewish prophets had long railed against idolatry, it was Islam's advance westwards, accompanied by the wholesale destruction of images, that encouraged some Byzantines to wonder if Leo was right in viewing the empire's difficulties as a result of divine disapproval of icons.

Many Byzantines opposed iconoclasm root and branch, but Leo was not deterred and his drive for religious conformity extended to the compulsory baptism of Jews. When the papacy convened councils to condemn the iconoclasts, Leo in 740 transferred Byzantine holdings in southern Italy from the papal diocese to that of the patriarch of Constantinople. Finding that Ravenna, the seat of Byzantine authority in the west, refused to accept the imperial edict against images, a fleet was dispatched to enforce obedience, but it foundered at sea. Afterwards the southern Italians also defied the Byzantine emperor, and a rival to Leo was proclaimed with popular support. Despite the pope urging loyalty to Constantinople and the would-be emperor's rebellion coming to nothing, a chasm opened between the Catholic and Orthodox churches. That religious and political confusion, aggravated by Lombard aggression, turned the pope into the equivalent of the Byzantine emperor in Italy only served to widen this theological divide. The independence of the papacy was finally confirmed by its siding with the Frankish usurper Pepin, whose oldest son Charlemagne was in 800 crowned by the pope at Rome as 'the Emperor of the Romans'.

Before his death in 741, Leo had strengthened Byzantium by marrying his son, the future emperor Constantine V, to the khan of the Turkish Khazar's daughter. She took the name Irene on her baptism and, we are told, 'learned Holy Scripture and lived piously, thus reproving the impiety of those men around her'. The chronicler means by this the iconoclasts at court, including her husband. For Constantine V was more than a competent soldier and administrator: he was well educated with a marked interest in theology which informed his own brand of iconoclasm. An opponent called him Antichrist, a man with the outlook of a Muslim and the heart of a Jew.

A pseudo-Roman coin struck to celebrate Charlemagne's coronation in 800, an act of defiance against the Byzantine emperor

Because contemporary critics of the emperor so greatly exaggerated their case against him, declaring for example that he was a devil-worshipper and a debauchee, it is hard to arrive at a balanced assessment of Constantine's reign. We know that he was inordinately fond of horses and spent a great deal of time in the imperial stables, an interest that was regarded as beneath an emperor's dignity. Claims that he indulged in child sacrifice are obviously untrue, as indeed are charges of casting magic spells and harking back to pre-Christian rituals. So intense is the criticism of Constantine in the historical record that his steady progress against the Arabs gets largely overlooked. It obliged the Abbasids to form a special province behind the actual frontier, the resources of which were entirely devoted to containing the Byzantines.

Iconoclasm was in tendency Monophysite, because images could be argued to turn Christ into a human being, thereby diminishing his divinity. When the patriarch Anastasius felt that Constantine's religious policy was weakening the accepted view of Christ's dual nature, he lent his support in 742 to an uprising in Constantinople. The rebels were easily crushed and, instead of being deposed as patriarch, Anastasius was flogged and paraded on an ass in the circus. This venue for chariot races had always acted as a forum for the public display of imperial decisions. Still traceable in Istanbul today, the racecourse was more than a place of entertainment: it played a key role in political ceremonial as well.

For three years, 744–7, Constantinople was devastated by plague, according to anti-Constantine chroniclers as a punishment for iconoclasm. Despite the emperor no longer taking the lead in the iconoclastic movement himself, a disdain for religious images was becoming widespread among his subjects. At a council held in Constantinople in 753 there was no complaint about iconoclasm: the three hundred bishops in attendance expressed no adverse comment at all. But a warning was given over the indiscriminate destruction of sacred vessels and vestments decorated with figures. Officials were also warned against robbing churches on the pretext of destroying images.

As the council chose to praise Constantine for 'delivering the world from idols', the emperor was now in an unassailable position, except for individual protesters such as the monk Calybites. This hermit came to the imperial palace in 761 and denounced Constantine as an apostate; he was flogged to death. The martyrdom revealed how opposition to iconoclasm resided mostly in the monasteries, and a ten-year period of persecution ensued. Monks were paraded in the circus, where the populace jeered them as enemies of the empire. The closing years of Constantine's reign were occupied by war in the Balkans, during which he died of fever in 755.

Constantine's son, Leo IV, abandoned his father's anti-monastic policy and took no active measures affecting religion. It seems that his mother, Empress Irene, had a moderating influence at court. With the early death of Leo in 780, the first iconoclastic era ended, since Irene acted as the guardian of the infant Constantine VI. Her regency was hailed with enthusiasm by the Church, whose praise knew no bounds. Irene was 'like a rose and a lily set in the midst of thorns'. A second outburst of iconoclasm occurred during the reign of Leo V, when military reverses afflicted Byzantium once again. It ended with his assassination in the palace chapel on Christmas Day 820, when Leo was unable to defend himself with the altar cross. The mildness of Leo's iconoclastic policy by comparison with Constantine V's, coupled with the shortness of his reign and the strength of the opposition, rendered the second iconoclasm too weak to last.

The Turkish empress Irene

A LIMITED REVIVAL

Byzantium enjoyed nearly two centuries of stability under the dynasty that Basil I established in 867. Having come to power through murdering his feckless predecessor, the new emperor's reign got off to an uneasy start; but Basil quickly revealed his excellence as a ruler, whose aim was to recover as much of the empire's lost territory as he could. He improved the Byzantine fleet by raising a permanent corps of marines. Its improved fighting capacity allowed Basil to take control of Cyprus, which the Byzantines had long shared with the Arabs; annex the heel of Italy; and curb Arab piracy in both the Mediterranean and the Adriatic. Basil's heir, Leo VI, continued

Emperor Basil I, the restorer of the Byzantine navy

with military improvements, one of which was to increase the number of horsemen in each regiment, with the result that the Byzantines moved onto the offensive in Asia Minor as well as Syria.

In the central Mediterranean, however, Byzantium experienced mixed fortunes. Berber converts to Islam had penetrated the imperial defences and set up an emirate in Bari, the only Muslim state ever to exist on the Italian mainland. From there raiding parties went out in search of loot, attacking towns and monasteries at will. The territory around Naples was ravaged and the great monastery at Monte Cassino stripped of its valuables. The abbot was struck down before the high altar. For a while in the ninth century it appeared that the Muslims were on their way to the conquest of the whole of Italy. Even though other Berbers and Arabs had occupied ports such as Taranto and Amantea on Calabria's western coast, from where they picked southern Italy clean, it was the aggression of Bari that worried Christian leaders most. Largely ignored by Arab chroniclers as an insignificant emirate, it was seen as a serious threat by both the Byzantines and the French.

Without any naval assistance from Byzantium, in 871 the Carolingian king Louis II managed to capture Bari. As part of a joint operation against the Muslim stronghold, a Byzantine fleet had duly arrived off Bari, but too late to assist the French. However, its admiral expected to convey Louis' daughter to Constantinople, but her proposed marriage to the Byzantine emperor fell through and the fleet sailed away empty-handed. Given that Louis had no male heir, Basil expected the marriage to transfer to Byzantium any Carolingian claims to southern Italy. Negotiations continued between the two rulers, but nothing was ever agreed. In contrast to Basil, the French king was described as 'a weak and unstable monarch'.

In 876, a Byzantine force drove from Bari a Lombard nobleman installed there after Louis' capture of the port. Together with Otranto, this gave the Byzantines two key bases on the Adriatic coast. But attempts to enlist the support of other southern cities in an anti-Muslim alliance failed, since Naples, Gaeta and Amalfi were heavily engaged in trade with the Muslims. Not even the pope could get them to sever their trade links with Muslim north Africa. In 879, Pope John VIII declared that he would anathematize everyone who failed to stop trading, but neither the local rulers nor the local bishops responded positively to this instruction. His warning totally ignored, John announced in 880 an all-embracing sentence of excommunication. Two years later, the pope made another attempt to coerce Amalfi without success. He was then assassinated, the first pontiff to suffer such a fate. A compromise was eventually reached, whereby the Amalfians were allowed to carry on trading in return for clearing the sea of pirates south of Rome. But they still preferred to use most of their ships on the profitable trade routes to north African ports rather than fight the Arabs or Berber marauders at sea.

Byzantium was back in the central Mediterranean, although Sicily was lost to the Arabs in 902. Its real successes during the tenth century lay elsewhere. In 962 Aleppo fell to a Byzantine army which numbered 30,000 horsemen and 40,000 foot soldiers. Offensives in Syria and Mesopotamia might have recovered more land from a weakened Abbasid caliphate had not a new people arrived in the form of the nomadic Oghuz Turks, driven westwards by their poverty and pressure from enemies on the Central Asian steppe. Another front where Byzantine arms triumphed was the Balkans, after a bitter contest against the Bulgarians concluded with the restoration of the Danube frontier, not held by Byzantium since the reign of Heraclius. Throughout the winter of 970–71, weapons and food supplies had been stockpiled and a fleet readied for action on the Black Sea and the river Danube. Difficulties in the Balkans arose from a Byzantine alliance with the Russians, who not only overwhelmed the Bulgars but also coveted their lands. Prince Svyatoslav of Kiev had impelled many Bulgars on stakes for the slowness of their surrender, but he met his match in the Byzantines and was defeated on several occasions. Svyatoslav therefore sent a peace envoy to the Byzantine emperor

John I, offering to withdraw across the Danube. The offer was readily accepted by the emperor so as to bring an expensive campaign to an end. And the opportunity was also taken to renew the old trade treaty which allowed Russian merchants to bring their wares to Constantinople as they had done in the past.

THE COMING OF THE SELJUKS

The only shadow that darkened this imperial revival was a final split between Orthodox and Catholic Christianity. In 1054, relations between the two churches reached rock bottom, when three papal legates had the temerity to place a bull of excommunication on the altar of Hagia Sophia, Constantinople's great cathedral. Even though in Europe it divided the Christian faith in what was called the Great Schism, the event did not leave the Orthodox church as isolated as Rome hoped it would, because Orthodox missionaries had already converted the Bulgarians, the Serbs and the Russians. Their pioneering activities permanently altered the religious map of Europe. The crucial conversion happened in 986 when Prince Vladimir, Svyatoslav's son, favoured the Orthodox faith, for both spiritual and political motives. Hearing of his wish to abandon paganism, missionaries converged on Kiev, where Vladimir was unimpressed by the lot of them. Islam attracted him until he realized that alcohol was forbidden. Judaism seemed to have little to recommend it since its followers had lost their land and were scattered all over the medieval world. Catholic missionaries left him cold, but he listened to a priest who had been sent from Constantinople. The prince's interest was confirmed when ten trusted envoys returned from that city, profoundly moved by the mosaics, frescoes and icons involved in Orthodox worship. 'We knew not whether we were in heaven or on earth', they reported to Vladimir. 'For on earth there is no such splendour or such beauty, and we know not how to describe it. We only know that God dwells there among men.' The enthusiasm of the Russians naturally put the iconoclasts on the back foot, a position from which they never recovered.

A more pressing problem than the theological dispute with Rome, though, was a Seljuk victory over the Byzantine emperor Romanus IV

St. Sophia in Kiev, built as a consequence of Byzantine missionary activity

Diogenes at Manzikert in 1071. An experienced general, Romanus had married the widow of Constantine X against the wishes of her relatives, who saw the purple as their own property. Dismayed though he was about the quality of the Byzantine army, which then included large numbers of mercenaries, the emperor whipped the troops into a fighting force and moved to defend Asia Minor. Romanus was the first emperor since Basil II to pay real attention to the condition of the army.

More than the Arabs perhaps, the Turks sank their identity in Islam, inaugurating a Sunni revival that eventually took them into Europe, where they lay siege to Vienna in 1526 and 1683. The Seljuk family were not the leaders of the Oghuz Turks during their journey westwards from the Aral Sea, but their own conversion to Islam ensured that, once recognized as the leading family, the Oghuz became Muslims too and were henceforth called the Seljuks. Without gaining any real advantage, the

Abbasid caliphs had recruited Turkish slave-soldiers from the ninth century onwards: they found these foreign troops were far from easy to handle since their machinations complicated the politics of Baghdad. The slave-soldiers had an agenda of their own. Given this history of Turkish involvement in the medieval Near East, there was no reason for the Seljuks to prop up the Abbasid caliphate. They preferred to let Alp Arslan establish an empire of their own, which extended from Samarkand to Damascus. Its capital was located at Rey, south of modern Tehran.

Loyal though they were to Alp Arslan, the Seljuks remained fiercely independent like other nomads, finding the discipline of an Islamic sultanate irksome. As a consequence of the reluctance to abandon traditional ways, the core of the Seljuk army consisted of slave-soldiers, Turkish in origin but from non-Oghuz tribes. Numbering at the most 15,000 men, this force was supplemented by Seljuk warriors whenever it needed extra strength on the battlefield. Although attacks beyond the borders of the Seljuk empire seemed no more than a continuation of nomad raiding, Alp Arslan regarded the expansion of its territory as tantamount to a holy war, a Sunni onslaught on Christians and Shia Muslims alike. The battle of Manzikert was essentially a sideshow for Alp Arslan, an engagement which happened when he heard of the Byzantine emperor's presence on the border of Asia Minor, while he was himself wresting Syria from Fatimid control. Alp Arslan's chief targets were Syria and Palestine, from which he intended to roll back Shia influence to Cairo.

Some of Romanus' commanders wanted to avoid a battle at Manzikert, but the emperor disagreed, probably appreciating how the frontier forts were in such poor condition that they could not be held in the face of a determined Seljuk advance. Romanus hoped instead to intimidate Alp Arslan by winning a decisive victory, and his offensive did catch the Seljuks by surprise. He was indeed on the brink of victory when disaffected relatives of the late Constantine X spread the rumour through the Byzantine army that Romanus faced certain defeat. The soldiers fled, leaving the emperor and his bodyguard stranded on the battlefield.

Alp Arslan never understood why the Byzantine army ran away. For him, it was Romanus having been taken prisoner that made Manzikert so memorable; for the Byzantines, it was the emperor's subsequent release by the Seljuks that made the battle unusual. One account of events afterwards informs us how Romanus was led through the Seljuk camp with a rope round his neck, so that he might be sold as a slave to the highest bidder. When he learned that the Byzantine emperor had been traded for a dog, Alp Arslan said: 'That is just, because the dog is better than he is! Give him the dog and set him free.' Considering Muslim dislike of dogs it was a prophetic remark, since on his return to Constantinople Romanus was indeed treated as less than a dog. The emperor's enemies seized power in Constantinople during his absence, defeated him in a civil war and then blinded him, causing his death.

In one form or another Byzantium lasted for four more centuries; but its army was less the direct descendant of the Roman legions, and more a ragbag of men collected together whenever an emergency arose. After almost eight hundred years of adapting to changing circumstances surprisingly well, the Byzantine army fell apart and left the once great bastion desperate to secure military assistance from western Europe, which came shortly after Manzikert in the guise of the Crusades.

Although the battle of Manzikert broke the Byzantine frontier defences, an achievement that had eluded Muslim commanders before Alp Arslan, the Seljuks did not push their military advantage. Alp Arslan died the next year, and within two decades the Seljuk empire disintegrated. But conflict between its successor states in the medieval Near East had no effect on the migration of Turkish people, more than a million of them settling in Asia Minor where they soon comprised not only the largest ethnic group but one that spread throughout the interior. As Byzantium's population at its height barely topped five million, this represented a formidable intrusion into the empire's heartland.

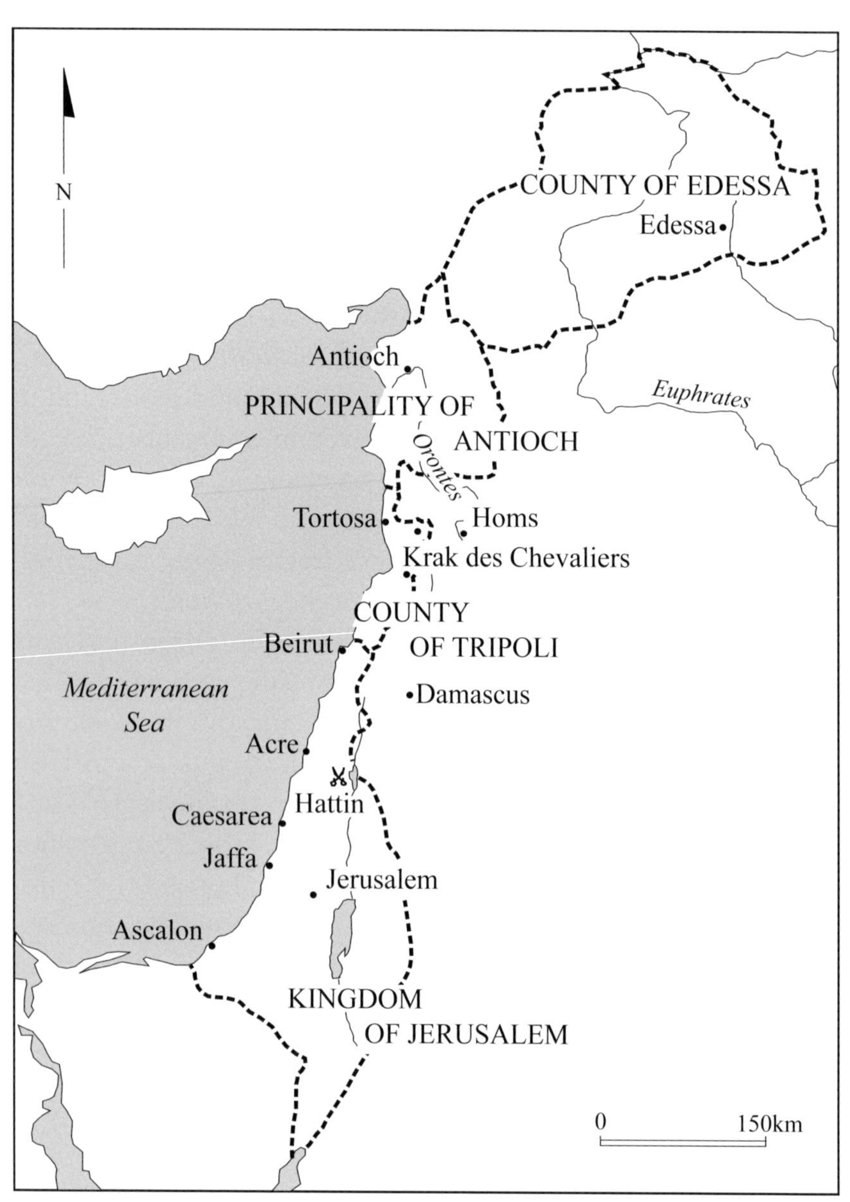

The Crusader states

9

THE CRUSADES

All who die by the way, whether by land or by sea, or in battle against the pagans, shall have immediate remission of sins. This I grant them through the power of God with which I am invested ... Let those who have been accustomed unjustly to wage private warfare against the faithful now go against the infidels and win the victory this war should accomplish.

Pope Urban II's call to arms at Claremont

The papacy of Urban II was a troubled one. His problems included conflict in Germany and France, a rival pope, and a threat to the survival of the Byzantines. At the end of the first millennium the medieval Near East had attained a kind of stability, with the Byzantines and the Arabs holding each other in a standstill. This balance of power was upset, however, by the arrival of the Seljuk Turks, who defeated the Byzantine army at the battle of Manzikert in 1071, and captured Jerusalem shortly afterwards. Although the word 'crusade' was not yet in use when, in 1095, Pope Urban called Europe to arms, it is transparent that he thought a combined effort against Islam might alleviate the continent's own chronic instability.

Worried by the Seljuk penetration of Asia Minor, Emperor Alexius I Comnenus sent an ambassador to Italy with an appeal for military aid. He requested an army that would recapture Byzantium's lost territories in Asia Minor and Syria and pay itself from the proceeds. He was not much interested in the Holy Land. But the pope was. A French nobleman who became

Pope Urban II preaching the First Crusade

a monk before his election as pope, Urban was stirred by a vision of an armed pilgrimage to regain the holy places associated with the life of Christ. It was obvious to some Muslims that military intervention by the Christian powers was likely to happen. One Arab commentator from Aleppo noted how 'the inhabitants of the Syrian ports often stopped Frankish and Byzantine pilgrims from travelling on to Jerusalem'. Another keen observer realized that the deliberate mistreatment of Christians in Antioch by the newly appointed governor, Yaghi Siyan, was bound to provoke a violent reaction.

So the pope's response to the Byzantine request for military assistance hardly came as a bolt out of the blue, since abused pilgrims returning home had already alerted their contemporaries to the unsatisfactory situation in Syria and Palestine. Understanding the value of joint action, however, Urban called a great council at Claremont, to which so many bishops came from Italy, France and Burgundy that it had to be held in the open air. An exact transcription of the sermon that Urban delivered there has not survived, but the words attributed to him at the start of this chapter were recorded by Fulcher of Chartres, a knight who was present. All accounts make clear that the pope told his listeners how 'Christ commands' armed intervention in the eastern Mediterranean. Urban died in 1099, just after the fall of Jerusalem to the Crusaders, but before news of the event had reached Italy.

THE FIRST CRUSADE

The assembly at Claremont was largely clerical, and therefore the pope set out to spread the crusader message more widely through a personal tour of

France and through the agency of his bishops. Within a year there were between 50,000 and 70,000 followers ready to move eastwards. According to Fulcher, they came from all the countries of western Europe, but they did not combine as a single army until they besieged Nicaea in 1097. A further 10,000 sailors and marines were also involved in what the Muslims quickly realized was an exceptionally large expedition.

Another surprise for the Muslims were the Tafurs, whose name appears to have meant 'vagabonds', a totally impoverished group which attached itself to the humbler members of the Crusade. A part of what was called the Peasants' Crusade, they were too poor to afford swords and spears, and wielded instead clubs weighted with lead, knives, axes, hoes and shovels. When they charged into battle they gnashed their teeth as though they intended to eat their enemies alive. The Muslims were terrified of the Tafurs, whom they called 'no Franks, but living devils'. Legendary though many of the exploits of the Tafurs undoubtedly were, these desperate people had their own king, a Norman knight who had discarded horse, arms and armour in favour of sackcloth and a scythe. Committed to poverty, this monarch expelled anyone who possessed money from the Tafur ranks. He said that only 'the poorest will take the Holy City, as God does not succour presumptuous and faithless men'. But this never prevented the Tafurs from looting captured Muslim settlements or raping Muslim women. When an emir complained about Tafur cannibalism, he was told by leading Crusaders: 'All of us together cannot tame King Tafur.'

The excitement that Pope Urban unleashed in his promotion of the First Crusade affected the poor as much as the nobility. Popular preachers like Peter the Hermit, a thin man with a flowing beard and a commanding presence, had an immense impact wherever he went in France and Germany. The pope may not have approved of all the people whom Peter inspired to 'take the cross', as joining the First Crusade was called, but the enthusiasm for wresting Jerusalem from Muslim hands was believed in Rome to be a sign of divine support. That the First Crusade was nonetheless an expedition designed to satisfy noble aspirations was apparent in the story about the discovery of the Holy Lance in Antioch. When St Andrew brought the glad tidings that this treasured relic was buried in one of the city's churches, it was to a poor French peasant that he appeared. And when the peasant, conscious of his lowly social position, hesitated to inform the noble leaders of the news, the saint reassured him: 'God has chosen you from all peoples, as ears of wheat are gathered from a field of oats. For in merit and grace you surpass all who have been before you, and all who shall come after you, as much as gold surpasses silver.' Such humility did not stop the massacre of European Jews as the Crusaders marched eastwards, nor the same treatment meted out to Muslims and Jews in Syria and Palestine.

Yet the pope's appeal attracted some of the most powerful individuals of the time, such as Robert II, count of Flanders; Raymond IV, count of Toulouse; and Robert, duke of Normandy. The most effective commander proved to be Bohemond of Taranto, head of the Normans from

The discovery of the Holy Lance at Antioch

southern Italy. Grateful though he was for their support, the Byzantine emperor reinsured himself by administering an oath which committed these leading Crusaders to returning to Constantinople all the reconquered lands that had formerly belonged to the Byzantines. When the Crusaders reached Syria in late 1097, they could not have come at a better moment. They found a politically fragmented land, where the local Muslim rulers could reach no agreement at all.

But it was only through treachery that they eventually took Antioch. Both the size of the city and its strong defences had given the Crusaders reason to pause. Located on the bank of the Orontes river, the city had been founded in 300 BC by Seleucus, one of Alexander the Great's commanders. Antioch prospered under both the Greeks and the Romans, becoming the third city of the empire after Alexandria and Rome itself. Lost during the initial Arab onslaught, it revived as a major centre of international trade after the Byzantines came back. Recaptured by the Seljuks in the eleventh century, Antioch settled down as an ordinary Islamic city, overshadowed by neighbouring Aleppo and Damascus. But its defences were still strong enough to fill the Crusaders with awe. The city walls rose out of low marshy ground and scaled the slopes of a steep hill, actually crowning its crest. In addition to this formidable defensive circuit, the inhabitants were so well supplied with stocks of food that they could defend the city as long as they liked. Antioch's governor, Yaghi Siyan, was so confident that he did little to oppose the arrival of the expedition; they therefore took advantage of his indolence to raid local vineyards, orchards, animal pens and cornfields to replenish supplies. These sources of food could not be expected to last long, and disease soon weakened the malnourished Crusaders.

A foraging party led by Bohemond and Robert of Flanders happened upon a large force sent from Damascus to relieve Antioch. In spite of the disparity in numbers, the Crusaders chose to engage the enemy and their determination not only shocked the relief force but forced it to fall back in disorder as well. Yet the siege of Antioch was almost put in jeopardy at the start of 1098 when an even larger army was sighted advancing from Aleppo. To block its advance, seven hundred knights moved against the Aleppo force, while the rest of the expedition stayed at Antioch in order to maintain the city's investment. Once again, the ferocious determination of Bohemond startled the Seljuks. He urged his fellow knights to 'fight valiantly for God and the Holy Sepulchre, for you know in truth that this is no war of the flesh, but of the spirit'. Inspired by his confident words, they charged the enemy without any thought of defeat, and caused the Seljuks to break ranks and split into small groups. Now was the time for Bohemond's *coup de grâce*: he led a hidden group of cavalry in another headlong charge that drove off the enemy in total confusion.

In the battles fought outside Antioch, Bohemond always took the lead and commanded a tactical reserve which intervened decisively at a critical moment in the action. Later the Catholic kings of Jerusalem usually exercised full control over their armies by personally commanding a similar reserve that could move to any part of the Christian lines where help was needed. Like Alexander the Great, Bohemond was more than a tactician, however. Always in the thick of the fighting, he 'charged the Turkish forces like a lion which has been starving for three or four days. Thirsting for blood, the lion falls upon flocks careless of its safety, tearing the sheep as they flee hither and thither.' As the Crusaders increasingly regarded themselves as being under divine guidance and protection, the tiresome investment of Antioch was borne with patience, although deserters were harshly punished when caught. One was obliged to lie on the floor of Bohemond's tent 'like a piece of rubbish' before being flogged in public.

Fortunately for the besiegers, Emperor Alexius sent 'wine, grain and large numbers of cattle' from Cyprus. Without this timely aid the Crusade would have faltered, if not failed. That is why any suggestion that the Byzantines left the Crusaders to starve in Syria is entirely unjustified. Alexius even placed an English garrison in Laodikeia, to safeguard this Syrian port through which his vital supplies were shipped. Capturing Antioch was not essential to the reconquest of Palestine, but the oaths sworn by the Crusaders in Constantinople seemed to require the clearance of Muslims from Syria first. Bohemond did not share this view and, arguing that the Byzantine emperor had not bothered to accompany the Crusaders in person, he said that Antioch should not be handed over to Alexius. Whoever breached the walls and delivered the city into Christian hands should be allowed to claim personal authority over it, something he intended to accomplish himself.

Bohemond's supreme ambition was about to be rewarded, since he made a secret arrangement with the officer in charge of the defence towers to let the Crusaders into the city. It is said that he was holding one of the officer's sons as hostage. So after a costly and frustrating eighteen-month siege, Antioch was betrayed. Fulcher was in the first party to enter the city and witnessed Bohemond raising his battle standard on the city wall to show that Antioch had fallen to the Crusaders. But it was also a declaration that the city belonged to him. Many of the inhabitants were killed in the sack of the city as the Crusaders ran amok, all their pent-up frustrations over the siege finding release in slaughter. The Tafurs especially enjoyed the indiscriminate shedding of blood. Yaghi Siyan fled in panic to the mountains where he was recognized by three Syrian Christians, who cut off his head with his own sword and brought it back to Antioch as a trophy for the Crusaders.

Once the fury of the sack abated, the Crusaders had to decide on their next move. They were encouraged, however, by the discovery in Antioch of the Holy Lance: it had pierced Christ's side during the crucifixion. Notwithstanding the existence of another lance at Constantinople with a longer established claim to authenticity, they accepted the find as the genuine article, perhaps in the hope that it showed how the Crusade was truly blessed. And divine assistance was urgently needed by the Crusaders, because yet another large relief force arrived and attacked them in Antioch. Exhausted though they were, there was nothing for it but to give battle, which they did outside the city walls. Groups of Frankish knights charged straight into the enemy and caused absolute havoc among the Seljuk soldiers. Victory over so many Muslim opponents was of course put down to supernatural support, either in the form of celestial knights or the terror of the Holy Lance itself. More probable than these explanations was Crusader discipline and a driving sense of purpose; the Seljuks were also handicapped by their much greater numbers, since poor communication between the different units made it appear that a defeat was imminent almost as soon as the two armies clashed. After the Seljuk army dispersed, the Crusaders took their camp and discovered Muslim women there. According to Fulcher, these women were not dishonoured but the Crusaders 'did drive lances into their stomachs'.

But the Crusade was no longer so united because Bohemond wanted to stay behind in Antioch. With a great deal of persuasion, this Norman wild man promised to go on, provided it was agreed that the oaths sworn in Constantinople were no longer valid. It may well have been the prospect of the Byzantine emperor arriving that spurred the Crusaders into action. Advancing southwards upon Jerusalem, they exploited the chronic divisions among their Muslim opponents which still prevented united resistance. The Arab rulers of Egypt, the Fatimids, were not at all displeased by the Crusaders' defeat of the Seljuk Turks in Syria, having in 1098 reoccupied Palestine themselves and placed a garrison at Jerusalem. And Arab enclaves, such as the coastal city of Tripoli which had long defied the Seljuks, were prepared to watch developments from the safety of their walls. Its emir even hastened to buy immunity from attack by releasing some three hundred Christian captives. He also provided guides for the Crusaders so that they could reach the border of Fatimid Palestine in safety. As the Fatimids only kept a few troops there, they were able to press on to the target of the Crusade, the city of Jerusalem.

The city of Jerusalem was one of the great fortress-cities of the medieval Near East. The walls beneath which the Crusaders camped had been originally laid out when the Roman emperor Hadrian rebuilt the city; and the Byzantines, Umayyads and Fatimids had in turn strengthened them with additional defences. Jerusalem's Fatimid governor was Iftikhar al-Daula, in command of a mixed garrison of Arab and Sudanese soldiers. Hearing of the approach of the Crusaders, Iftikhar expelled all the Christian residents from the city, drove off all the flocks and herds from nearby pastures, and poisoned all the wells. The only non-Muslims allowed to remain in Jerusalem were the Jews. At the same time the governor sent to Egypt for armed support.

Discovering as at Antioch that they could neither fully invest the city nor take it by storm, the Crusaders fell back on penance. To the mockery of Jerusalem's defenders, the entire army walked barefoot round the city and then listened to a sermon preached on the Mount of Olives. A subsequent assault then miscarried through the shortage of siege towers, but assistance was at hand when six Christian vessels put into the harbour at Jaffa, which they found deserted by the Muslims. These Genoese and English ships were carrying food supplies and military equipment including the ropes, nails and bolts necessary for making assault towers. Once enough timber had been collected, the Crusaders set to work in spite of the summer heat, hoping to take Jerusalem before a Fatimid army arrived from Egypt. The construction and placement of the assault towers was closely watched by the defenders, who reinforced the threatened defences accordingly. Following a second barefoot procession round Jerusalem, accompanied by crosses and holy relics, and the preaching of three sermons on the Mount of Olives, the Crusaders were ready for a final two-day assault, which succeeded. By then, their fighting strength was down to 1,300 knights and 12,000 foot soldiers. It was a close-run victory at the end of a previously unimaginable overland trek from western Europe.

The sole survivors of the sack were Iftikhar and his bodyguard, who sought refuge in the Tower of David. In return for a large amount of gold, they were escorted out of the city and allowed to reach Ascalon. The wholesale massacre of Muslims and Jews, who were held to have assisted in the city's defence, shocked Muslim opinion, but Catholic observers described it approvingly in apocalyptic terms. The subsequent defeat of the Fatimid relief force at Ascalon seemed to confirm this view, because a single charge by Frankish knights was enough to secure victory. Both Muslim and Christian chroniclers agree that the battle was a surprisingly brief one.

The Arab and Berber horsemen of the Fatimid army did not fight in the same way as the Seljuk Turks. Superior numbers would have enabled them to outflank the Crusaders, but they were not mounted archers like the Seljuks, their principal weapons being the lance and sword. At Ascalon, they therefore chose not to spread out, so providing the Frankish knights with an ideal target to an all-out charge—a compact body of enemy cavalry.

Because the First Crusade was described as following 'in the footsteps of Christ', the bloodletting on the fall of Jerusalem obliged churchmen to explain the event in theological terms. 'In our time', reflected Gilbert, the Benedictine abbot of Nogent, 'God has instituted holy warfare so that

The Tower of David, the last refuge of its Muslim governor, Iftikhar al-Daula

the knightly order and the errant mob', rather than engaging in mutual slaughter, 'might find a new way of deserving salvation.' Within two centuries, this idea of divinely approved warfare was deployed to justify any action against Islam, for the refusal of Muslims to embrace Christianity rendered them worthy of destruction.

THE CRUSADER STATES

After the First Crusade's establishment of bridgeheads at Antioch and Jerusalem, four Christian territories were carved out of Syria and Palestine: the kingdom of Jerusalem, the principality of Antioch, the county of Edessa and the county of Tripoli. They were known as the Outremer, 'the land overseas'. Later Crusades were intended to expand, defend or restore these territories. They failed because in western Europe the sheer good fortune of the First Crusade was always underestimated. At the close of the eleventh century, the task of capturing Jerusalem was comparatively easy. Muslim disunity, Byzantine logistics and Crusader commitment were sufficient to guarantee military success. But in the early thirteenth century an entirely different situation prevailed. The Muslims had discovered in Saladin a general capable of mastering the Crusader states by the time of his death in 1193, and shortly afterwards Venice wrecked Byzantium by turning the Fourth Crusade into an attack upon the city of Constantinople. It no longer seemed Christ's wish that the Muslims should be driven from the Holy Land, and the old Crusader optimism evaporated with the realization that Islam was perfectly capable of defending itself.

Bohemond succeeded in establishing at Antioch a principality much stronger than the kingdom of Jerusalem. Well situated strategically and better resourced as Syria was, Bohemond still faced two serious enemies: the Byzantines and the Muslims. His descendants managed to hold on to the principality until 1291, when the Mamluks sent an army from Egypt to take Acre, the last Crusader stronghold in the medieval Near East. Bohemond's own luck ran out in 1100, when he was ambushed and taken prisoner by the Seljuks. Ransomed three years later, Bohemond was again badly defeated as he led an eastwards thrust towards Mesopotamia and, despairing of his military resources, he returned to Europe in order to enlist adventurous knights.

So charismatic a leader was he that the English king Henry I prevented him from entering his kingdom and, instead of recruiting English knights, Bohemond had to concentrate on France, where the expensive presents and holy relics he freely distributed made him immensely popular. He even married the French king's sister. With his newly raised army, however, Bohemond decided to attack the Byzantines rather than defend Antioch, but by 1108 he had achieved nothing at all, because Emperor Alexius was too strong for such an adventure to work, once the Venetians allied themselves with Constantinople in return for trade concessions. Their ships disrupted Bohemond's logistics and, in 1111, the Norman warrior died a broken man. He was buried at Canosa in Apulia, where his Romanesque-style mausoleum can be seen today.

The first Crusader to rule Jerusalem, Godfrey of Bouillon, the duke of lower Lorraine, in 1099 refused the title of king on the grounds that 'he could never wear a crown of gold where his Saviour had worn a crown of thorns'. Here a most odd legend intrudes, claiming that it was King Tafur who gave Godfrey a branch of thorns in memory of the crown placed on Christ's head at his crucifixion, and that Godfrey held Jerusalem as 'a fief of King Tafur and God alone'. Like Peter the Hermit, the reported utterances of the leading Tafur were often bordering on the prophetic. But Godfrey's brother Baldwin I was formally crowned in the Church of the Holy Sepulchre in the ensuing year, after which he took up residence in a palace next to the Tower of David.

At first, the Outremer was regarded by Catholic Europe as a permanent acquisition. Pilgrims arrived in their thousands along with settlers, while high-born nobles combined military service for the Crusader states with personal pilgrimage. Increasingly, the model of a penitential campaign was used against Muslims on other frontiers, such as Spain, and against papal opponents within Europe, like the crusade launched against the Albigensian heretics in southern France.

From the perspective of Cairo, the Franks were the enemy of Islam. Having already lost what tenuous hold they had on Sicily, after the Normans crossed the Strait of Messina from southern Italy in 1061, the Fatimids became obsessed with the containment of the Crusaders in Palestine. The defeat at Ascalon seemed to threaten an invasion of Egypt itself, although the comparatively small number of Crusaders ruled out any such enterprise. Further clashes around the city of Ascalon failed to allay the fear of invasion, and in 1103 the Fatimids invoked the duty of jihad and arranged with the Seljuk ruler of Damascus for a joint campaign against the kingdom of Jerusalem. But once again the Crusaders took advantage of their enemy's continued divisions, and aided by renegade Muslim allies from Damascus, King Baldwin I triumphed by killing the governor of Ascalon and scattering the Arab–Seljuk forces. But the city of Ascalon still did not surrender, and remained a useful base for future Fatimid operations.

Egypt's contribution to the coffers of the Umayyads and the Abbasids had made it the second most valuable province after Iraq, but its wealth was slow to translate into political power. With the steady decline of the Abbasid authority, though, Egyptian governors were able to assert their independence in the early tenth century, from which period another caliphate emerged under the Fatimids, whose name derives from Fatima, the daughter of the Prophet. This claim of descent undoubtedly assisted their takeover of Egypt in 969, the culmination of a conquest which had begun in present-day Algeria and spread along the north African coast.

Previously count of Edessa, King Baldwin I greatly expanded his kingdom, capturing Caesarea with the assistance of a Genoese fleet, but Acre eluded his grasp. To strengthen the Crusader states against Muslim counter-attacks, the pope set up a military order, the Knights Templar. The Knights Hospitaller was already in existence before the First Crusade as an order of volunteers caring for sick pilgrims in Jerusalem. They took monastic vows and followed the Benedictine rule, adopting as their symbol the white Maltese cross. After the expulsion of the Muslims, the Hospitallers became more active militarily as they policed the pilgrim routes in Palestine. Established in 1118, the Templars were recognized by their red crosses, taking their name from the Dome of the Rock, which was believed to be Solomon's Temple and not the creation of the Umayyad caliph Abd al-Malik.

The Hospitaller stronghold of Krak des Chavaliers

A kind of Christian response to jihad, both these two religious orders frequently battled against Muslim intruders, with whom they concluded their own truces when necessary. The secular authorities had no control over their actions, nor their military strongholds like the Krak des Chavaliers, a massive fortress occupied by the Hospitallers. Yet the idea of an order of monks dedicated to the use of force in the cause of Christ only became a reality with the Templars, despite a small number of clerics voicing their concern about the violence necessarily involved. One critic pointed out how they were 'a new monster composed of purity and corruption namely a monk and a knight'. Even though this trenchant criticism was not specifically directed at the Templars, the implication was inescapable—except for someone like St Bernard of Clairvaux, an eager promoter of the Second Crusade. This famous French monk travelled as far as Germany to recruit Conrad III, king of the Germans and the Romans. Never actually crowned as the Holy Roman emperor, Conrad's prestige drew his fellow countrymen fully into the Crusades for the first time.

In 1144, the Turcoman capture of Edessa and the massacre of its Frankish inhabitants startled western Europe, which in reply launched the Second Crusade. The precedent of the previous Crusade ensured that another call to arms received widespread support, with the result that the Second Crusade was the largest Western response to the needs of the Crusader states since their foundation. The addition of German arms to the expedition seemed to augur well for its success, but the German Crusaders found themselves as welcome in Byzantine lands as a plague of locusts. Cities along the route east closed their gates and would supply food only by letting it down from the walls in baskets, after cash payment. Angered by this lack of sympathy, the Germans pillaged defenceless villages and farms, and even attacked a monastery. In Constantinople the Germans were received coolly by the Byzantine emperor, who had come to see the Crusades as Western imperialism by other means. The formation of independent states in Syria and Palestine encouraged this view, which in 1204 the Fourth Crusade would fully confirm through the capture of the city of Constantinople and the partition of the Byzantine empire.

The Second Crusade met with disaster. The German army was virtually destroyed by the Seljuks at Dorylaeum, south-east of Nicaea; a wounded

Conrad narrowly escaped from falling into enemy hands. Leading no more than 2,000 survivors, the German king joined up with the rest of the Crusaders in Syria and participated in the abortive siege of Damascus. The subsequent retreat merely added to the casualty list.

THE ADVENT OF SALADIN

Until Saladin's campaigns, there had been nothing to make western Europe seriously reconsider the Crusades. The variety of motives and ambitions which lay behind them had been held together in a single purpose so long as there were victories on the battlefield, and resistance to Muslim counter-attacks appeared comparatively easy.

Known as Salah ad-Din Yusuf ibn Ayyub, Saladin was a Kurdish Muslim who rose to prominence in Fatimid Egypt. His obvious military talents were displayed in the blunting of Crusader attacks from Palestine; and despite being a Sunni, he was swiftly promoted by the Shia Fatimids. In 1171 Saladin took over the government in Egypt, abolished its caliphate, and renewed the province's allegiance to the Abbasids. Having put down pro-Fatimid rebellions in Egypt, he sent forces to conquer Yemen. The dynasty which Saladin founded as its first sultan was the Ayyubids, named after his father.

The Muslim conqueror Saladin

Saladin had grown up in Damascus, a city he always remembered with affection. One tradition relates how as a young man he was more interested in religion than joining the military. But he soon distinguished himself as a soldier and travelled to Egypt with a Syrian force sent to assist the weakened Fatimids. Al-Hakim's legacy of misrule at the start of the eleventh century had been followed by famines resulting from poor Nile floods, the collapse of the caliphate's finances, and finally bloody disorder in Cairo as mercenary and slave troops battled it out in the streets. The Berber soldiers who had brought the Fatimids to power were no longer in the caliphate's service. This breakdown of authority explains not only the end of Fatimid rule, but also its ineffective defence of Muslim lands in the central Mediterranean. The Normans had conquered the whole of Sicily by 1090.

Having come to power in Egypt, Saladin is said to have given up a soldier's pleasure in 'wine drinking and turned from frivolity to religious observance'. Instead of attacking the kingdom of Jerusalem, however, the new sultan of Egypt began a campaign against his Muslim rivals, because Saladin realized that previous wars against the Franks had been hindered by Muslim disunity. It was an issue that needed to be sorted out before he attacked them in strength. One campaign that Saladin directed from Syria against the Templars on the Jordan river, however, was in fact a preparation for the future conflict with the kingdom of Jerusalem. In spite of a truce between Saladin and the Franks, the construction of a powerful fortress at the strategic river-crossing of Jacob's Ford simply could not be tolerated. Protected by a ditch and strong walls, its Templar garrison was of considerable size, amounting to sixty knights. After a victory at nearby Marj Ayyun in the summer of 1179, Saladin besieged the fortress, undermining a portion of the wall and then making it collapse with fire. Although the Templars put up a desperate fight, they were overcome—with the exception of the fortress' commander who preferred to jump into the flames rather than be taken prisoner. Saladin razed the fortress to the ground.

This action aside, Saladin was under growing pressure to cease fighting Muslim opponents and concentrate on the Franks instead. A failed assault on the Krak des Chevaliers in 1184 was in all probability a response to this criticism, but his critics did not have long to wait for the destruction of the kingdom of Jerusalem. Three years later at Hattin, close to Lake Galilee, Saladin destroyed the kingdom's army and reduced Crusader holdings to Tyre, Tripoli and Antioch. Harassing attacks on its line of march by mounted archers, and especially against the rear of the column, had forced the Crusaders to give battle in a place where there was hardly any water available. The night before the battle, Muslim soldiers lit fires so that choking clouds of smoke drifted across the Christian camp intensifying the misery of thirst.

The response to Saladin's crushing victory at Hattin was immediate, with the kings of Germany, France and England taking the cross. A special tax, called the Saladin Tithe, was instituted in France and England to help finance the Third Crusade, which aimed to liberate Jerusalem. Only the army that Frederick Barbarossa, the Holy Roman emperor, led overland failed to arrive in strength, because Barbarossa drowned in 1190 trying to cross a river in Asia Minor.

The English and French monarchs did not embark until this date, and on the way Richard the Lionheart took the opportunity to wrest Cyprus from the Byzantines, the island remaining in Catholic hands until 1571, when the Ottoman Turks annexed it. Despite the port-city of Acre falling to the Crusaders, it was merely a staging post for the assault on Jerusalem. Having repulsed Saladin's efforts to drive them back into the sea, King Richard twice marched within a few kilometres of Jerusalem—only to withdraw each time, concluding that he had insufficient men either to take or hold the city. Because Richard could not strike at Saladin's power bases in Syria and Egypt, the military stalemate led to negotiations which left the Crusaders in control of the coastline and allowed pilgrims access to Jerusalem.

As Saladin was recognized for his clemency, which he demonstrated on the fall of Jerusalem by choosing to ransom rather than slaughter the defenders as Islamic custom allowed, it seemed possible to negotiate a satisfactory peace, once Christian and Muslim positions became clear. Richard wrote to Saladin, pointing out how warfare had ruined Palestine, since 'property and lives on both sides are destroyed ... All we have to talk about is Jerusalem, the Holy Cross and these lands. Now Jerusalem is the centre of our worship which we shall never renounce, even if there were only one of us left. As for these lands, let there be restored to us what is this side of Jerusalem. The Holy Cross, that piece of wood has no value to you, but is important to us. Let the sultan bestow it upon us. Then we can have peace and have rest from this constant hardship'. The English king was probably unaware that Saladin had placed part of the

Holy Cross at the entrance to his tent, so that visiting Muslims would tread on it as they entered. In reply, Saladin said that 'Jerusalem is ours as much as it is yours ... As for the land, it is also ours originally. Your conquest was an unexpected accident due to the weakness of Muslims there at the time.' In a sense, this analysis was largely correct because the Crusader states were a unique phenomenon, carved out of a part of the Near East which had been fought over more times than anywhere else since ancient times. Even though Saladin would have liked to carry jihad as far as Rome, the instigator of most Christian attacks on the Muslim world, he knew that this was impossible and that a compromise peace offered the best way of defending Jerusalem. From this practical decision sprang in large measure Saladin's worldwide fame: not unlike Erwin Rommel in World War Two, the Kurdish commander came to be seen as a gallant foe.

THE FOURTH AND FIFTH CRUSADES

Dissatisfied with King Richard's peace agreement, Pope Innocent III promoted yet another expedition, the lamentable Fourth Crusade, whose chosen target was Egypt but turned out to be Constantinople. The absence of kings denied the Crusaders access to national taxes and fleets, obliging them to seek help from Venice. By the summer of 1202 it was clear that the expedition, now gathered at Venice, could never raise the fare demanded by the Venetians. The shortfall was solved by the blind eighty-eight-year-old Venetian doge, Enrico Dandolo, agreeing to provide transport in return for the Crusaders capturing the city of Zara in present-day Croatia. That the city belonged to Hungary deterred nobody.

Shortly afterwards the doge, who accompanied the expedition, persuaded the Crusaders to meddle in Byzantine politics as well. Many of them were disgusted by this diversion of effort and withdrew, but the bulk of the Crusaders sailed to Constantinople, which was taken by force in the spring of 1204. Within weeks Count Baldwin of Flanders had been appointed emperor in place of the Byzantine incumbent, who was pushed off the top of a high marble column so that his execution 'should be seen by everyone'. Frankish knights then became lords of lands in

Greece and Macedonia, while Venice picked up choice possessions among the Aegean islands. For the Venetians it marked a new departure into territorial instead of simply commercial imperialism. The excuse given out by the Venetians to the effect that Dandolo was taking revenge for his blinding, a favourite Byzantine punishment, fooled very few people. His eyesight might have deteriorated as a consequence of a blow to the head, received in a brawl during his merchant days in Constantinople, but he would never have been elected doge if he were sightless.

The capture of Constantinople was not an accident; it had been on the agenda ever since the Second Crusade of 1145–9. Successive popes had voiced their disappointment at the Byzantine failure to become actively involved in the recovery of Jerusalem. Crusader cynicism was of course the decisive factor in the attack of 1204, not least because Constantinople represented a much easier conquest than facing the Muslim forces of Egypt.

The Fifth Crusade of 1213–29 was altogether different. This final attempt to reoccupy Jerusalem failed, although its leader, the Holy Roman emperor Frederick II, gave the impression of success. This most extraordinary of all European monarchs was called *stupor mundi*, 'the marvel of the world'. Born in 1194, he grew up in Palermo, the neglected heir to the Sicilian throne. He learned in that cosmopolitan city half a dozen languages, including Arabic. After being crowned king of Sicily, Frederick schemed to unite Germany with Italy and succeeded in becoming the Holy Roman emperor in 1220, having gained papal support by offering to yield Sicily to the pope as a fief. Despite his promise, he could not bring himself to meet his side of the bargain and give up the island. He antagonized Rome even more by not joining the Fifth Crusade until 1228, over a decade after it was launched. Pope Gregory IX excommunicated Frederick, an occupational hazard for medieval emperors.

Few Christians living in what was left of the Crusader states were unduly disturbed by Frederick's relations with the papacy, nor did they express much surprise at his arrival with a bodyguard of Arab troops and a Muslim teacher for his own instruction. They were less pleased with his conduct as a Crusader, when he exploited the rivalry between the rulers of Syria and Egypt in early 1229 to conclude a peace treaty with al-Kamil

Emperor Frederick and Sultan al-Kamil

Muhammad al-Malik, the fourth Ayyubid sultan of Egypt, that made Jerusalem open to Christian pilgrims except for the Temple Mount, which was to remain under Islamic religious authority. A narrow corridor linking Jerusalem and the coast was guaranteed as a means of safe passage. In addition, Bethlehem and Nazareth were returned to the Christians, who thus regained control of the holiest shrines of their religion: the places of the annunciation, nativity and crucifixion. So concerned was al-Kamil to reach a settlement with Frederick that he instructed the muezzins in Jerusalem not to make their call to prayer in the night, for fear of offending the Holy Roman emperor during his pilgrimage there. Frederick himself was just as keen to reach a quick agreement, because he needed to get back to southern Italy before the pope launched a planned invasion of Sicily.

It was an extraordinary spectacle to have a Crusading emperor arrive amid fanfares, and then, hardly unsheathing his sword, have him reach an agreement with the Muslims by diplomacy. What few understood was Frederick's chief objective: securing access to Jerusalem for pilgrims, rather than winning glory on the battlefield. That Jerusalem was left half-empty and without walls hardly mattered. For Frederick had achieved an advantage in his bitter struggle with Gregory IX, who held that the emperor was subordinate to the papacy. With the treaty signed with the Muslims, an excommunicated Frederick could now style himself as Defender of the Church and King of Jerusalem, but local Christians were not at all satisfied. So unpopular was he with them that when the Holy Roman emperor embarked from Acre for home, he was pelted with offal. As Philip of Novara recorded, 'he sailed from this port hated, cursed, and vilified'.

The agreement lasted until 1244, when Jerusalem was seized by freebooters from Egypt. The rollback of Christian power in the medieval Near East had less to do with Muslim heroics than European exhaustion: the Outremer was simply too far beyond the sea. The mood in Europe no longer favoured war against Muslims as a way of salvation. At first the Crusades had strengthened the papacy, but eventually the sponsorship of warfare came to undermine its spiritual leadership. In Germany anyone seen wearing a Crusader's cross was likely to suffer personal injury. Yet the preaching of holy war was not so readily forgotten, especially among the population at large, and anxiety about a Muslim counter-attack triggered a number of popular movements. The oddest of these was the Children's Crusade of 1212. Large groups of youths led by Nicholas of Cologne marched from Germany to Italy with the aim of freeing the Holy Sepulchre, in the belief that innocence and purity were strong enough weapons against Islam. Some of the children reached Genoa, where they were disappointed that the waves did not divide like Moses' experience during the escape of the Jews from Egypt. Others went to Rome and ports on the Adriatic coast of Italy. None of Nicholas' followers actually reached Palestine, although some unfortunates may have ended up in the slave markets of north Africa.

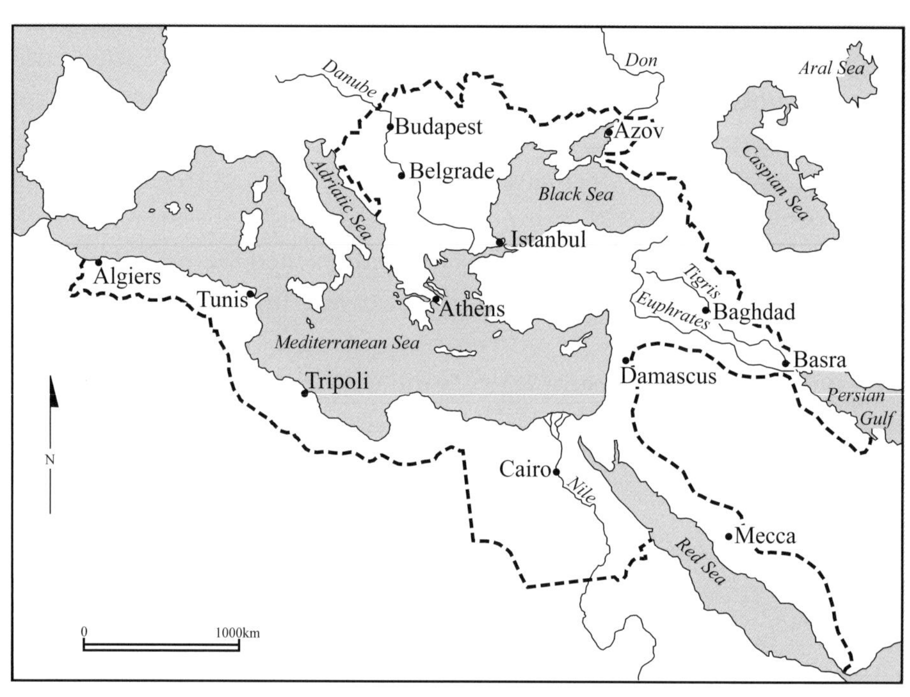

The Ottoman empire at its fullest extent

10

THE OTTOMAN EMPIRE

The early Abbasids eventually were succeeded by al-Rashid's descendants. Among them were good and bad men. Later on, when power passed to their descendants, they gave royal power and authority their due. They became enmeshed in worldly affairs of no value and turned their backs on Islam. Therefore, God permitted them to be ruined, and the Arabs completely deprived of their power, which he gave to others.

The Muqaddimah *of Ibn Khaldun*

Thus the north African scholar Ibn Khaldun explained the passing of the Abbasid caliphate in his universal history, the truly remarkable *Muqaddimah*. Here Ibn Khaldun is making a fundamental distinction between a caliph and a king. Whereas a caliph acts as a substitute for Muhammad and ensures that 'all worldly conditions are to be considered in their relation to their value for the other world', a king's rule on the contrary relies on nothing more than force, so that people are constantly in danger of having their property confiscated and suffering from other forms of injustice, such as forced labour, the imposition of duties not required by religious law, and the collection of unjustifiable taxes. That was the reason, Ibn Khaldun asserts, for the decline and fall of the Abbasids, once they forfeited religious leadership in the eyes of their subjects and came to depend solely upon troops recruited from frontier regions to maintain their position.

What also exercised Ibn Khaldun was the surge of Mongol power, which resulted in the loss of Arab conquests in most of Asia. It was the greatest clash ever between the nomadic culture of the steppe and the civilization of intensive agriculture: within a couple of generations, Mongol arms created an empire that stretched from China to Hungary. Once its founder, Genghis Khan, asked two learned Turks about the puzzling phenomenon of the city, something quite alien and a threat to the world of the nomads. And only with great difficulty was Ogodei Khan, the successor of Genghis Khan, persuaded to tax the inhabitants of northern China rather than slay them and turn their fields into pasture for Mongol horses. Like father like son, Ogodei Khan remained a nomad in temperament throughout his life.

The same was true of the Ilkhanate, or 'lesser khanate', established by Genghis Khan's grandson, Hulegu, after the capture of Aleppo in 1260. This Mongol leader was helped by the Armenian king Hethum, whose Christian kingdom was surrounded by Muslim enemies. That Hulegu's wife was a Christian was no doubt a factor in Hethum's decision to offer assistance. Yet Hulegu did not abandon his nomadic lifestyle for residence in a city, preferring to live outside city walls in a tented encampment, with the rich pastures of Azerbaijan a favourite location.

After the success at Aleppo, Hulegu believed that he could return with confidence to Mongolia for the election of the new khan. His second-in-command, Ked Bukha, was told to conquer Damascus and then occupy the rest of Syria. But Hulegu miscalculated badly. During his absence Ked Bukha was defeated at Ain Jalut, to the south of the Sea of Galilee, by Mamluk forces from Egypt; the Mongols, totalling perhaps 10,000 horsemen, were outmanoeuvred and Ked Bukha killed. The Mamluk sultan's instinct to attack then was prescient, because the Mongol advance in the medieval Near East was temporarily halted. The next target would have certainly been Egypt. Not that this reverse, which Muslim commentators lauded as the saving of Islam, was more than a temporary setback, for only a fraction of the total Mongol strength was engaged. It was only a question of time before the Mongols returned but, for a variety of reasons, no serious Mongol attempt to conquer Syria and exact revenge on the Mamluks was made for twenty-one years. Hulegu had his hands full dealing with the Golden Horde, a rival Mongol state located to the north of the Black and Caspian seas. After the accession of Kublai Khan in 1260, relations between the Ilkhanate and the Mongol homeland remained close, but there was never any question of the Great Khan actually nominating a new Ilkhan. The Mongol empire had broken into separate states, with Kublai Khan gaining the lion's share.

Although Nestorian Christians were influential in the Ilkhanate, as indeed they were in Mongolia, it was Islam which was finally adopted as the state religion by Ghazan on his accession as the seventh Ilkhan in 1295. His principal wife was the Mongol princess Kokochin, whom Marco Polo escorted from Kublai Khan's court in China to the Ilkhanate. Even though Ghazan Ilkhan continued fighting the Mamluks, his prede-

Ghazan Ilkhan studying the Qur'an

cessor had lost an important battle at Homs in 1281, when the Mamluks had reinsured their foreign policy through cooperation with the Golden Horde. Under Ghazan 'the people of the book' were able to worship freely, although Jews and Christians became second-class citizens as was standard practice in Muslim states. But Buddhists who refused to convert to Islam were expelled from the Ilkhanate.

Ghazan's conversion led to a tremendous change in Mongol attitudes. The Ilkhans began to rebuild neglected cities, restore the irrigation schemes on which agriculture depended and construct at Tabriz a permanent capital of their own. This eventual accommodation with settled ways was cut short by Tamerlane, a ferocious warrior from Central Asia, whose people were of Mongol stock but had become Turkish in speech and had adopted Islam. In a repeat of Hulegu's conquest of the medieval Near East, Tamerlane spread terror wherever he went. Most of all he enjoyed raising pillars of human heads. At Baghdad in 1401, a sack left 90,000 dead, their heads being cemented into 120 towers.

THE TURKISH RESCUE OF ISLAM

Ibn Khaldun met Tamerlane shortly after the city of Baghdad was captured, when the Central Asian conqueror asked him to write about north Africa. Tamerlane seems to have been impressed by Ibn Khaldun's view of history. 'On the surface', Ibn Khaldun told him, history 'consists of reports of eras and dynasties and past events', but a real understanding of history involves 'a search below the surface of events, a profound knowledge of underlying causes, a determination of the subtle origins and causes of existing things'. While outlining how this more scientific approach explained the rise and fall of states, Ibn Khaldun must have mentioned Damascus, since not long afterwards the city surrendered and its inhabitants were put to the sword. Before leaving for home, he requested that Tamerlane should in future spare scholars and officials when taking a city by force of arms. For Ibn Khaldun was sure that Allah had rescued the faithful by sending: 'from the Turkish nation and from among its great and numerous tribes, strong rulers to defend them and utterly loyal helpers, who were brought from the House of War to the

House of Islam under the rule of slavery ... They entered Islam with the firm resolve of true believers and yet with their nomadic virtues undefiled by the ways of civilization'. Here we have Ibn Khaldun's perspective on social development: the fundamental difference between the urban and the primitive, which produces tension between merchants and nomads, between the written script and verbal communication. Even though Tamerlane turned Samarkand into a splendid capital with mosques, libraries, observatories and parks for the scholars, scientists, poets, philosophers and artists he gathered from the countries he conquered, he was still a nomad at heart whose followers were only one remove from a nomadic existence themselves. Like Genghis Khan, he had achieved military success by a retinue system whereby ex-nomads pledged their undying loyalty to him. Yet the violent nature of both leaders was apparent in the Gok Sarai, 'the blue palace', the seat of Tamerlane's power in Samarkand: it consisted of a heavily fortified residence that included his court, treasury, armoury and, last but not least, his prison.

Ibn Khaldun did not live long enough to see the Ottoman Turks fulfil the role he envisaged for the Central Asian saviours of Islam, although Osman son of Ertugrul had founded in 1326 the Ottoman empire by his capture of Bursa, not a great distance from the Sea of Marmara. In 1261, the Byzantine emperor Michael VIII Palaeologus had recovered Constantinople from the descendants of the Fourth Crusade and then concentrated on driving the rest of them out of mainland Greece. It was to prove a mistaken policy, because Byzantine neglect of Asia Minor gave the Ottomans scope for territorial gain. Osman gave his name to the Ottoman or Osmanli dynasty, but it was his son Orhan who first established Bursa as a proper capital. Its great mosque, the Ulu Cami, was not completed until 1399; the costs were defrayed by spoils from the defeat of King Sigismund of Hungary at Nicopolis, a fortress on the Danube. Ulu Cami was the grandest mosque built in Asia Minor during the two centuries before the Turkish capture of Constantinople. Sultan Bayezid I actually lifted the siege of that city to march in 1396 to the relief of Nicopolis, where the Frankish knights in Sigismund's army determined the outcome of the action, once their impetuous charge left the Hungarian infantry exposed to a counter-attack by a far stronger body of Ottoman cavalry.

Sigismund managed to escape, but other Western leaders were not so lucky and their ransoms provided the funds for building Ulu Cami.

Although the attempt to expel the Turkish garrison from Nicopolis proved a costly failure, this Christian advance into Romania had the effect of drawing the sultan's attention away from hard-pressed Constantinople, which was already surrounded on all sides by Ottoman territory. Shortly after 1361 the Ottoman capital had been moved from Bursa to Edirne, over 200 kilometres west of Constantinople. Bursa was still revered as the first seat of Ottoman government, the burial place of

The Ottoman triumph at the battle of Nicopolis in 1396

Osman and the first five sultans, but the shift into Europe marked the direction of future Turkish ambitions. Extending control beyond Budapest was as much a priority for the Ottomans as their advance in medieval times to the Persian Gulf, and in north Africa along the Mediterranean coast. It was annoying to have the Byzantines still holding out in Constantinople, meagre though their armed forces now were, but the city's land and sea walls made it difficult for the Ottomans to overcome them.

The Ottomans followed the traditional Islamic policy of tolerance towards 'the people of the book', so that Christians, Jews and others who accepted monotheism were thus entitled to protection as long as they lived quietly under Muslim rule and paid a special head tax in lieu of military service. A few Balkan Christians did convert to Islam: either to take advantage of the benefits of full membership of Ottoman society, or to escape the persecution they had suffered as heretics under Christian rulers. But there was no major effort to enforce mass conversion, perhaps for no other reason than a desire to retain the head tax as a source of revenue for the treasury. The resettlement in Europe of Muslims from Asia Minor was restricted to areas which put up most resistance to the Ottomans. In these places the local population was enslaved and their property confiscated for the benefit of the new settlers. The steady expansion of Ottoman dominion obliged the sultans to devise a system of government which would maintain their armies and at the same time administer the conquered peoples. Inevitably this moved the Turks farther away from their Central Asian roots, despite the continued arrival of thousands more nomads driven westwards first by the Mongols and then Tamerlane. The Sunni tradition of the caliphate offered the Ottomans a useful political prop, although it was not until the 1540s that Suleyman the Magnificent dared to claim that he was indeed the caliph; thereafter the Ottoman sultan acted as the representative of Muhammad and his four immediate successors. From the accession of Selim II in 1566 onwards, each sultan was always acknowledged as the Muslim caliph.

It proved invaluable for this far-reaching religious claim that in Eyup, a suburb of Istanbul on the Golden Horn, the body of Abu Ayyub al-Ansari was buried. Discovered by the dervish Akshemseddin, the spiritual guide of Mehmed II who took Constantinople in 1453, this close companion of the Prophet had offered timely accommodation to Muhammad when he moved Medina. The Prophet's camel was supposed to have chosen Abu Ayyub's house when it sat down by the doorway. Admired by Shia and Sunni Muslims alike, Abu Ayyub asked to be interred under the walls of Constantinople when the Arabs reached the city. Constructed to incorporate Abu Ayyub's tomb, the Eyup Sultan mosque became the most popular site of Muslim pilgrimage near the Ottoman capital. And a royal pilgrimage to Eyup was always seen as an essential element in the ceremony of installation for a new sultan.

THE FALL OF CONSTANTINOPLE

So desperate did the Byzantines become when they were cut off from the rest of Europe by land, and depending entirely upon communication by sea, that in 1369 Emperor John V went to Rome in the hope of obtaining

The renowned Eyup Sultan mosque in Istanbul

papal support by converting to Catholicism. Orthodox bishops repudiated this act, deeming it as no more than a personal conversion, but the emperor's unilateral action divided his subjects and made it even more difficult to unite them against the Ottomans, whose advance into Europe seemed without end. When Sultan Bayezid I saw how isolated Constantinople was, he sent envoys in the spring of 1402 to demand the city's capitulation. But the Byzantine emperor replied with pious determination: 'Tell your master that we are weak, but that we trust in God, who can make us strong and can pull down the mightiest from their seats. Let your master do as he pleases.'

The Byzantines felt more confident about Constantinople's survival because news was coming through from the east that Tamerlane was about to invade Asia Minor. This Central Asian conqueror resented the existence of another Turkish power, fearing that it might endanger his own control of the medieval Near East. After sacking Aleppo, Damascus and Baghdad, Tamerlane was ready to challenge the Ottomans and a battle was fought at Ankara in 1402. Tamerlane's army was larger, strengthened by war elephants from recently conquered northern India; when they charged the Ottomans, Bayezid's soldiers broke and fled, leaving the sultan and his second son, Musa, as prisoners of war. Apart from a Serbian contingent in the Ottoman army, whose heavy plate armour offered protection from the arrows fired by Tamerlane's mounted archers, no one else stood their ground. After the battle, Tamerlane marched around Asia Minor and sacked cities, including the old Ottoman capital of Bursa. Despite his title, 'the sword of Islam', Tamerlane was by no means inclined to behead non-Muslims. In comparison with his Muslim enemies, Christians, Jews, Buddhists and Hindus escaped lightly. But on rare occasions, almost as though to appear even-handed, Tamerlane would unleash his fury against them too.

Bayezid was well treated as a captive, and when he died in 1403 his son Musa was freed and allowed to convey the corpse to the family mausoleum in Bursa. The seventy-two-year-old Tamerlane went back to Samarkand, dying in 1405 as he was launching an invasion of China. Some historians argue that Tamerlane's humiliation of the Ottomans was the moment to push the Turks out of Europe, quite overlooking the fact that hundreds of thousands had already settled in the Balkans. By 1410 more Turks were living in the European provinces of the Ottoman empire than those in Asia Minor. The ensuing struggle for supremacy between Bayezid's sons lasted for over a decade, before Mehmed II finally inherited a rebuilt empire in 1451. It was in far better condition than when Bayezid left it to his father in 1403. Mehmed's father Murat II was one of the great Ottoman sultans, and reformed the army as well as the administration in such a way that his son could make new conquests and enlarge the empire on both its eastern and western frontiers. Conscious of the conflict that had almost destroyed Ottoman rule after the defeat at Ankara, Murat made sure that the accession of Mehmed was undisputed in spite of the quarrels which had initially broken out over his candidacy.

Arguably Mehmed II's success at Constantinople derived as much from his peaceful succession as the great cannon which he commissioned for the siege. Two years earlier, by means of a written will, Murat II had managed to prevent the violent struggles that tended to accompany each sultan's elevation. According to traditional lore, Osman alone was peacefully succeeded by his son Orhan, after his brother Ali Pasha had voluntarily renounced his claim to the throne and retired to a life of contemplation. Despite Orhan never having a brother, the story is accurate in that he became sultan with none of the bloodletting which characterized the start of so many subsequent reigns. Such civil wars were the inevitable result of the Ottoman acceptance of almost any legitimate heir as ruler, irrespective of precedence. In spite of his father's will naming him as the next ruler, Mehmed took no chances and executed his infant half-brother as soon as he entered the place.

Sultan Mehmed II, the conqueror of Constantinople

The Ottoman Turks secured their lasting foothold in Europe with the capture of Constantinople. There was consternation in western Europe, but the Venetians had been persuaded to do nothing in return for a trade treaty, as indeed had Hungary, which was pleased to enjoy a respite from fighting the Turks. The actual siege lasted from February until May 1453, when the Theodosian land wall was breached and the Ottoman soldiers poured into the city. The opening was made by a monstrous gun, the invention of a Hungarian engineer named Orban. This man had offered his services to Emperor Constantine XI, but the Byzantine ruler could not pay him the salary he thought to be his due, nor could he provide the raw materials required for his powerful artillery. Orban therefore went to the Ottoman sultan, who was delighted at the prospect of a cannon that was capable of firing balls heavy enough to shatter masonry.

Although the monster which Orban created for Mehmed could only be fired seven times a day, its impact was devastating and weakened whole sections of Constantinople's landward defences. Realizing that nothing could be saved, the Byzantine emperor Constantine discarded his imperial insignia and died fighting in the breach. His body was never identified, in spite of a stuffed head supposedly belonging to him being sent round the leading courts of the Islamic world by a triumphant Mehmed. Cut off from all outside help, Constantinople's defenders were simply worn down. While Islamic law would have justified a full-scale sack of the city in view of its resistance, Mehmed kept his troops under strict control, killing only those Byzantines who continued to resist and doing all he could to keep the city intact so that it could be the great centre he planned for his empire. He even forgave the Genoese colony of Galatea, across the Golden Horn, which had forfeited its agreed neutrality by taking in Byzantine fugitives. The colony would in future be unwalled and become part of the Ottoman empire, but its inhabitants still retained the right to trade throughout the provinces. Earlier the Genoese had flown Tamerlane's colours in true opportunist style.

With the prestige brought by the conquest of Constantinople, now called Istanbul by the Ottomans, Mehmed became the absolute ruler of a centralized empire, which comprised most of the old eastern Roman empire plus Muslim additions. Powerful Ottoman families were deprived of political influence and relatives who might threaten his position were executed. Mehmed's next move was to restore Istanbul to its former greatness, rebuilding the city and importing as settlers people from all parts of his empire. Muslims, Armenians, Jews, Greeks and Slavs were all warmly welcomed. Many Jews came from as far away as Spain, where they were suffering renewed Christian persecution. Between 1478 and 1502, Isabella of Castile and Ferdinand of Aragon took three related decisions. They persuaded the pope to create the Inquisition; they expelled the Jews; and they forced Muslims living in the kingdom of Castile to convert to Catholicism. The old Iberian tradition of tolerance, established by the fugitive Umayyad prince Abd al-Rahman, was over for good.

In a sense, the Ottoman sultan had a golden opportunity to reshape the city because large areas had been left empty as Byzantine fortunes steeply declined. Even though Istanbul's development as a leading metropolis only reached its peak in the middle of the eighteenth century, Mehmed's visionary resettlement and rebuilding programme gave the city a critical impetus as a renowned pleasure resort. The glitter of gilded palaces in the Bosphorus, the elaborately carved fountains and kiosks, the sounds of musical bands, and the colourful spectacle of public life in gardens and squares captured the imagination of residents as much as visitors. The Ottoman empire may have been under intense pressure along its frontiers, but there was no faltering of self-confidence among Istanbul's inhabitants. The caliphate shared their enthusiasm, so that within the decade of 1718–28 new palaces were commissioned for the imperial family, senior courtiers and high officials. The most celebrated of palatial projects was the so-called Abode of Happiness, which was built for Ahmed III on the Golden Horn.

Yet the most conspicuous buildings were the waterfront palaces constructed along the Bosphorus in order to satisfy a fashion for luxurious hideaways. Caliph Ahmed's transfer of the court back to Istanbul from Edirne, where it had been located for a number of years, obviously stimulated the building frenzy. The pavilion of Humayunabad, or 'the imperial abode', at Bebek on the European shore of the Bosphorus, was but one of several erected for the benefit of Ahmed's family. A downside of this particular construction was the confiscation of all the property belonging to Greek, Armenian and Jewish residents there. The Armenian chronicler Incicyan, writing at the end of the century, reported that the village of Bebek had been flourishing, thanks to an ever-growing population, until the pavilion was finished. After that, the only residents were members of the ruling class and their servants.

Outside Istanbul, the Fatih or 'conqueror', as Mehmed was now called, chose to extract from the surviving pockets of Byzantine power a fixed amount of tribute rather than overwhelm them. The fate of Mistra in the Peloponnese was not untypical. Following the Fourth Crusade, which in 1204 had resulted in Constantinople's first capture, Frankish lords divided Greece between themselves and William of Champlitte was made the master of the Peloponnese. Within a year he received letters from the pope addressing him as 'Prince of all Achaea'. But his early death opened the way for Geoffrey of Villehardouin to assume a leading role, and it was his descendants who converted the natural fortress of Mistra, to the west

The Humayunabad pavilion on the Bosphorus

of ancient Sparta, into their stronghold. The Greek revival led by Emperor Michael VIII, founder of the final Byzantine dynasty, regained Mistra in 1261 and made it the centre of a new despotate named Morea.

By the fall of Constantinople, Morea was administered by Demetrius and Thomas, two close relatives of the last Byzantine emperor; their quarrels hardly abated when the Ottomans intervened and warned them to keep the peace. In 1460 the sultan himself appeared at the head of an army and, after some hesitation, Demetrius surrendered himself and Mistra while Thomas fled to the Venetian island of Corfu. It is not so easy today to envisage Mistra as it must have been under the despots, but

Mistra, the last Byzantine stronghold in the Peloponnese

its majestic location and surviving buildings still charm the visitor. Of its original 20,000 inhabitants, the only current residents are the nuns who live in the convent of the Pantanassa. The frescoes in Mistra's churches dramatically reveal the religious conviction of the Orthodox faith, beset though it was during the Middle Ages by intense opposition from both Catholicism and Islam. For most of the period that Greece was part of the Ottoman empire, however, the Peloponnese remained a quiet backwater. There was no serious effort to incorporate the Mani, the middle peninsula of the three southern prongs of the Peloponnese, despite its stubborn refusal to pay the Ottomans any tribute at all. The vengeful Maniots were left to pursue their own private feuds.

THE OTTOMAN ZENITH

The sixteenth century witnessed the apogee of the Ottoman empire. After disposing of his brothers in 1512, Selim I continued the expansion which had started immediately after the capture of Constantinople. Selim's first campaign was directed against Safavid Persia, whose ruler Shah Ismail was encroaching upon Ottoman holdings in the east. In 1514, Selim's army won a crushing victory at Chaldiran in Azerbaijan, from which it took the Persians a generation to recover. The Safavid cavalry could not withstand fire from the artillery positioned in the centre of the Ottoman battle line. After the defeat, the Persians manufactured 2,000 muskets with the aid of Ottoman deserters, and they produced copies of an Ottoman canon recovered from a river bed. They also used diplomatic contacts to obtain up-to-date weapons from abroad.

Selim consolidated Ottoman defences in the east and then focused his attention on the Mamluks, whose authority stretched from Egypt as far as Syria. Had his Janissaries not baulked at spending a winter in Tabriz, the sultan might have continued with the campaign against Safavid Persia. The Janissaries, the Yeni Ceri or 'new troops', were the most obvious example of non-Muslim recruitment in the Ottoman empire. Agents went periodically through the provinces, conscripting the strongest and brightest Christian boys, while Christian captives formed the other source of recruits. Once they entered the corps, which provided the sultan with his engineers and technicians as well as his soldiers, they were forbidden to marry and, like the ancient slave-troops of Sumerian kings, they had to devote themselves entirely to the service of the state. At first the boys were taken at the age of six or seven, only one from each family, never an only son, but in the late sixteenth century these rules were discarded and recruits might be in their teens. It was only in the next century, when the Janissaries were allowed to marry and so turned the corps into a hereditary body, that compulsory conscription faded away. Some Christian parents were not adverse to their boys joining the Janissaries, as these soldiers could rise to riches and power, and often help their relations. A solitary uprising against conscription occurred, when in 1565 Albanian Christians expressed their resentment over the compulsory conversion to Islam of every Janissary.

In 1515, Selim moved into Mamluk Syria. Within three years he had reached Cairo, expanding Ottoman territory right round the eastern Mediterranean. Back in Istanbul, the sultan extended the naval arsenal and prepared a large fleet, since as long as the island of Rhodes remained in the possession of the Knights of St John, the sea route between Istanbul and the newly conquered province of Egypt would never be secure. When Selim died in 1520, his eight-year reign had doubled the size of the empire and given it a navy. During Selim's stay in Cairo, we are told that the sultan had already augmented Ottoman power at sea by ordering the construction of fifty warships.

Hearing the news of this unexpected maritime initiative, the Muslim merchant community in Gujarat rejoiced, because in 1498 the Portuguese had rounded the Cape of Good Hope and reached India, where they endeavoured to dominate seaborne trade. The Portuguese had a clear run until Ottoman warships arrived as the Mughals, who controlled most of the subcontinent, were a land-oriented people. The third Mughal emperor, Akbar the Great, had responded with puzzlement when in 1486 he stood on a beach and saw waves for the first time. Although the Ottoman navy never drove the Portuguese from Asian waters, the pressure it exerted in the Indian Ocean hindered Portugal's attempted monopoly over the spice trade. Farther east the Ottomans even provided Aceh, a sultanate in western Sumatra, with military assistance in response to the diplomatic mis-sions it sent to Istanbul, by dispatching technicians capable of casting guns, and artillery men to fire them. By the 1620s, Aceh possessed 5,000 cannons for its confrontation with Portuguese Malacca. Yet it was in the Mediterranean that the Ottoman navy was really deployed in order to thwart the Venetians and their Hapsburg allies.

The succession to Selim I was peaceful in 1520, since his only son Suleyman had no brothers to dispute the throne. He did face a rebellion by the governor of Damascus, though, which was soon suppressed. 'The Magnificent' or the 'Grand Turk', as Suleyman I was called, had another advantage and that was the Janissary corps which he could use to control difficult members of the Ottoman ruling class. Above all, the new sultan was concerned with justice: he declared that soldiers should pay for all provisions they consumed during a campaign, whether in Ottoman or enemy territory, and he insisted that taxes were only levied according to the ability to pay, with no more of the arbitrary taxes and confiscations imposed by his father. Suleyman also reminded officials about their duty to protect the lives, property and honour of his subjects regardless of their religious beliefs. And finally, he compensated those who had been deprived of their property and released the poor who were imprisoned for debt, by paying off their creditors with funds from the treasury.

Suleyman the Magnificent, the conqueror of Hungary

Even though Suleyman also devoted his energies to a series of campaigns, he always avoided fighting on different fronts in the same year. Suleyman's primary ambitions were in Europe, where he cleared the Balkans of Christian enclaves and conquered the kingdom of Hungary. Buda and Pest surrendered in 1526. Yet Hapsburg interference in Hungary obliged Suleyman to conduct two more campaigns and, in 1529, even attack the city of Vienna. This threat to a major Christian city shocked western Europe, but it did not result in another crusade. Given Hapsburg problems with the Protestant Reformation, all that Archduke Ferdinand of Austria, the brother of the Holy Roman emperor Charles V, could hope for was a successful defence of Vienna, which he achieved through strengthening the city walls and adding earthen bastions along with an inner rampart. Probably never more than an opportunist thrust after his decisive defeat of the Hungarians, Suleyman decided not to settle down for a thorough investment of Vienna but to return instead to Istanbul and continue with his reform programme.

Suleyman was able to relax his guard against the Christian powers of Europe, since in 1522 the troublesome island of Rhodes had been neutralized after a prolonged siege. By the terms of the surrender, all inhabitants wishing to leave the island could go, along with the Knights of St John who moved to a new base in Malta. Although they could harry Muslim vessels from there, the eastern Mediterranean was now safe. The defeat of the Ottoman fleet at Lepanto in 1574, not long after Suleyman's death, made little difference to the strategic situation. Commanded by Don Juan of Austria, the bastard son of Charles V, the Christian fleet surprised the Ottomans in a large bay in the western Peloponnese, close to the ancient city of Pylos. Celebrated though the naval victory was throughout Christian Europe, the Ottomans were not weakened at sea, so that Venice soon signed a new peace treaty accepting the permanent loss of Cyprus, while Spain withdrew its troops from Tunis, where they had supported anti-Ottoman sultans.

Suleyman's legacy was immense. Not only did he enlarge the Ottoman empire in Europe and Asia, but even more his sponsorship of education raised the standard of its administration. The interest that he took in justice more than balanced his claim to the caliphate: following Abbasid practice, the caliph was an absolute ruler but his decisions were always subject to religious scrutiny. In no manner, however, were religious critics ever a drag on scientific speculation under the Ottomans. At the Suleymaniye mosque, the largest ever built in Istanbul, the Ottoman sciences received a major boost with its opening of a school that for the first time placed emphasis on mathematics and medicine rather than Qur'anic studies. The Janissary engineer and architectural genius Mimar Sinan built the great mosque at Suleyman's command. The development of geography was of course a natural consequence of growing Ottoman naval power, with the Ottoman admiral Seydi Ali Reis relating the experiences of sailors in the Red Sea, Persian Gulf and Indian Ocean. He also wrote books on astronomy and mathematics.

Selim II, the only surviving son of Suleyman, enjoyed in 1566 an undisputed succession. He was very different from his father in that he had a distaste for affairs of state as well as military campaigns. Selim's own son, Murad III, endured a less peaceful reign at the close of the sixteenth century. Renewed conflict with Safavid Persia and Hapsburg Austria, plus the need to halt Russian encroachment in the Crimea, inaugurated a period of decline for the Ottomans.

IMPERIAL TROUBLES

Difficulties on the battlefield were replicated in the palace, when in 1621 a rebellion by the Janissaries ended with the execution of Caliph Osman and his replacement with another ineffective ruler by the name of Mustafa, who had been forcibly retired four years earlier because of his mental illness. Dethroned for a second time in 1623, Mustafa was replaced by Osman's twelve-year-old brother Murad IV. Buying the loyalty of the Janissaries and other regular troops proved expensive, but at least it returned a degree of stability to Ottoman rule. The engagement of Austria in the Thirty Years War, essentially a struggle between Catholic and Protestant Europe, removed a great deal of pressure from the Ottoman empire and allowed its army to concentrate on Safavid Persia, which had occupied Baghdad. Fighting on the eastern front did not go well and Murad's replacement of the Ottoman general displeased both the Janissaries and other regular soldiers, who in 1632 demanded the heads of the caliph's closest associates. They even contemplated dethroning Murad, but some of the soldiery remained loyal and this gave him scope for a counter-attack. The defeat of the uprising saved Murad's throne, but it was a sign of the troubles then facing the Ottoman empire.

The troubled Ottoman caliph, Murad IV

Now increasingly suspicious of anyone at court, Murad executed family members and precipitated a succession crisis as he had no surviving sons of his own. Besides sanctioning executions which encompassed courtiers as well, the caliph fell under the influence of Muslim fundamentalists, who persuaded him to ban coffee and tobacco, the latter on pain of death. The recovery of Baghdad, which the caliph triumphantly entered in 1539, appeared to have restored Ottoman military glory and stabilized the empire once more, but it would soon be tested again under his brother, known as Ibrahim 'the Mad'. Another war with Venice resulted from the Ottoman invasion of Crete, during which the Venetians blockaded the Dardanelles. After disagreement between Venice and its European supporters over the conduct of the island's defence, the Ottomans were able to annex Crete in 1669. Ibrahim's descent into madness coincided with this campaign and he was deposed before its successful completion. His successor in 1648 was his seven-year-old son, Mehmed V.

The conquest of Crete was not the only Ottoman military success. Imperial expansion west of the Black Sea, at the expense of the Ukraine, made it an Ottoman lake for the first time. Yet Russian intervention was a worrying sign for Istanbul, although the Dnieper river became the recognized northern boundary of Ottoman dominion; but it was not long before renewed conflict with the Hapsburgs undermined these advances, since it involved the disastrous Ottoman siege of Vienna in 1683. A relief force of 25,000 cavalry led by King Sobieski of Poland ended the sixty-one-day siege in a single charge. The political consequences of this Ottoman reverse were no less dramatic because it led to the formation of the Holy League, a coalition of anti-Ottoman powers in Europe. During the sixteen years that followed, the Ottoman empire suffered defeats on both land and sea. By the Treaty of Karlowitz in 1699, Caliph Mustafa II ceded Hungary to the Austrians, and Athens and the Peloponnese to Venice. Within two decades the Ottomans had recovered the lost territory in Greece, but Suleyman the Magnificent's prized conquest of Hungary was lost forever.

The Ottoman empire was first and foremost a Muslim power, a fact emphasized by Suleyman's assumption of the caliphate; yet this bold step could not disguise the presence of a large non-Muslim population that, in most of the European provinces, actually comprised the majority. Yet even in the Near East, the Muslim population was far from homogeneous. Kurdish hill-tribes had little in common with Arab bedouin roaming the deserts of Syria and Arabia. And there were also substantial Christian and Jewish communities in towns and villages. Although Islamic courts acted as the primary ones of the empire, Ottoman officials were inclined to let different peoples settle their affairs at the local level as far as possible. Punishment for unresolved non-capital crimes usually meant fines or the lash, or a combination of both.

For most of the Ottoman empire's existence, individuals who were of minority status enjoyed fuller rights and more legal protection than they would have been accorded in either contemporary France or Austria, not to say Spain once the Inquisition set to work. It is true that inter-communal relations worsened during the nineteenth century, but this had much to do with the rise of nationalist sentiment among minority peoples. A case in point is the tragic Armenian massacre of 1915–16, when more than 600,000 perished as they were being deported out of the battle zone with Russia. The presence in the Russian invasion force of Armenian Russians, and some Ottoman Armenians who had defected to the enemy, led to this draconian decision to move a whole population. The Armenian trek westwards consisted of a non-stop programme of neglect and violence, despite official orders to protect the refugees. Particularly aggressive were displaced Muslims from the recently lost Balkan provinces.

This aberration marked the nadir of Ottoman rule. Trouble had been brewing ever since European pressure increased at the close of the eighteenth century. In 1783 Catherine the Great annexed the Crimean khanate, depriving Istanbul of a valuable source of manpower at a time when the Janissaries ceased to be of much use as a fighting force. Just as bad was Napoleon Bonaparte's invasion of Egypt in 1798. Even though the French were checked by the British, after Horatio Nelson's destruction of the French fleet anchored in the Nile and Ralph Abercromby's defeat of veteran French regiments in a hard-fought campaign, it was the tempting offer to transport the exhausted French soldiers back home that finally tipped the scales, especially as Bonaparte had already slipped back to seize power in France. Not only did the French attempt to turn Egypt into a colony end in a dismal failure, but it provided a rare opportunity for

The court of the would-be reformer Selim III

British soldiers to match themselves against the most experienced French troops. As one commander put it: 'Our service regained its ancient standing in the estimation of the British people.' The turmoil of the invasion, however, gave Muhammad Ali the chance to set himself up as ruler of Egypt. This Ottoman officer from Albania effectively ended Istanbul's direct influence in this rich province, although it remained the caliph's nominal possession until the First World War.

Selim III, who reigned from 1789 to 1807, appreciated that the Ottoman empire needed to be reconstructed on new principles. For him reform was an absolute necessity: growing separatist tendencies had to be held in check, the armed forces swiftly modernized, and diplomatic relations established with foreign countries. Starting in 1793, Selim opened a permanent embassy in London and others followed in European capitals. Along with the Iranians, as the Persians were now known, the Ottomans were deeply concerned about the Russians, whose expansion had already made them all-powerful among the Turkish-speaking peoples of Central Asia. Because Russia was also determined to control the Balkans, it failed to notice that the British and the French were intent on preserving the integrity of the Ottoman empire, with the result that the Crimean War was fought in 1853–6.

Until the mid-nineteenth century, Istanbul had resisted European loans since they could lead to foreign domination and control, but Ottoman participation in the Crimean War had to be financed by this method. Predictably, it led to more loans and, by the mid-1870s, the Ottoman empire was mired in debt and largely controlled by a public debt administration run by its foreign creditors. In a last effort to regain caliphal authority, Mahmud II had moved against the Janissaries, whom he called 'nothing more than a great disorganised body into which spies have penetrated to foster disorder and to incite rebellion', and also against powerful families in the provinces. A rebellion of Janissaries stationed at Istanbul was put down in 1826 by loyal troops, and then Janissary garrisons were overcome in other cities. Although Mahmud's efforts laid the foundation for an Ottoman revival, the empire acquired neither an up-to-date army nor a modern administration. The burden of debt was already crippling the imperial government before the Balkan

Wars of 1912–13 liquidated its remaining European possessions, except the coastal plain between Edirne and Istanbul. Provinces that in the sixteenth century had stretched almost to Vienna now ended a few hours' train journey from the capital.

PART 4

THE MODERN NEAR EAST

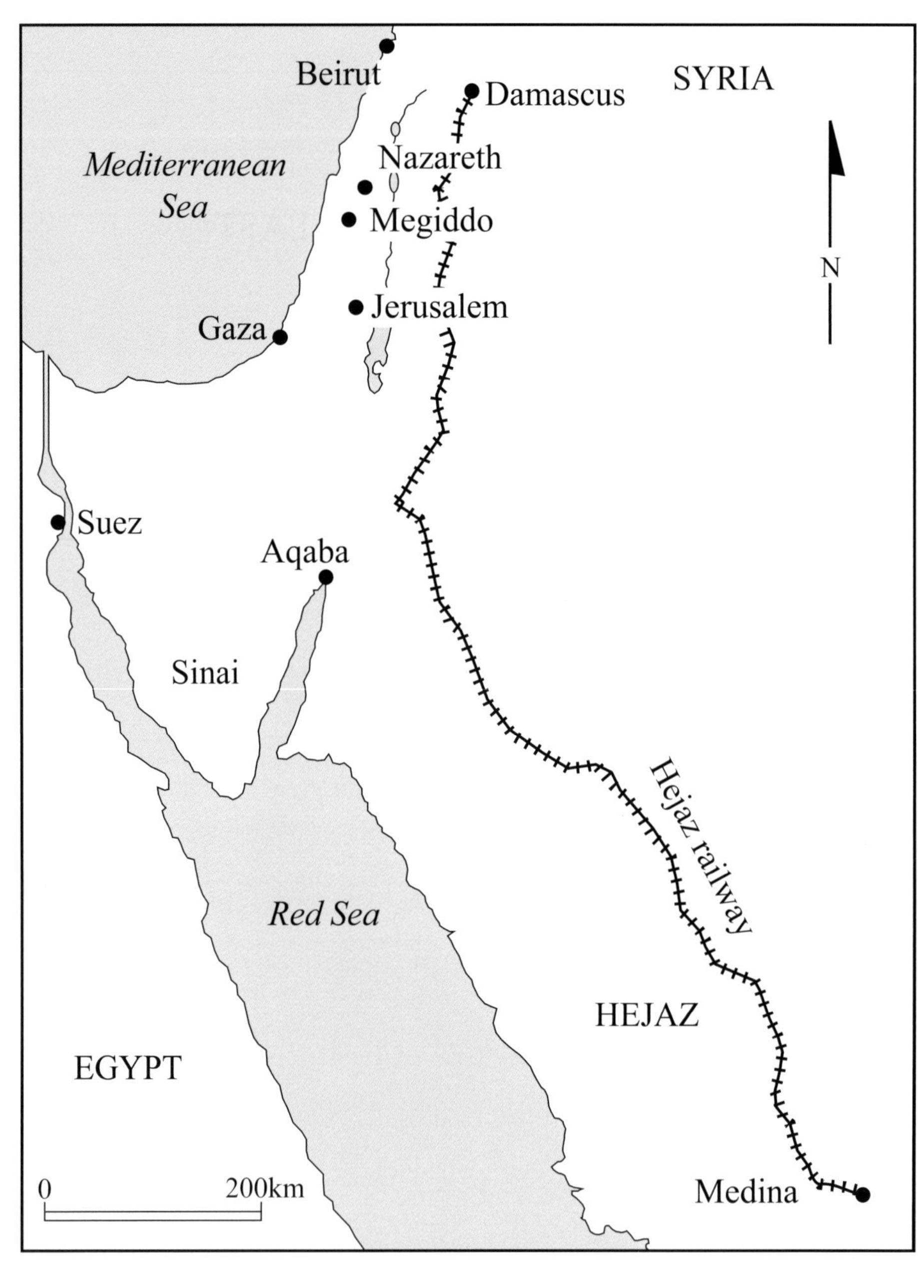

The scene of the Arab Revolt

11

THE FIRST WORLD WAR AND THE ARAB REVOLT

I did not rise in revolt except to champion the truth and to aid the oppressed. The Arabs were Arabs before Moses and Jesus and Muhammad. We are Arabs before all else.

Faisal ibn Hussein on the liberation of Aleppo in 1918

From his vantage point as a member of parliament, Faisal ibn Hussein, briefly the future king of Syria and afterwards the king of Iraq, observed the decline of Ottoman power. Since the deposition of the caliph Abdulhamid II in 1909, the Young Turks had replaced his absolute rule with a parliamentary system of government in the belief that only a modernized empire could hold its own during the twentieth century. Already Armenian and Arab activists sought greater autonomy within a weakened Ottoman state, while European imperial powers and the newly emergent Balkan countries, such as Serbia, Montenegro and Bulgaria, endeavoured to annex Ottoman lands in Europe. When in 1912 Greece also joined the anti-Ottoman coalition in the First Balkan War, the combined forces of the Balkan states totalled 715,000 men as compared with only 320,000 Ottoman soldiers in the field. The surrender of Edirne's garrison closed a chapter in the Turkish involvement with the European mainland, because in the subsequent Treaty of London the Ottoman government was obliged to sign away more than 80,000 square kilometres of territory and nearly 4 million inhabitants, surrendering all its possessions in Europe except for a small area around Istanbul itself.

Losing Libya to newly united Italy was nothing compared to ceding Albania, Macedonia and Thrace, because they ranked among the most prosperous and developed provinces in the empire. The sudden loss of tax revenues was compounded for the Ottomans by the sheer expense of the First Balkan War, which did not quite work out as the victorious Balkan countries anticipated, for the sharing out of the spoils was upset when Austria and Italy recognized Albania's declaration of independence. During the subsequent conflict between Serbia, Greece and Bulgaria in the Second Balkan War of 1913, Ottoman forces took advantage of the general confusion to liberate Edirne, whose inhabitants had suffered Bulgarian atrocities almost equal to the later Ottoman treatment of the Armenians.

The recovery of Edirne, an earlier Ottoman capital than Istanbul, was hailed as a triumph for the Young Turks as the movement's leader, Enver Bey, had taken the initiative in the campaign. Largely composed of middle-ranking army officers, the Young Turks sought to reform the centuries-old empire in order to halt territorial haemorrhaging, but continued losses prompted in 1913 a Young Turk dictatorship. How involved Mustafa Kemal was in these changes remains a matter of speculation, although there can be no doubt that Ataturk, or 'Father Turk', as he would soon be called, gained from the German-inspired reorganization of the Ottoman army on the eve of the First World War. With German support and military aid, the Young Turks hoped to regain lost territory in both Egypt and eastern Asia Minor. They were confident in their soldiers' ability to prevail, and rather naively expected local Muslims to rise up against the British and the Russians in the wake of their victories.

ENTERING THE WORLD WAR

After the Ottoman declaration of war in November 1914, Ataturk had asked for an immediate transfer to active duty. At the time he was a military attaché to Bulgaria, Serbia and Montenegro, but his open dislike of the Ottoman–German alliance prevented such an appointment until 1915. Mehmed V, the half-brother of the deposed caliph, did not approve of Enver

Caliph Mehmed V declared a jihad against Britain, France and Russia in 1915

Bey's pro-German policy either. Yet he and his successor Mehmed VI, whose reign lasted until the abolition of the Ottoman sultanate in 1922, were mere figureheads. All that Mehmed V could do as caliph was to declare jihad against Britain, France and Russia. The declaration failed to garner worldwide Muslim support for the Central Powers, but it had an effect in odd places like Singapore, where in 1915 an Indian regiment mutinied when its Muslim rankers learned of it.

At the start of the same year, Ataturk finally left Sofia to take command of an Ottoman division that as yet existed only on paper. By this point in the war, the Ottomans were already in trouble because an offensive led by Enver Bey in the Caucasus turned into a disaster, with most of the ill-equipped troops freezing to death even before they could confront the Russians. Asia Minor thus lay open to a Russian advance.

Even greater was the threat looming closer to Istanbul itself. At the instigation of Winston Churchill, a seaborne assault was being planned for the Dardanelles. With most of its land borders in Europe sealed off by Germany and Austria-Hungary and its Baltic Sea outlet blockaded by the German navy, Russia urgently needed access to the Mediterranean so as to receive supplies from Britain and France. Perhaps recalling the forcing of the Dardanelles by a British squadron in 1807, the Admiralty thought it was possible to reach the Ottoman capital with a combined expedition on land and sea. Since 1807, however, the Ottomans had taken the defence of the Straits more seriously, as the attackers were to find to their cost.

Ataturk had just begun forming his new division in early 1915, when the British bombardment of Ottoman fortifications in the Dardanelles obliged Istanbul to dispatch him there at once. Its defence was a matter of life and death ever since the British premier Herbert Asquith had said upon the Ottoman empire's entry into the war that Britain was determined to end its dominion in Europe as well as Asia. The German general Otto Liman von Sanders was given command of the Ottoman forces in the Dardanelles, whose slowness to react to the Allied landings Ataturk firmly believed had denied his troops the chance of driving the invaders into the sea. As it was, his own steadiness under fire had prevented a precipitate Ottoman retreat and effectively thwarted the advance on Istanbul. His counter-offensive led to trench warfare reminiscent of the Western Front before the final withdrawal of the Allied expeditionary force at the end of 1915. There were extensive casualties on both sides, with the Allies suffering 132,175 killed and wounded.

Even though Enver Bey tried to limit Ataturk's popularity as the saviour of Istanbul, there was nothing the Young Turk leader could do to damp down public enthusiasm for his successful defence of the Dardanelles. Only the profound disagreement of Ataturk with high-ranking German officers in general, and with Liman von Sanders in particular, pushed him to the sidelines. Ataturk disliked Germany's exploitation of the Ottoman army for its own purposes and he realized that it was in fact on the losing side in the First World War. His recall to command was caused by Russian successes in Asia Minor, where in the north they swiftly captured the key cities of Erzurum and Trabzon, and in the south, supported by Armenian volunteers, they seized Mus and Bitlis. Ataturk halted the Russian advance and, once the Russian Revolution of 1917 took hold, the threat from the east seemed over. It was not, however, as the Arabs were already in revolt. Again differences with German commanders prevented Ataturk's transfer to Syria and Palestine in order to prepare a defensive position against a British attack from Egypt. It hardly helped his situation when he submitted a memorandum to the government criticizing Germany: he cautioned against its domination of the empire which could only lead to it becoming a German colony if the Central Powers were victorious.

THE ARAB REVOLT

The Arab rebellion against Ottoman rule was launched by one man: Sharif Hussein. Despite worrying about its unforeseen consequences, Faisal had no choice but to accept his father's action. Yet he was certain of British support in the ensuing conflict because, in response to the Ottoman use of Islam to stoke up anti-British sentiment in Iran, Afghanistan and India, Britain desperately needed Arab allies to undermine the caliph's declaration of jihad. An alliance with Sharif Hussein, the emir of Hejaz, the province in which both Medina and Mecca were located, was therefore priceless.

At the age of thirty-four, Faisal was thrust into a series of events that were unmatched for their audacity in modern times. Initially, he had much to learn as the Ottomans fought as a modern army, unlike the hit-and-run tactics of bedouin warfare, but his most pressing problem was a lack of weapons and ammunition. Even accepting such military aid from the British was not without its complications, for there was a danger of the Arabs escaping Ottoman control only to fall under the yoke of a European power. So Faisal had the difficult task of keeping Arab tribesmen actively involved in the rebellion, while ensuring that too close a relation with Britain did not develop into a political burden. His father shared these concerns, writing to the High Commissioner in Egypt, Sir Henry McMahon, with a demand that Syria, Palestine and Arabia should all be independent countries in the event of an Ottoman defeat. Subsequent correspondence between McMahon and Hussein focused on British attempts to limit the post-war gains that the Arabs could expect in return for their military contribution. In the end, the High Commissioner was assisted by the creation of the Arab Bureau, a Cairo-based unit that was responsible for the collection of information and the formulation of policy on Arab issues.

Britain needed room for manoeuvre because of the separate negotiations it was simultaneously conducting with the French about the shape of the post-war Near East: negotiations which would entail well-defined spheres of influence quite different from the impression given to Sharif Hussein by Sir Henry McMahon. Not wishing to face Ottoman reinforcements, the Arab revolt broke out in Medina in June 1916. The uprising

Emir Sharif Hussein, the first Arab leader to rebel against the Ottomans

here was initiated by Faisal, who led an assault on Medina's defences. Some 30,000 men were involved, although only 6,000 were armed with rifles. Sharif Hussein himself commanded a force dispatched to Mecca, which fell after a short siege. Elsewhere the Arabs found themselves up against machine guns, artillery and aircraft.

Well-entrenched Ottoman positions denied Faisal an easy victory at Medina, and his tribesmen were driven southwards by an Ottoman counter-attack. The city would continue to defy the Arabs until early 1919, more than two months after Britain and Ottoman Turkey had signed an armistice. Although the British were not unduly impressed by the Arab uprising, they recognized that the fighting in Hejaz was likely to draw off a sizeable number of Ottoman troops who would otherwise be deployed in Sinai against any British advance towards Palestine. What would really transform the military situation was use of the port of Aqaba, the only port of present-day Jordan. But its capture could only be achieved by a seaborne assault upon which the Ottoman guns defending the port were bound to inflict damage. The Arab Bureau was also opposed to the Arabs taking the port themselves, since after the war it was likely to be essential to the defence of Egypt.

It was a target that T. E. Lawrence, later known as Lawrence of Arabia, realized the Arabs would have to take if they were to have any claim to territory beyond Arabia. As he said to Faisal, when they first met, Hejaz 'is far from Damascus'. Lawrence saw that Faisal was the only one of Sharif Hussein's sons who had the necessary qualities to carry the Arab revolt to a successful conclusion. Having persuaded his superiors in Cairo that the Arabs needed more military supplies, Lawrence returned to Hejaz and remained a liaison officer with Faisal for the rest of the war. Once he revealed how the French would take over Lebanon and Syria unless the Arabs captured at least Damascus and Aleppo themselves, Faisal was ready to risk a surprise land attack on Aqaba, after yet another failed effort at Medina. Lawrence was particularly critical of Faisal's brother Abdullah, whose lethargic approach to warfare seriously weakened any Arab advance northwards. He could not even be relied upon to cut the railway to Medina.

Without the knowledge of his superiors in Cairo, Lawrence left with Faisal for the attack on Aqaba with fewer than fifty Arabs. As they progressed northwards, he hoped to recruit extra men from the Howeitat and other tribes, using the £20,000 they were carrying with them. Among the highlights of the advance were the demolition of a section of the railway, and crossing a vast desert beyond it. How taxing the desert crossing was can be glimpsed in Lawrence's notebook, where he records the way that the 'sun reflects like a mirror flame-yellow, cutting into our eyes, like the glare of burning glass on closed lids. Heat waves and eyes often black. Camels exhausted and foot-burnt.' By the time the attackers reached Aqaba their numbers had grown to some 2,000 men. Faced with the choice of surrendering or being massacred, the 300-strong Ottoman garrison raised the white flag. The seizure of the port was actually welcomed in Cairo as a means of reinforcing the Palestine front, where the British were struggling to make headway across Sinai.

Lawrence's report of the capture of Aqaba may have exaggerated his own role in the operation, but the newly appointed commander-in-chief Edmund Allenby was prepared to overlook any showmanship as long as Lawrence could keep the Arabs on side. He knew that he would shortly invade Palestine, and so any assistance he could get on the inland flank of the enemy was well worth having, since few reinforcements were likely to be sent to Egypt. The Western Front remained Britain's priority, although there was a desire to avenge the humiliating defeat at Kut-al-Amara, south of Baghdad. There a besieged British force, weakened by disease and without supplies, had been compelled to surrender to the Ottoman army in 1916. Nearly 11,000 troops, largely from India, were taken prisoner.

The Aqaba fortress, whose capture in 1917 boosted the cause of Arab independence

General Allenby entering Jerusalem in December 1917

Lloyd George, who had replaced Asquith as British prime minister, did not believe that all the country's military resources should be concentrated in Europe, and he authorized the renewal of hostilities in Mesopotamia, where Baghdad was soon captured. Lloyd George intended that the oil resources of Mesopotamia should be within a British sphere of influence after the war. He also regarded Palestine as an objective of special significance, both because of its historical appeal and because it could serve as a protective buffer to the British position in Egypt. As a result, Allenby had been transferred from France to Egypt with the instruction to capture Jerusalem 'as a Christmas present for the British nation'. Like Bernard Montgomery during the Second World War, Allenby moved his headquarters close to the front, and within weeks of his arrival visited the majority of the units under his command. According to the Australian Official History, 'he went through the hot, dusty camps of his army like a strong, fresh, reviving wind'. The relative independence of his new role, away from an uneasy relationship with Douglas Haig, the British commander-in-chief on the Western Front, seems to have had a tonic effect on Allenby.

THE CONQUEST OF PALESTINE AND SYRIA

Lloyd George was a firm advocate of Britain's imperial destiny. He believed in the largest possible measure of local home rule within the empire, and was happy to see the development of dominion status; but in his view, they were still backward peoples not yet fit for self-government. His ambivalence about the Arabs was not, however, the reason for his wish to see the Jews reunited in the land of their ancestors. Lloyd George had been brought up on the Bible, and the story of the ancient Jewish people was as familiar to him as the history of England. And he seems to have expected the Jews in Palestine to form a lively, distinct community under British rule. That is why he was in full agreement with the Balfour Declaration of providing a 'national home' for the Jews.

It was to be Allenby's victory in Palestine which would allow the implementation of this policy. Fully aware of the usefulness of the Arab advance northwards in tying down a considerable number of Ottoman troops, Allenby knew that the campaign would be decided close to the Mediterranean coast. Rather mischievously, Lloyd George had recommended that Allenby should read Sir George Adam Smith's *Historical Geography of the Holy Land*, suggesting that it probably contained more practical advice than could be found in War Office papers. Overcoming the Ottomans at Gaza, where previous British attacks had failed, Allenby pushed his troops forward with such energy that on 11 December 1917 the British had taken Jerusalem—well in time for Christmas.

But it was Allenby's masterly imitation of the Egyptian pharaoh Thutmose III's tactics at Megiddo the following September which effectively knocked the Ottomans out of the First World War. Back in 1460 BC the pharaoh had marched to the southern slope of the Carmel mountain range with an army of 20,000 men, and then decided to advance upon the city of Megiddo, situated on its northern slope, by means of a direct, narrow pass: modern Wadi Ara. At a conference the pharaoh was warned by his senior officers of the dangers involved because 'our vanguard will be engaged in battle while there are still troops to enter the pass'. Not for the sake of prestige did Thutmose reject their advice, though the campaign account carved on Amun's temple at Karnak gives this impression, but for the good reason that his enemies would also assume that he was unlikely to choose to advance through a pass which shrinks in places to a width of less than 10 metres. Except for a minor skirmish, the Egyptian negotiation of Wadi Ara was as uneventful as it was unexpected: Thutmose was right and his opponents were unable to concentrate their forces fast enough to resist his chariot charge.

Some 3,400 years later, Allenby also caught the Ottomans off-guard. Just as the surprise emergence of the Egyptians had won the day, so the Fourth Cavalry Division disconcerted Liman von Sanders, Ataturk's bête noire. Writing a decade later, Archibald Wavell, a rising officer who was destined to become the British commander-in-chief in the Near East during the Second World War, marvelled at Allenby's exploitation of the terrain. He explains how his horsemen reached the end of Wadi Ara: 'just in time. A small body of Turks were surprised and rounded up ... As the leading troops moved out ... the Turkish force, of which the captured detachment was the advance guard, was seen approaching. This was a column in six companies with twelve machine guns. It received short shrift from the leading regiment of the Division, the Second Lancers. Supported by the fire of armoured cars, the Indian squadrons were into the enemy infantry with the lance before they even completed their deployment. Forty-six Turks were speared, and the remainder, about 500, surrendered. The whole action had lasted only a few minutes'.

The German general had sent this column to block the pass the day before. Its slowness in covering the short distance from Nazareth gave Allenby's cavalry its chance. The Fourth Cavalry Division covered an astonishing 100 kilometres in less than a day, losing only twenty-six horses on the way. The unexpected thrust beyond Megiddo amazed Allenby, who wrote to his wife how he was 'almost aghast at the extent of our victory'.

Just as amazed was Liman von Sanders: he had to make a desperate escape from his quarters in Nazareth, wearing his pyjamas. Street fighting alone saved him from capture, as mounted troops were not the best equipped for that kind of combat. While the German general engaged immediately afterwards in the thankless task of rallying demoralized Ottoman soldiers, the situation was beyond repair. By the time Damascus fell, fewer than 20,000 Ottoman troops out of a total of 100,000 serving in Palestine and Syria were not prisoners of war. Not quite the biblical Armageddon, the last battle of all between the nations of the world which was supposed to take place at Megiddo, but Liman von Sanders still knew the position was hopeless and soon returned to Germany.

General Allenby told the American archaeologist James Breasted that 'they wanted me to add "Armageddon" to my title, but I refused to do that. It was much too sensational and would have given endless opportunity to all the cranks in Christendom. So I merely took Megiddo.' Then he added how curious it was that the cavalry advance should have been similar to 'old Thutmose's experience in meeting an outpost of the enemy and disposing of them at the top of the Pass leading to Megiddo!' But it should be noted how Allenby did not exactly follow the ancient Egyptian dispositions. Whereas the pharaoh only used a single pass, Allenby sent cavalry forces through two of them, and also pushed another force behind the Ottoman lines near the coast, in places employing the beach itself for rapid movements. But it was the speed of the horses which gave both Thutmose and Allenby their sweeping triumphs.

As the Ottomans fell back on Damascus, Allenby's troops and the rebel Arabs joined forces for a final push, which resulted in the city's capture at the beginning of October. As a reward for their efforts, the British conceded the honour of accepting the surrender of Damascus to Faisal's followers. What should have been a moment of jubilation was overshadowed by the politics of partition, as Allenby, with Lawrence as his interpreter, spelt out the new administrative arrangements to Faisal. In line with the Balfour Declaration, the Arabs would have no say in the running of Palestine, nor would they have a role in Lebanon, which France would administer. Despite this unwelcome news, Faisal went to the town hall to receive the acclaim of the Damascene public. One can only wonder how he felt.

AFTER THE OTTOMAN DEFEAT

The defeat of the Ottomans resulted in the total loss of their empire and its replacement by new governments whose boundaries bore little resemblance to the provinces of the Ottoman empire before the war. Britain's immediate post-war concern was to consolidate its position in the modern Near East and fill the political vacuum left by the collapse of the Ottoman empire after four centuries of continuous rule. As keen to gain their share of Ottoman territory, the French landed troops at Beirut late in 1918, occupying the surrounding coastal area. As the supreme imperial power, Britain could pay lip-service to the principle of self-rule while doing everything in its power to obstruct Arab nationalism. Instability would persist for much of the period before the outbreak of the Second World War, but there was little the Arabs could do to alter the new arrangements. The League of Nations formally acknowledged the Anglo-French ascendancy when it agreed in 1920 to the creation of five new states—Syria, Lebanon, Transjordan, Iraq and Palestine—which were to be administered under a British or French mandate in cooperation with the Arabs.

Although in 1921 Sharif Hussein's sons Faisal and Abdullah became kings of Iraq and Transjordan respectively, he himself gained little personally from the Arab rebellion. His claim to be king of all the Arabs was never accepted by the British or the French, and his consequent refusal to acknowledge the post-war settlement deprived him of support from Britain when, in 1924, Abdulaziz al-Saud overran Hejaz. Sharif Hussein's long-standing quarrel with Ibn Saud, whose power base was in central Arabia, intensified when the former claimed to be the caliph. During his exile in his son's kingdom of Transjordan, Sharif Hussein continued to use the title but it was not generally accepted. Ibn Saud went on to become the king of Saudi Arabia and presided over the discovery of petroleum in 1938 and the start of large-scale production after the Second World War. From his forty-five sons have descended all the subsequent kings of Saudi Arabia.

Sharif Hussein was sympathetic to the plight of the Jews in Europe, as indeed was Faisal, and welcomed Jews' presence in, as well as their migration to Palestine. But this generous outlook had no sympathy with the Zionist desire for a separate Jewish state covering the whole of Palestine. Arab-speaking Jews were for Faisal no different from other Arabs. Lawrence was impressed by this attitude, but understood why Faisal was also concerned about British promises to the Zionists. He was reassured in 1918 when a prominent member of the Arab Bureau informed him that 'the Jewish settlement in Palestine would only be allowed in so far as would be consistent with the political and economic freedom of the Arab population'.

In 1919, an attempt to make Faisal king of Syria failed. Britain evacuated its troops from Syria, handing over the province to France and the Arabs. The French were pleased with the evacuation but not with any Arab entitlement to rule. Lukewarm towards the Arab uprising against the Ottomans, the Syrians themselves were never going to rally to Faisal's defence, choosing to accept a French mandate instead. In Damascus, Faisal discovered that he could no longer enthuse its inhabitants, nor prevent a French occupation, so that the Arab kingdom of Syria came to a premature end. Because of this challenge, France did not follow the same approach to its mandate as Britain adopted in Transjordan and Iraq. On the contrary, France brought the African colonial model to Syria, which comprised collaboration with local power-holders and a respect for traditional customs and institutions. Such indirect French rule was backed by a force of 15,000 Frenchmen and colonial troops.

The French occupation of Syria in 1920

The creation of the Arab kingdom of Transjordan, the present-day Hashimite kingdom of Jordan, was meant to placate Arab opinion. Awarded in 1921 to Abdullah, Sharif Hussein's second son, it took the new king several years before he managed to loosen the British mandate and unify his kingdom. Zionists hated its creation because by crossing the river Jordan to what is now called the West Bank, Transjordan reduced the size of a potential Jewish state. Even after Abdullah established his position as ruler, his kingdom with a half-nomadic and half-settled population of 250,000 was hardly a major player in modern Near Eastern politics. Even with an influx of Palestinian refugees, Jordan still had only 1.3 million people in 1947. That the Jordanians remained loyal allies of the British is quite remarkable considering the problems that Jewish emigration caused them on the West Bank.

Not until 1988 would Jordan be prepared to abandon its claim to that part of the old mandate of Palestine. By then King Abdullah I had been assassinated by a Palestinian Arab in Jerusalem. Against the advice of his advisers, Abdullah met his end there in 1951, quoting the Arab proverb:

'Until my day comes, nobody can harm me; when my day comes, nobody can save me.'

Money was at the root of Britain's desire for an independent Iraq. Struggling to maintain their imperial role in the aftermath of the First World War, the British could not afford costly territorial additions to their empire. Colonial Secretary Winston Churchill was acutely aware of the need for economy and so in 1921, at a conference held in Cairo, he listened to T. E. Lawrence who argued for Faisal's candidature. Even though Churchill dubbed the Arab delegates 'the forty thieves', Faisal was given Iraq as his kingdom. Ignoring the provincial arrangements of the Ottomans, which had recognized how the Kurds, Shia and Sunni comprised totally different entities, the British announced the creation of a unitary state with its capital at Baghdad.

Churchill and Lawrence were initially opposed to including the Kurds, for whom they sought to establish Kurdistan between Iraq and Turkey. Other delegates disagreed, possibly because they regarded this oil-rich region as an economic necessity for Faisal's kingdom. The sad history of modern Iraq bears witness to the wisdom of the view of Churchill and Lawrence. The Kurdish people, divided among Turkey, Iran, Iraq and Syria, have been embroiled in conflict with their host governments over the past century in pursuit of their cultural and political rights. Iraq itself has never known enduring peace either: it suffered conflict with Britain during the Second World War, a revolution in 1958, almost continuous war with Iran from 1980 to 1988, and since Saddam Hussein's 1991 invasion

Arab rebel leader Faisal ibn Hussein, who became the king of Iraq in 1921

of Kuwait conflict with the United States, Britain and their allies. Now it faces a threat from the Islamic State, a home-grown enemy which has extended its activities into neighbouring Syria. The Syrians themselves remain annoyed at the creation of Lebanon, which they believe to be an integral part of their country. They intervened in a Lebanese civil war in 1976, and remained in occupation of Lebanon for thirty years.

Whereas Britain seemed initially to have succeeded in Iraq with Faisal's kingdom becoming in 1932 a sovereign state, it soon discovered that there was no easy solution in Palestine. The conflicting ambitions of the Jews and Arabs eventually erupted in open warfare and led to the British abandonment of the mandate in 1948. Even without the support of President Harry S. Truman for a Jewish state, the enormity of the Holocaust had put Britain in an impossible position. Needing an American loan to recover from the ravages of the Second World War, the British could not afford to antagonize Zionists in the United States, nor lose the goodwill of the Arabs, who could easily disrupt the sea route to India and their other Asian colonies. The consequences of this dilemma remain very much with us today.

12

THE RISE OF MODERN TURKEY

By complete independence, we mean of course complete economic, financial, judicial, military, cultural independence and freedom in all matters. Being deprived of any of these is equivalent to the nation and country being deprived of all its independence.

Mustafa Kemal Ataturk

Turkey is one of the wonders of today. Even its boundaries are those that its nationalist leaders managed to fix in the aftermath of the First World War. Although contemporary Turkish historians like to give the impression that their country's emergence as a modern state resulted from some grand plan, the truth is that the period from 1919 to 1922 was so fraught with danger that its survival was by no means certain. Fortunately for the Turkish people they found a saviour in one man, Mustafa Kemal Ataturk.

The Young Turks had tried to prepare the Ottoman empire for modern times, but made its dissolution almost inevitable by siding with the Central Powers during the First World War. They deposed Abdulhamid II in 1909 because this sultan was an out-and-out autocrat, who had prorogued the Ottoman Chamber of Deputies in 1878 and then ruled without reference to anyone else. The so-called Young Turks were a diverse group, although its backbone comprised middle-ranking army officers. Many of its members subscribed to a German philosophy popularly known as Vulgar Materialism, which rejected religion and explained

Ataturk, the saviour of modern Turkey

social development through Darwin's notion of the survival of the fittest. In its birthplace, this simplistic philosophy had little impact: in the Ottoman empire, however, it touched a nerve among the Young Turks whose activities would eventually turn Turkey into a secular nation-state.

Although Ataturk was never really an active member of the Young Turk movement, in large measure because he regarded the alliance with Germany as an unmitigated mistake, Ataturk did take the view that modern science was critical for the Turkish nation's future development. As far as he was concerned, science promoted progress while religion retarded it. He could say that 'seeking any guidance other than science is thoughtlessness, prevarication, and ignorance'. Anything that could not be readily explained was not worth considering. As for Islam, Ataturk believed that it had not 'arisen as a result of the national evolution of the Arabs, but as a consequence of the emergence of Muhammad'. He was equally realistic about western Europe: it was the epitome of material progress, yet at the same time Ataturk saw its blatant desire to profit from the break-up of the Ottoman empire, especially after the defeats it had suffered in the Balkan Wars.

DIFFICULT TIMES 1919–22

During the summer of 1918, the dramatic German advance on the Western Front ground to a halt. Peace with Russia had enabled the Central Powers to redeploy forces from the eastern front to Belgium and France, giving them a local numerical advantage. German commanders decided to act before the United States, which had entered the war the previous year, was able to field enough troops to redress this manpower imbalance. But the failure of the German army to achieve a decisive victory spelt the beginning of the end for the Central Powers, who were in terminal decline when Allenby successfully invaded Syria.

As soon as the Young Turks learned that their German ally had approached the American president Woodrow Wilson to mediate a ceasefire with Britain and France, they knew that the Ottoman empire had no choice but to sue for peace too. From Istanbul the most senior British prisoner of war was dispatched to open discussions about an armistice. As a result of this contact, an Ottoman delegation was invited to the Aegean island of Lemnos to receive armistice terms. After four days of negotiations, the British and Ottoman delegates signed the armistice agreement aboard HMS *Agamemnon*, a battle-scarred veteran of the Dardanelles campaign. The terms were mild, possibly because the British officers actually involved were aware that the politicians would impose the punishment for Ottoman belligerency at a subsequent peace conference. Yet there were already signs of impending partition, with the French and the Armenians staking claims to territories in Asia Minor.

Even worse, the British premier Lloyd George was prepared to back Greek claims for at least the Aegean seaboard of Asia Minor. What was called by the Greeks the 'Great Idea' comprised a burning desire to complete the 1821–33 War of Independence by annexing all the territories in which there were still resident Greeks. Those living in western Asia Minor were a prime target, since their ancestors had settled there centuries before the birth of Christ. As the Athenian philosopher Socrates had remarked: the Greeks lived 'like ants and frogs around the pond between the Pillars of Herakles' at the western end of the Mediterranean 'and the river Phasis' on the eastern shore of the Black Sea. It was during the Greek War of Independence that Lord Byron died in 1824, between the two Ottoman sieges of Mesolongi, a town located on the northern edge of the Gulf of Patras. The poet's stalwart support of the cause of Greek independence was never forgotten in Britain, nor in Greece where Byron actually paid for the service of foreign volunteers who came to fight at Mesolongi.

The attitude of the British government towards Greece had changed during the course of the First World War. Reluctant initially to become involved in its internal affairs, Lloyd George finally agreed with the French in 1917 that the patriotic Venizelos should be assisted in his opposition to the pro-German policy of King Constantine, who firmly believed that the Central Powers would be the victors. Eleftherios Venizelos' provisional government at Salonica, and the Greek military supporting his pro-Allied stance, made it seem less likely that the deposition of the king would provoke a civil war. Constantine had dismissed Venizelos from office in order to keep Greece neutral, since his country was too exposed to British seapower to risk joining the Central Powers. In the event, there was no civil war after the deposition of the monarch, although the Greeks were henceforth split between royalists and republicans. Lloyd George had got to know Venizelos before he moved from 11 to 10 Downing Street. They instantly liked each other, perhaps because both of them had moved, geographically speaking, from periphery to the centre—Lloyd George from Wales, Venizelos from Crete. These two outsiders enjoyed an instant rapport and their mutual admiration was to have disastrous consequences a few years later for both of them. The Greco-Turkish War of 1919–22 was to contribute, in no small measure, to Lloyd George's political downfall.

Promised territorial gains at the expense of the defeated Ottomans, Venizelos landed 20,000 soldiers at Smyrna, modern Izmir, in early 1919. This city was to be the bridgehead of a Greek advance in Asia Minor, despite most of the port's inhabitants being Muslims. An otherwise peaceful occupation of Smyrna took a violent turn when a Turkish journalist in the crowd fired a shot, killing the Greek standard-bearer. After the death of several hundred Turks, the Greek army launched an offensive inland, which by the end of 1920 had secured an area of occupation extending over most of western Anatolia. Lloyd George was ready to encourage the advance as increased Greek pressure would oblige the Ottoman sultan to sign the punitive Treaty of Sèvres. It was also believed that it would force Ataturk to follow suit.

Never intending to do any such thing, Ataturk simply played for time. Whilst he had no wish to provoke the British into an active role alongside

Greek soldiers falling back on Smyrna in 1922

the Greeks, he needed to find new friends abroad. Now based in Ankara, where he gathered like-minded Turks to form an alternative national government, Ataturk deployed all his diplomatic skills to establish an unlikely alliance with the Soviet Union. Overcoming his personal loathing for communism, he made territorial concessions to Moscow in return for arms and financial aid. It was indeed the steady flow of Russian weapons, ammunition and money that made possible the prosecution of the war against the invading Greeks, thereby securing the independence of modern Turkey.

Sultan Mehmed VI was so despondent that he was prepared to accept almost anything that the victorious Allies demanded in the Treaty of Sèvres, which consigned him to rule a small state in the centre of Asia Minor, whereas possibly he envisaged an international role as caliph. From Ankara, however, Ataturk challenged the sultan's action. The atrocities committed by the Armenians in eastern Anatolia, where even the Kurds threw in their lot with Ataturk, and by the Greeks in the west, where Prince Andrew, father of the Duke of Edinburgh, was astounded by Greek cruelty, could not but stimulate a Turkish backlash. This Ataturk used against Mehmed VI, and by the end of 1920 he had assembled an army of patriots. Having repelled the Armenians and forced the French in Syria to agree to a more reasonable border, Ataturk judged in mid-1922 that the moment had come to deal with the Greeks, who had over-extended their lines in the mistaken belief that Britain would always come to their rescue.

During a twenty-one-day battle on the Sakarya river, the Greeks were stopped and pushed back westwards. The ferocity of the battle exhausted both sides, but it completely undermined Greek morale. By September 1922 the Greeks were back in Smyrna where a Turkish general, whose sons had been killed by the Greeks, sanctioned a massacre. Non-Muslim and non-Jewish Smyrna was put to the torch, while thousands of Christian refugees cowered on the coastal road and the harbour. Realizing that the terms of the treaty which the sultan had signed could never be enforced, the Allies reluctantly accepted the Turkish nationalist victory. When Ataturk arrived in smouldering Smyrna, he was invited to walk over a Greek flag, but he refused on the grounds that respect should be shown to the men who had died fighting for it. Lloyd George was less interested in honour and sent a telegram to the commander of a British force in Istanbul, ordering him to prevent Ataturk's men entering the city. The commander chose to ignore the order: he lacked the troops necessary to put up an effective resistance and, more tellingly, he had come to respect the Turks and sympathize with their aspirations.

Exhausted by the First World War, no Allied power had the will to engage in a renewed conflict with Turkey anyway. The French had made a separate peace with Ankara, while the British were concerned with repercussions in India where the Khilafat movement expressed its sympathy for the nationalist Turkish government. As this Muslim organization put it: 'Mustafa Kemal Pasha has done wonders and you have no idea how people in British India adore his name.' Among other reasons, Lloyd George's complete mishandling of the crisis caused his political eclipse.

Fearing for his life, Mehmed VI was smuggled onto a British warship and taken with his five wives to Malta, where he was presented with a bill for the voyage. He never returned as ruler because Ataturk seized the opportunity in 1923 to establish Turkey as a republic. The national assembly unanimously accepted his proposal and elected him as the first president of the new republic. In the same year, the Treaty of Lausanne fixed Turkey's present-day borders, although these were extended in 1939, when the French handed back a portion of their mandated territory in Syria. Perhaps the most unexpected move that Ataturk oversaw was the compulsory exchange of populations: about half a million Turks, some of them Greek-speaking, crossed over to Turkey, while a million Greeks, many Turkish-speaking, left Asia Minor for Greece. Just as Garibaldi had to accept, however reluctantly, the sacrifice of his birthplace Nice in 1860 so that Piedmont Sardinia could gain French military assistance against Austria in northern Italy, so in 1922 Ataturk gave up all hope of Turkey ever recovering Salonica, the cosmopolitan city in which he had been born.

THE SECULARIZATION OF TURKEY

The permanent loss of Salonica, present-day Thessaloniki, revealed Ataturk's pragmatism. What could not be obtained without dire consequences for Turkey was not worth contemplating. In a similar manner, Ataturk moved with caution in ending the Ottoman heritage. There was a strong religious element to Turkish nationalism, and he was very careful not to alienate it. Ataturk had a fight even to have Mehmed VI deposed, and so he made a concession: the sultan's cousin Abdulmecid was allowed to stay in the palace as the spiritual leader of the Sunni Muslims, but he was forbidden from wearing a sword, thereby underscoring the absence of secular authority. This shrewd move even caused the Indian Khilafat leadership to designate Ataturk 'the Sword of Islam' and 'the Renovator of the Caliphate'. However, he soon gave Muslims outside Turkey reason to think again, telling them not to expect anything from the caliphate but rather 'to strive toward saving themselves', going on to condemn the caliphate as 'a calamity' for the Turkish nation. Nonetheless, Ataturk still trod with great care and waited a year before, in 1923, abolishing the caliphate altogether. Intent on eliminating Islam from public life, he sent the surviving members of the Ottoman dynasty into exile the next year and, in 1926, put on trial the remaining Young Turks who objected to the end of the caliphate and the downgrading of religion. They also went into exile.

Such was Ataturk's charisma that no one would now oppose him, and he went on to form a new political party which would encompass all members of society, including farmers, workers, capitalists, industrialists and intellectuals, and would serve as a vehicle for the transformation of the Turkish state. It was, in effect, one-party rule. A landslide victory in the 1923 elections meant that Ataturk had an absolute mandate for reform. That he himself became the object of a cult, not unlike the adulation of the Soviet leader Lenin, had no effect upon him since his reforms were all that mattered. Not even a foiled attempt on his life prevented him from pressing ahead with the revolutionary programme he intended to implement, which ultimately aimed at Turkey becoming a multi-party democracy.

Although he remained on his guard throughout the early years of his political supremacy, Ataturk's outlook was clear enough to thoughtful observers. When a senior cleric tried to advise the national assembly, Ataturk told him to return to a mosque because 'we did not win the war of independence with prayers, but with the blood of our soldiers'. Islam was simply being written off as a burden, which the move of the capital from Istanbul to Ankara was expected to lessen. The great mosques of the Ottoman era were left behind and a new, secular centre of government would assist with the creation of a modern Turkish republic. Privately Ataturk confided in his closest associates how absurd it was that a seventh-century bedouin should be dictating the smallest details of people's personal lives. By closing religious schools and banning expensive gifts at saints' tombs, he tried to put a distance between Turkish nationalism and Arab religion. The Qur'an was translated into Turkish and the call to prayer was also delivered each day in the same language, not Arabic. Religious conservatives hated all this, but dared not speak out openly.

The idea behind this initiative was a programme of religious reform similar to that of the Protestant Reformation in Europe which would liberate Turkish energies after long years of stagnation and apathy. Ignoring the religious enthusiasm which had powered the Reformation in Europe, Ataturk sought rather to secularize religious observance, leaving belief as a matter for each individual's conscience. Charles Sherrill, the US ambassador, compared him to Martin Luther and John Wycliffe, the medieval philosopher who was dismissed from his teaching post in Oxford in 1379, largely for condemning the luxury and pomp of the clergy. Ataturk said he was no Luther, but he did in fact share some of Wycliffe's attitudes about institutional religion. And like the English philosopher, who personally translated the Gospels into his mother tongue, Ataturk was prepared to let ordinary people make up their own minds about religion, without priestly interference. A Turkish version of the Qur'an was the essential means for this to happen. After the separation of the religious establishment from the secular government, Sherrill was informed by one of Ataturk's followers: 'Turkey is now a Western power.'

ATATURK'S NATIONALISM

Ataturk had taken a society in which religion played an important role and led its transformation into a society run on secular lines. But the major shortcoming of this unprecedented change was its initial failure to engage the Turkish people as a whole. Despite saying privately that he would like to have seen religion 'at the bottom of the sea', Ataturk realized that the reduction of Islam's influence in daily life had left a void which urgently needed to be filled. His solution was Turkish nationalism.

Although at first his authority derived from military success and seemed no more than a dictatorship, Ataturk tried very hard to create a republic based on civilian legality. His speeches were never state-managed before large crowds as were the rallies of Mussolini and Hitler, for Ataturk always sought by reasoned argument to convince the Turkish people of the benefits of social reform. He accepted the need for liberal institutions such as political parties, trades unions, a free press and freedom of speech, but he was under no illusion that a fully modern Turkey would appear overnight. What he made absolutely clear, however, in the 1920s was that 'the successes that our army has gained up to now cannot be regarded as having achieved the real salvation of the country'. That required 'new victories in science and economics', and he added that these should take place in Asia Minor, the heartland of the Turkish nation.

Calligraphy in the Ottoman palace at Istanbul, whose script Ataturk ignored

The new republicanism laid emphasis therefore on reason, in the same way that it had been instrumental in shaping both the French and American revolutions. Perhaps its most Turkish feature was the cult of Ataturk himself, the inspiration and guide of the new republic. School children still promise each academic year to strive for the progress that Ataturk expected every Turk to regard as a personal target. The intellectual roots of Ataturk's nationalism are to be found in late-nineteenth-century attempts to formulate a Turkish identity, but he added a scientific element by embracing Darwin's theory of evolution. The Turks were told to 'rectify their thoughts by abandoning superstitions' that were based mainly on 'Jewish myths' and appreciate that their own development stemmed from 'deep ethnic roots', because Turkish identity was not based on such an alien import of Islam, but rather on the historical evolution of the Turkish peoples. So intent were Ataturk's followers to give the Turks a star role in world history that they even claimed that the cradle of human civilization was Central Asia, from where the Turks migrated to establish ancient states like Sumer and Hatti. Apparently it was also the impulse of Turkish culture that stood behind Greco-Roman civilization. Claiming that on Crete the early achievements of the Minoans were a result of Turkish migration was of course an island too far.

Absurd though these historical claims undoubtedly were, they had something in common with the Nazi view of ethnic determinism. In vain, Heinrich Himmler spent a fortune looking for archaeological proof of the German people's Aryan ancestry, while Benito Mussolini maintained an archaeological team at the Greco-Roman town sited at Butrint for a similar purpose. In order to strengthen Italy's territorial claims in Albania, Mussolini sought to prove that Trojan refugees, the ancestors of the Romans, once lived in Butrint. Even though no evidence was unearthed to show that Aeneas ever strayed there, one of the city's gates was obligingly named by its excavators as the Scaean Gate, after the famous gate at Troy.

The latent racism of Turkish nationalism was actually the tail end of European prejudice, first articulated during the era of Iberian exploration overseas. A powerful reinforcement of this outlook came from the Christian orders themselves, as they tended to uphold white supremacy. Clerics indeed pointed out how it was divinely ordained that black people should be enslaved; they bore the burden of Noah's curse as supposed descendants of Ham. This insidious notion of racial inferiority provided a convenient cloak for the slave trade. Whereas Noah's other sons Japheth and Shem were believed to have settled in Europe and the Near East respectively, Ham dwelt in Africa. One of the descendants of Shem was none other than Jesus Christ, a circumcised Jew, whose life and death brought about the conversion of Japheth's offspring, the uncircumcised Europeans. Entirely outside the Christian faith, and the protection of Christ, were the heretical descendants of Ham. For St Augustine, the ancient interpreter of the Christian world, the division between Japheth, Shem and Ham, between European, Jew and African, was not a question of ethnicity, but rather a matter of those who lived according to divine will and those who lived according to human desires. This is not an unreasonable interpretation of the biblical story when it is recalled that St Augustine was of Berber stock himself.

That Noah's curse was invoked at the very moment when the Spaniards and the Portuguese sailed off to dominate the spice trade is hardly a surprise, for the superiority it implied was a useful means to justify aggressive imperialism. As yet, this attitude was not the fully-fledged racism of the late nineteenth century, when pseudoscientific evidence was adduced to shore up European dominance in world affairs. It is somewhat ironic that the Turks drew upon this pernicious tradition in order to justify their own existence as a distinctive people. That their linguistic experts additionally claimed in the 1930s that the Indo-European and Semitic languages derived from a proto-Turkish language once spoken in ancient Central Asia shows how insecure modern Turkey still felt itself to be. Simplifying the Turkish language was one thing, as indeed was the adoption of the Latin alphabet, but quite different were such far-reaching assertions that had no historical basis in fact. The extravagant claim of the Turkish origin of world civilization was advanced at a time of public uproar over the abandonment of the traditional Arabo-Persian script. Ataturk obviously hoped that a Turkish nationalism resting upon modern science, historical speculation and language reform would serve as the foundation for a new belief in the value of a civil society.

After Ataturk's death in 1939, the more outlandish historical and linguistic assertions were either watered down or dropped altogether. Gradually, the Turkish government switched its attention to early Ottoman history and recognized how the final years of the Ottoman empire were a prelude to the rise of modern Turkey. A similar move took place to reduce the hostility of government policy towards Islam. In 1944, several leading Turkish racists were even put on trial. But Ataturk's personality cult has remained strong enough for some patriots in other Near Eastern countries to wish they had produced a similar leader themselves.

TURKEY AND THE WEST

Ataturk instinctively sided with the European democracies against German aggression, but during the Second World War the British premier Winston Churchill was to discover that Turkey could not be persuaded to join the Allied cause. Not even the possibility of recovering Mosul was sufficient to tempt the Turks, who saw no advantage in becoming involved in another European power struggle. Yet Turkey did maintain a strict neutrality. When in early 1941 the Allies invaded Vichy Lebanon and Syria, the local commander Henri Dentz asked the Luftwaffe for assistance as well as reinforcements from Vichy forces in Africa and France. Having sacrificed his paratroopers in Crete, there was nothing Hitler could do but watch Syria's reduction. He did allow French troops with anti-tank guns to travel by train through the occupied Balkans to Salonica, then by ship to Syria. Because the Royal Navy would be able to intercept these troop transports, the French asked to continue the journey by train, but Turkey refused transit rights point blank, and by so doing decided the fate of Lebanon and Syria, both of which passed under Free French control.

One reason for Turkish reluctance to give active support to Britain was the threat posed by Russia, then still on peaceful terms with Nazi Germany. That Turkey had as much to fear from the Russians as the Germans was apparent at the end of the Second World War, when Joseph Stalin demanded the right to garrison the Bosphorus, Soviet Russia's only means of moving its warships between the Black and Mediterranean seas. At this early stage in the Cold War, the United States hurriedly sent naval forces of its own to thwart Stalin's plans. In gratitude for this timely intervention, Turkey dispatched a contingent to the Korean War in 1950 and, two years later, became a member of the North Atlantic Treaty Organization, whose primary aim was to deter Russian aggression in Europe.

There was a price to pay for the American aid which Turkey now received, and that was a democratic system of government which soon pushed Ataturk's admirers from power. Even though the great man had always hoped that his country would develop into a fully-fledged democracy, he would have been disappointed in the so-called Democrats whose new party espoused religion so as to ensure a majority. It was a sign of things to come, as were the anti-Greek riots that the Democrats did little to stop in Istanbul. As the government also lost control of the economy, impoverishing civil servants and army officers on fixed salaries, the scene was set for the first of a series of military coups. Overthrown in 1960, the Democrats were excluded from politics and their prime minister, Adnan Menderes, was hanged.

Turkey's international reputation was the chief casualty of the military takeover, which solved none of the country's problems. A population explosion and a drift from the countryside to the cities witnessed the development of ugly shanty towns around them. The number of inhabitants in Istanbul jumped from 1 million to the present-day total of 15 million. As a result, the political spectrum widened to include left-wing secularists who wished to continue with Ataturk's programme; centralists whose sympathy for the army was paramount; and right-wing groups inclined towards religion. A further complication was that disaffected young Turks started to favour terrorism. In spite of another military coup in 1971, rampant inflation, national debt and energy shortages only added to Turkey's woes, making violent political confrontations a feature of everyday city life.

Into this confused situation came yet another cause of instability, the Cyprus problem. With the agreement of the military junta in Athens, the president of Cyprus, Archbishop Makarios, was almost killed by Cypriot Greeks intent on the island becoming a part of Greece. Makarios escaped from his would-be assassins through the back door of the presidential palace and fled to Paphos, where he was taken first to Malta and then London. Seeing how EOKA, a Greek nationalist group led by Nikos Sampson, was not only hostile to the island's Turkish residents but had also declared a new government for Cyprus, the Turkish army intervened. Its two-stage invasion in 1974 resulted in the partition of the island with forty per cent being occupied by the Turkish Cypriots in the north. The United States had stopped Britain from pre-empting the Turkish landings, so concerned was Washington to keep Ankara as an ally in the Cold War.

The acceptance of Greek Cyprus as a member of the European Union before the issue of partition had been settled was a diplomatic error of the first order, because it put a potential stumbling block in the way of Turkey's own admission. Another difficulty for the Turks was the political role played by their armed forces. In 1980 a military coup seemed to return the country to direct rule, although within two years parliamen-

An EOKA slogan calling for the union of Cyprus with Greece

tary democracy was restored as a result of American and European pressure. The ensuing economic upsurge based on devaluation, the scrapping of currency controls, greater freedom for banks, lower taxes and labour mobility turned Turkey into one of the fastest growing countries in the world. Foreign distractions were largely ignored, despite the rise of the Islamic State and the civil war in Syria. A consequence of this self-imposed detachment from the rest of the modern Near East was a widening economic gap between Turkey and other Muslim states as the pace of modernization increased.

The logical conclusion of this trend was the anticipated request from Turkey to join the European Union. But the request presented Brussels with a double problem: the apparent revival of Islam in Turkish society and an army strictly wedded to the secular order. In 2010, however, Recep Tayyip Erdogan managed to forestall military intervention when plans came to light in Istanbul. Despite a chequered past and brief imprisonment, Erdogan gained wide acceptance of his policies, including accession to the European Union. His Islamist background was not seen as a threat to the republic, suggesting that the generals had badly misjudged the situation. Since then, though, Erdogan has tried to stifle criticism through arresting vocal opponents and censoring the press. The narrow win Erdogan achieved in a 2017 constitutional referendum, called to enhance his presidential position, dangerously divided Turkey. That he visited the Eyup Sultan mosque after the result was declared caused many Turks to wonder if the president viewed himself as a modern caliph.

Quite possibly some of the European-style freedoms which Ataturk bequeathed to the Turkish nation will be eroded in future, but there is no question of his profound impact on its outlook. Whether or not Turkey joins the European Union, its emergence as a potential member is a sign of how far the country has come since the difficult years of 1919–22. Not only is it a tribute to the determined leadership of 'Father Turk', but even more it marks a realization in Europe that Turkey might well function as a modern Byzantium, a bastion against Islamic extremism.

13

THE SECOND WORLD WAR AND DECOLONIZATION

President Harry S. Truman told a meeting of Arab ambassadors: 'I have to answer to hundreds of thousands who are anxious for the success of Zionism. I do not have hundreds of thousands of Arabs among my constituents.'

The White House in 1949

From the First World War onwards, Arab nationalist movements profited from the rivalries among the European powers, but they gathered pace after the liquidation of their colonial empires, once Britain granted India, Pakistan and Burma independence in 1947. Decolonization was to a large extent a result of external pressures and the impact of changing world politics. In the Far East, the British, French and Dutch all failed to recover from Japan's brief triumph between 1941 and 1945. The poor state of defences in Malaya and Singapore was repeated elsewhere, including the great American naval base at Pearl Harbor, which succumbed to a surprise attack by the Imperial Japanese Navy. Only in the Philippines were the Japanese invaders resisted by the local people, because the United States had already fixed a date for the colony's independence. President Franklin D. Roosevelt noticed this singular event and accordingly made plans for a very different post-war world.

Even if Singapore's surrender in early 1942 was insufficient to bring down the curtain on European colonialism, the sweeping election victory of the Labour Party in Britain certainly had that effect. The 1945 landslide ensured that the British were spared the agony of colonial wars, unlike the Dutch in Indonesia and the French in Indochina. Prime Minister Clement Attlee's early decision to end British dominion in India ensured that decolonization soon followed elsewhere. In the Near East, however, this was to prove far from straightforward, especially in Palestine where unrest had troubled the mandated territory in the 1920s as well as the 1930s.

THE SECOND WORLD WAR

The loss of Mosul to British-mandated Iraq after the First World War only served to confirm Ataturk's view of Near Eastern politics. He turned away from his Arab neighbours, not out of hostility to the Arabs, but for the reason that they had patently lost their independence to Britain and France. The British now dominated Iraq, Palestine, Jordan, Aden and the states along the Persian Gulf, while the French dominated Syria and Lebanon. An exception to this European supremacy was Arabia, where the bedouin remained tribal and an Arab monarchy was acknowledged just as long as it suited them. Never really under Ottoman control, the bedouin tribesmen had revolted in 1916 and then lent support to the British offensive in Palestine and Syria. Faisal, one of the sons of Sharif Hussein, the emir of Hejaz, had led the Arab revolt against the Ottomans, reaching Damascus in late 1918, where an Arab administration was formed. Faisal's triumph proved short-lived, however, as Britain had already agreed that Syria would belong to France.

Arab ambitions were not then Britain's prime concern. What worried London, and indeed Paris, was the political vacuum caused by the disappearance of the Ottoman empire after centuries of continuous rule. The search for stability must explain the Balfour Declaration of 1917, which endorsed the creation of a Jewish homeland in Palestine. This response to the growing political importance of the Zionist movement in Europe and North America was seen at the time as a means of extending British influence. The declaration stimulated the migration of Jews to Palestine, gave rise to Arab–Jewish conflict during the inter-war years, and led to the creation of Israel in 1948.

By creating the Arab kingdom of Transjordan, the present-day Hashimite kingdom of Jordan, London hoped to placate Arab opinion, but this state was never a major player in modern Near Eastern politics. That the Jordanians remained loyal to the British was quite remarkable considering the problems that Israel caused them on the West Bank. Not until 1988 would Jordan abandon its claim to any territory west of the river Jordan. Although Britain's imperial presence ceased shortly after the Second World War, its legacy in the Near East was an unfortunate one because it left the Arabs feeling that their legitimate interests had been sacrificed for the sake of Zionism. Referring to the replacement of the Ottomans as 'the Last Crusade' was incredibly short-sighted: it only served to strength the position of hard-line Muslim clerics, who said that Christian cynicism underlay both French and British policies.

One of the most trenchant critics of Britain was the mufti of Jerusalem, Amin al-Husseini, who organized Arab opposition to Zionism in Palestine. Stirring up Arab fears through such extravagant claims as that Jewish settlers were planning to take back the Temple Mount, al-Husseini did much to foment riots in the late 1920s. Several hundred Arabs and Jews were killed in Jerusalem, Hebron, Jaffa and Haifa; many more suffered wounds. These disturbances were minor, however, in comparison with the 1936–9 Arab uprising, which received financial assistance from fascist Italy. Al-Husseini issued dire warnings, threatening the wrath of Allah unless Jewish immigration stopped. Before the rebels were finally crushed by the British authorities, the mufti quit his post in Jerusalem and fled first to Lebanon, then Iraq. In the 1939 White Paper, Britain limited Jewish immigration to 75,000 people over the next five years, but this concession did not entirely satisfy the Arab Palestinians, even when coupled with the promise of a Muslim-majority state and an end to the idea of a Jewish national home.

A factor in the change of British policy in Palestine was undoubtedly Nazi Germany's preparations for a European war. Berlin had not missed al-Husseini's virulent anti-Semitism, nor his impatience with Britain's administration. Refuge in Iraq was more promising for al-Husseini, once Rashid Ali al-Kailani came to power and made secret contracts with the Nazis. He even issued a fatwa for a holy war against Britain, when

Winston Churchill moved to prevent Iraq along with its oilfields falling into German hands. In 1941 al-Husseini had sent a letter to Hitler in which he requested help in solving the Jewish question in Arab lands.

For years, the Nazis had experimented with the best method for exterminating Jews and other undesirables. But it was not until 1941 that mass destruction was perfected through the development of camouflaged gas chambers at Sachsenhausen near Berlin, and to this prototype concentration camp Germany's Arab sympathizers paid a visit in 1942. Hitler had already given al-Husseini an extended audience the previous autumn, so pleased was he to learn that the mufti wanted to cooperate in destroying the Jewish people. Immediately afterwards, Hitler ordered leading Nazis to meet at Wannsee in order to arrange for the final solution.

The visit in June 1941 to Sachsenhausen was organized with such meticulous attention to detail that Himmler personally took the planned tour himself. Apart from the gas chambers, the camp possessed four new crematoria to speed up the disposal of corpses. The Arab guests had a practical

The entrance to the children's memorial at Yad Vashem in Jerusalem

interest, since they wanted similar facilities built at Tunis, Baghdad and Jericho, as soon as Nazi Germany won the war, which al-Husseini believed it would. Hitler said of the mufti, he is 'a realist, not a dreamer'. The German dictator even came to regard al-Husseini as an Aryan, something confirmed by a doctor to whom he went for a check-up.

After the fall of France, and the Vichy regime headed by Philippe Pétain drew close to Nazi Germany, Britain resorted to its traditional strategy of peripheral warfare, with the result that in the Mediterranean it appeared to be on the losing side. That Ermin Rommel at one point reached the border of Egypt only added to the illusion. Yet Britain had always relied on its maritime strength and on coalitions to maintain the balance of power in Europe. Not until the Americans became allies, thanks to Japan and Hitler's declaration of war, would Winston Churchill contemplate an invasion of mainland Europe. Even then, he was reluctant to cross the Channel in force before the Soviet Union's victories on the eastern front were stretching the German army to breaking point. Stalin might complain that Britain wanted the Russians to bear the brunt of the fighting, but this was hypocritical in view of his hope in 1940 that the Western democracies and the Germans would bleed each other to death.

Dealing with Vichy enclaves outside France took time: Syria was not captured until 1941, Madagascar surrendered in the ensuing year, as did north Africa after Anglo-American landings in Morocco and Algeria. Having cleared the southern and eastern shores of the Mediterranean, the Allies were ready to invade Italy and then France, whose liberation would unhinge Nazi Germany's western defences. Again the slow Allied advance northwards in Italy was generally misunderstood, except by generals like Bernard Montgomery who recognized that the primary purpose of the Italian campaign was to tie down as many German divisions as possible, and to use the Foggia airfield to bomb the Germans in Bavaria, Austria and the Danube river valley. The mountainous terrain of central Italy favoured the German defenders and the few Italian units remaining loyal to Mussolini. Only in 1944 was it clear that Hitler's empire had no chance of survival.

For Jewish people living in Palestine, the defeat of Nazi Germany was vital. With Britain totally opposed to its dominance, the Jews decided in the words of David Ben Gurion that 'they would fight the war as if there

Australian forces in Syria in 1941

were no White Paper, but at the same time continue to fight the White Paper as if there were no war'. Considering that al-Husseini was busy recruiting Balkan Muslims for Himmler's SS, this attitude comes as no surprise. On a tour of Yugoslavia, he told recruits that: 'The lands suffering under the British and Bolshevist yoke impatiently await the moment when the Axis will emerge victorious. We must dedicate ourselves to unceasing struggle against Britain—that dungeon of peoples—and to the complete destruction of the British empire. We must dedicate ourselves to unceasing struggle against Bolshevist Russia because communism is incompatible with Islam'. Now it appears incredible that this fierce enemy of the Allies should have managed to slip through the net after the war and find asylum in newly independent Egypt.

As late as Adolf Eichmann's trial in 1961, al-Husseini could assert that in the killing of Jews 'the Nazis needed no persuasion or instigation either by me or anybody'. Al-Husseini's political machinations after the British withdrawal from Palestine came to naught and in 1974 he died a disappointed man in Beirut. His final request was to be buried in Jerusalem, which Israel had captured during the 1967 Six-Day War. It was refused.

POST-WAR DECOLONIZATION

At the end of the Second World War, the leading powers in the Near East were the Soviet Union and Britain. Germany and Italy were defeated; France was unable to hold onto Syria and Lebanon and its influence was restricted to the western Mediterranean; and the United States was initially slow to become involved until Stalin's attempt to control the Bosphorus brought its navy post-haste to the defence of Turkey.

French colonial rule always depended upon finding local collaborators. In Lebanon, the Maronite Christians performed this function: named after the Syrian saint Maron, they maintained a semi-independent existence as well as their faith after the Arab conquest. But in Syria the French had to choose among the Arab notables who had been involved with the Ottoman administration, which tended to set one group against another. It did not help when one of the French governors showed a marked indifference to local religious sensitivities, whether Christian or Muslim. The Syrian rebellion of 1925–7 began as a tribal disturbance among the Druze, who inhabited a mountainous area south of Damascus, but it spread to other parts of the colony. After the rebels were defeated, Paris decided to adopt the British policy in neighbouring Iraq, which isolated extremists, conciliated moderate members of society, and worked towards genuine independence. When this experiment failed, the French fell back on direct rule, well before the Vichy governor, Henri Dentz, arrived in 1940 following the defeat of France. It was left to Britain to end this unreal situation a year later, when it installed a Free French administration. General Georges Catroux, the Free French commander, issued a proclamation in which he stated that 'I come to put an end to the mandatory regime and to proclaim you free and independent.'

The reality of Israel's relations with its neighbours. The border with the West Bank

But Syrian nationalists were not prepared to accept anything short of a complete severance of the link with France, and clashes after the end of the Second World War between French soldiers and Syrians only ceased when, in 1946, Britain obliged France to withdraw altogether. But a post-war slump undermined the Syrian economy and paralysed its government. Scaling back on military expenditure after the failure of Syrian troops in Palestine, where the Jews drove them headlong from Galilee, was bound to provoke a coup; egged on by the Americans, Colonel Hosni al-Za'im, the chief of the army staff, seized power in 1949 with little bloodshed. Installed as president, al-Za'im increased the size of the army; enfranchised women; disapproved of traditional Arab headgear; and abolished feudal titles. When he endeavoured to negotiate with newly established Israel, another officer took al-Za'im's place until 1954, when he was in turn overthrown. Whatever the benefits to Washington of these military interventions, they set a poor example to the Arabs, who were henceforth the victims of their armed forces as the arbiter of political power. In Syria this tendency led to the establishment in 1970 of Hafez Assad's repressive regime, which continues today under his no less ruthless son.

Although Paris had been inclined to unite Lebanon with Syria, the Maronites insisted on its continued separation; but they complicated matters by demanding additional territory. The result was the transfer to Lebanon of land inhabited by Sunni Muslims who bitterly resented their separation from Syria. Reconciled to some extent by a power-sharing agreement, the Muslims living in Lebanon acquiesced in the arrangements for an independent state, which down to the late 1950s flourished economically. But discontent over the distribution of the new wealth, especially in booming Beirut, led to demonstrations, strikes and violence. As the Lebanese army refused to suppress these popular expressions of discontent, the government sought help from the United States, which sent a force of marines. In Washington the intervention was of course explained in terms of the Cold War.

What the Americans overlooked was how Palestinians living in refugee camps around Beirut had unbalanced Lebanon's population. Christians were anxious about the camps being used as bases for attacks on Israel, while Muslims welcomed these activities. The situation reached crisis point when the Palestine Liberation Organization transferred its headquarters to southern Lebanon. In 1982, the Israelis drove it out, hoping to find an ally in the Maronite Christians, but the civil war that had begun in 1975 intensified and a shaken Menachem Begin resigned as Israel's prime minister. US marines had no chance of enforcing a ceasefire, 241 of them dying when a vehicle packed with explosives was driven into their barracks in Beirut. After the Americans left in 1984, the continuing civil war in Lebanon almost destroyed its society as militias fought each other for territory. Beirut was reduced to a ruin, its population in 1989 sinking to 150,000.

No country in the modern Near East endured greater territorial changes after the Second World War than did Jordan: yet no country remotely approached the internal stability enjoyed by the Jordanian people. Politics were dominated by King Hussein ibn Talal, Abdullah's grandson, whose astute handling of affairs during a period when monarchies were no longer esteemed by most Arabs was masterful. He avoided entanglement with the Arab–Israeli conflict, absorbed as many refugees as Lebanon, and put his kingdom on the road to prosperity. King Hussein settled the issue of succession by designating his brother Hassan as heir. Even though this meant bypassing his own children, whose mother was English, the king believed that the dynasty could only survive through an emphasis on its Hashimite heritage, which stretched all the way back to Prophet Muhammad himself. While in 1999 the gravely ill monarch was receiving treatment abroad, news arrived that Hassan's Pakistan-born wife was already redecorating the palace. An angry Hussein returned to Jordan to die, but not before pushing Hassan aside and designating a new successor, Abdullah II, his eldest son by his English wife. Hussein's dying wish was that the next in line should be Hamzah, his son by his Arab–American wife, Queen Noor. But Abdullah made his own son the heir in 2004. Despite this royal discord, the Hashimite kingdom of Jordan remains an island of comparative calm amid the growing turbulence of the present-day Near East.

THE KINGDOM OF IRAQ

Even though Colonial Secretary Winston Churchill was not entirely satisfied with the borders of the new kingdom of Iraq, he knew that Britain's interests there were not territorial. 'Apart from its importance as a link in the aerial route to India ... and apart from the military significance of the oil deposits,' he noted, 'the General Staff are not pressing for the retention of Mesopotamia ... on strategic grounds of Imperial security.' So at the 1921 Cairo conference, Churchill was willing to listen to T. E. Lawrence and risk annoying the French by giving the throne to Faisal ibn Hussein. And within a couple of years the Iraqi kingdom appeared a good gamble. Churchill commented that 'our difficulties and our expenses have diminished every month that has passed. Our influence has grown while our armies have departed.' But popularity eluded King Faisal, and he wondered just before his death in 1939 whether it was ever possible for Iraq to become a single nation.

As soon as the new king arrived in Iraq, he immediately encountered the opposing expectations of his people. Disembarking at the port of Basra from a British ship, Faisal was greeted by the flag of the Arab revolt, but also banners hailing the 'Iraqi Confederation' and proclaiming 'Long live Basra'. Besides recognition of his leadership in the cause of Arab freedom, the other banners indicated the power struggle behind the scenes between the advocates of an autonomous status for Basra and those calling for a centralized Iraq. Whatever misgivings Faisal might have had about the fervour of his reception in southern Iraq, they were soon overcome by the immense crowds and displays of support and affection which greeted him when he reached Baghdad. As the city had not been a capital since the collapse of the Abbasid caliphate in 1258, its inhabitants were delighted to have a ruler who would restore its status. Moving into the residence of the former Ottoman governors of Baghdad, Faisal was visited by poets in time-honoured fashion, welcoming him in verse and competing in praise of his virtues.

Faisal wasted no time in approaching the Shia community, the people whose ambivalent welcome at Basra still worried him. So he went to nearby Kadhimain, a town where the shrines of two Shia saints were located, and won over the people living there. But he also attended Friday prayers at the main Sunni mosque in Baghdad. There was in fact no doubt about his illustrious family line, which could be traced back to Hassan, the eldest son of Muhammad's son-in-law Ali ibn Abi Talib. The young imam had been forcibly retired by Ummayads to an estate near Medina, where he mysteriously died in 669. His younger brother Hussein was not prepared to be so easily shunted aside and, refusing to acknowledge the Ummayad caliphate, he was ambushed and killed in 680 on his way to Mesopotamia. Hussein's severed head was sent to Caliph Yazid in Damascus where it was put on display as a reminder of Allah's approval of Ummayad rule. Today in the main mosque in Damascus stands Hussein's shrine, to which Shia pilgrims come from both Iraq and Iran.

Having established his religious credentials with both Sunni and Shia Muslims, Faisal won a plebiscite and was crowned in 1921 as king of Iraq. Opposition to his reign was not long in showing itself, however: first over the slowness of ending the British mandate, and then through the diverse expectations of the Iraqis themselves. It did not help that the king fell ill and required an abdominal operation. That the British High Commissioner Sir Percy Cox tried to get Faisal to agree to the arrest and exile of his political opponents would have slowed the recovery of a lesser man, but the king was determined not to die and leave Iraq in disarray. Thereafter he rarely referred to the mandate, treating it in an ostrich-like manner as if it did not exist. Added to the political uncertainties troubling his kingdom was the threat of Turkish intervention in the north, when Ataturk's forces attacked British garrisons in the borderlands between Iraq and Syria. Turkish propaganda in Iraq stressed the continued subjugation of the kingdom to the 'infidel British'. Once the Royal Air Force had halted the Turkish advance, the external threat receded and Faisal could concentrate on the formation of a properly elected government. But this move to more secular rule displeased Shia religious leaders, who moved to Iran from where they launched a campaign against Faisal. It set the pattern of Iraqi politics down to the present day and involved Iraq and Iran in a conflict that only mutual exhaustion ended in 1988.

Finally, the Anglo-Iraqi Treaty of 1934 ended Britain's mandate and allowed Iraq to become a member of the League of Nations two years later. In spite of Faisal's detractors expressing their lack of enthusiasm for this achievement, there was rejoicing and celebration in most parts of the kingdom. But the Kurds were unimpressed by the failure of the treaty to make reference to Kurdistan, an autonomous ideal cherished by the Kurdish population. That was the reason for elections being so tightly managed by Faisal's favourite prime minister, Nuri al-Said. The growing autocracy of the throne at this time was not motivated by any personality trait, but by the desire of Faisal to control growing unrest in his volatile kingdom.

That the Iraqi kingdom should have depended upon its army for its existence was therefore inevitable and, in 1936, its first political intervention not only brought down the elected government but introduced an unprecedented degree of instability into the central administration. Even though the Second World War and a British invasion in 1941 apparently excluded the Iraqi army from the political process, the death of King Faisal I just before the start of hostilities removed an accomplished operator from the scene. With justice, Faisal's reign has been compared to the superhuman strength of someone who swam towards the goal of complete national independence 'while there was a ball and chain tied to one of his legs'.

After the Second World War, decolonization rode in tandem with Arab nationalism and especially in Egypt, where Nasser's nationalization of the Suez Canal in 1956 provoked a severe political crisis in Iraq. Four years earlier, the Egyptian revolution had begun with a military coup that marked the beginning of the end of the old order in the Arab Near East. British troops were no longer stationed in the country and so there was nothing to stop the Egyptian monarchy being swept away. At the heart of the revolution was Lieutenant Colonel Jamal Abd al-Nasir, more generally known as Nasser, who said 'my parliament is the army', the instrument of the radical changes which he intended to make in Egypt's economy and society. Pro-Nasser demonstrations in Baghdad provoked the royal government to suspend the constitution and imprison hundreds of activists. Prime Minister Nuri al-Said so detested Nasser that he even joined Britain and France in plotting the overthrow of the Egyptian leader. After the abortive Anglo-French occupation of the Suez Canal zone in late 1956, however, Nuri was politically isolated inside and outside Iraq. The climax came in 1958, when troops loyal to Brigadier Abd al-Karim Qassim stormed the palace and machine-gunned the royal family, including the twenty-three-year-old King Faisal II. Disguised as a woman, Nuri nearly escaped until someone in the crowd recognized him. The fourteen-times premier was stripped, killed, castrated and then dismembered, his legless body dragged through the streets of Baghdad behind an army lorry.

SADDAM HUSSEIN AND THE GULF WARS

The 1958 revolution was the work of a small group of army officers, a circumstance that made the new republican government appear a minority affair. Even though a three-man sovereignty council was formed, comprising a Sunni, a Shia and a Kurd, it lacked real power and disappeared in 1963, when Qassim's regime was overthrown. Its secularization policies had offended religious leaders and split the armed forces as well. The subsequent uncertainty was a gift for Saddam Hussein al-Tikriti, who swiftly rose through the ranks of the Ba'ath party, a socialist movement founded in the 1930s by two French-educated Syrian teachers. Its basic aim was the inclusion of the Arabs in a single state, but only in Syria and Iraq were those who took the same view ever influential.

The rise and fall of Saddam Hussein proved disastrous for Iraq and indeed the modern Near East. Before the Gulf Wars, Iraq's principal foe was Iran, an Islamic republic under the control of hard-line clerics, whose declared aim was to 'extend the sovereignty of Allah's law throughout the world'. Between 1980 and 1988 the Iraqis and the Iranians fought each other to a standstill, with more than a million battlefield casualties altogether. Cynicism marked both of the belligerents, but perhaps Iran most of all. At the height of the conflict young Iranians destined for the front were given plastic keys as the means of entering paradise. Few noticed that these celestial instruments had stamped upon them 'Made in Hong Kong'. When the Iran–Iraq war

Najaf, south of Baghdad. The largest and busiest cemetery in the modern Near East

Superior military equipment gave the Allies a decisive edge during the two Gulf Wars

ended in 1988, Iraq was burdened with a large foreign debt, the onus of high defence spending, and a devastated economy.

To overcome this economic crisis, Saddam Hussein gambled on oil: it brought about his own downfall and inaugurated the present-day conflict in both Iraq and Syria. When Saddam Hussein failed to get Arab oil states to cut production and thus increase oil prices and his own national income, he decided to lay claim to Kuwait's oilfields. By seizing this tiny state through a lightning campaign in 1990, Iraq came to control twenty per cent of the world's known oil reserves. When playing the anti-Israel card failed to gain Arab support, Saddam Hussein faced a coalition made up of the United States, Britain, Saudi Arabia, Syria and even Israel. Britain's hawkish premier Margaret Thatcher egged on President George Bush, and in 1991 hundreds of US bombers and missiles forced Iraq to evacuate Kuwait. Fearful of an Arab backlash, Saddam Hussein's forces were not pursued to Baghdad, at least not until the Second Gulf War of 2003 ended his regime. The sheer extent of the damage inflicted then, plus the absence of a considered plan for post-war Iraq, plunged Mesopotamia into total chaos. Saddam Hussein himself survived until the end of 2006, when his hideout was discovered and he was hanged.

The Gulf states had been drawn back into the Anglo-American sphere of influence by the sabre rattling of Saddam Hussein and the Islamic pressure of Iran. The United Arab Emirates from its foundation in 1971 relied on an abundance of oil revenues, with Abu Dhabi the main producer. Less successful was Dubai when, in the late 2000s, it began to turn itself into a hub of finance and tourism. Notwithstanding large-scale American support for Israel, these oil-rich states cannot compare with its economic progress, a diminutive power though it remains in the modern Near East.

Had the Labour government had less decolonization to handle in 1945, then it is quite possible that a fairer outcome would have resulted in Palestine. As it was, Britain's attention was taken up by Burma and India, so that the opportunity for a more reasonable settlement in the mandated territory was missed. In 1946 Jerusalem's King David Hotel was blown up by Zionist guerrillas who wanted nothing less than a separate state in their ancient land. Ninety-one British, Arab and Jewish lives were lost in the explosion. During the following year all-out fighting began, after a vote by the UN General Assembly decided to partition Palestine into Arab and Jewish sectors, with greater Jerusalem to be under international control. By the time of the ceasefire at the end of 1948, the newly declared state of Israel controlled eighty per cent of the former mandate. Ever since, its citizens seem to have lived on borrowed time as they were besieged by their Arab neighbours and such groups as Hezbollah and Hamas, the aggressive successors of the Palestine Liberation Organization. One of the key factors in the continued political turmoil today is the unresolved issue of Israel's right to exist as an independent Near Eastern country.

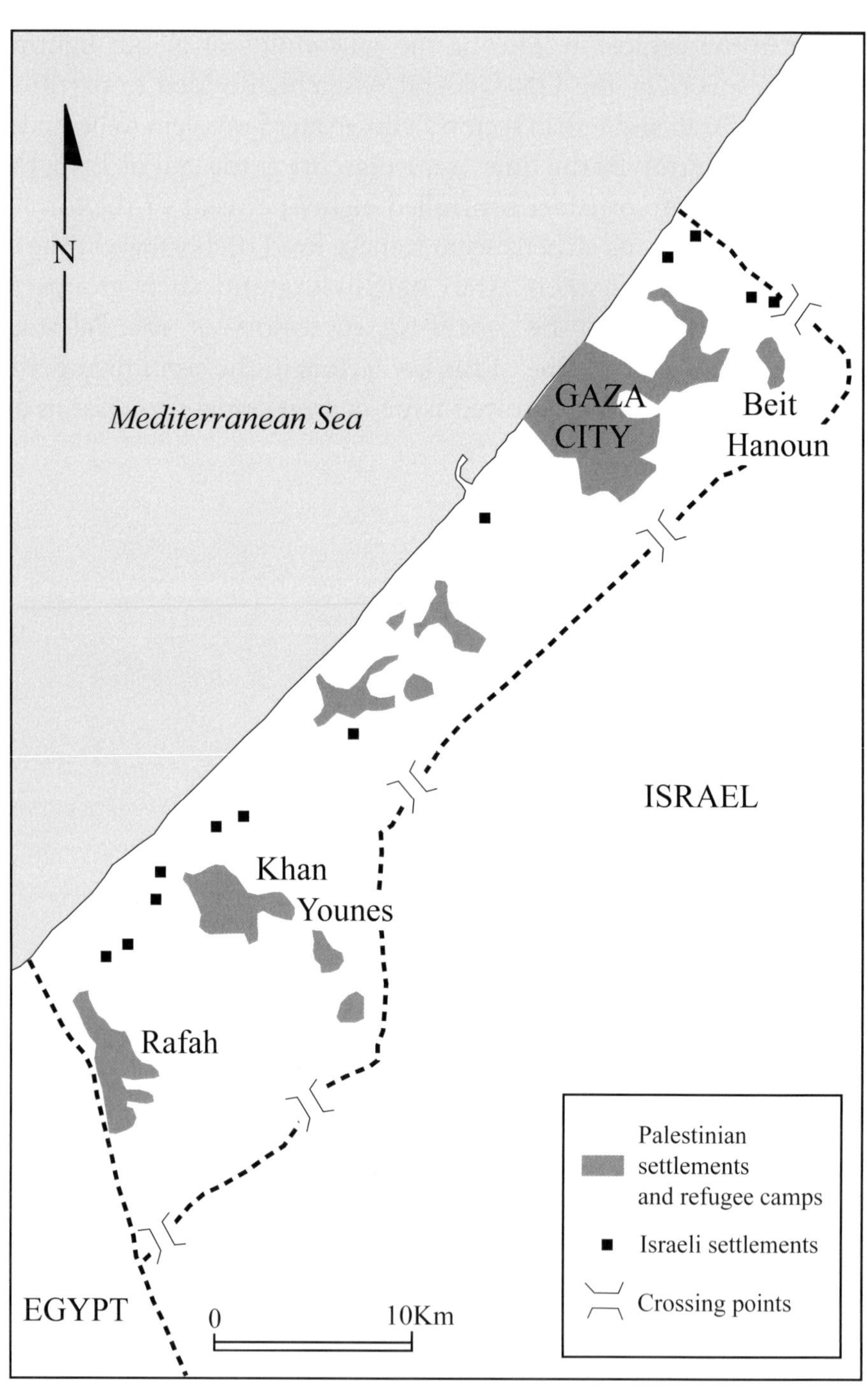

The Gaza Strip

14

A TIME OF TURBULENCE

Nimrud's systematic destruction by Islamic State ... is the worst act of vandalism since the Nazis blew up Russian cultural monuments and razed Warsaw to the ground during the Second World War.

The Times, *13 April 2015*

The 'orgy of destruction' by Islamic militants, smashing statues and bas-reliefs with sledge hammers, and even bringing to the site of ancient Nimrud a bulldozer in order to level the archaeological remains, shocked the world in 2015. This iconoclasm was justified by reference to Muhammad's removal of idols from the Ka'ba, and his prohibition of statues in general. The Islamic State of Iraq and Syria took no notice of Ban Ki-moon's condemnation of the destruction as a war crime. The view of the UN Secretary-General was brushed aside with the comment that the Islamic State was 'removing every statue and idol that could be worshipped alongside God'. When later in the same year attacks on the Near East's rich cultural heritage shifted from Iraq to Syria, archaeologists and historians around the world wrung their hands in horror.

At Palmyra, the ancient oasis city in the Syrian desert, another burst of vandalism reduced long-preserved structures to ruins. The blowing up of Baal Shamin's temple in particular was an appalling action. Explosives planted around the well-preserved temple destroyed its inner chamber, causing the external columns to collapse. Originally dedicated to the

A reconstruction of the Baal Shamin temple at Palmyra, destroyed by Islamic State militants in 2015

West Semitic storm god Baal, the temple was later converted for Christian worship, containing frescoes that were like red rags to Islamic militants. So angry were these iconoclasts that they beheaded Khaled al-Asaad, the curator of Palmyra, as a punishment for apostasy, protecting idols, and his links to the Syrian regime. A photograph was published showing the eighty-two-year-old archaeologist bound to a lamppost with his head placed beneath his feet. It would appear that the real reason for his execution was a belief that he had hidden Palmyran treasures to save them from destruction. Khaled al-Asaad had spent half a century at Palmyra, where he lived in a house overlooking the ruins.

THE ARAB SPRING

Although not directly connected with the so-called Arab Spring, which started in December 2010 in Tunisia, the violence sponsored by the Islamic State was the most extreme version of what became known as

Islamism, a political ideology that came into its own during the wave of uprisings. In essence, Islamism was an attempt to turn the clock back to the heady days of the Arab conquests following Muhammad's death in 632. Then Arab tribesmen set out to carry Allah's message far and wide, since they believed it was the final dispensation to humanity. For Islam was nothing less than a 'reformation of a world sickened by ignorance and injustice'.

The revolution in Tunisia marked the beginning of a series of demonstrations and protests which challenged the existing Arab governments as far east as Saudi Arabia. A common slogan was 'the people want a change of regime'. The first political casualty of the upsurge of protest was the Tunisian president Ben-Ali, who fled to Saudi Arabia in January 2011. The spread to Egypt of popular protest against long-standing and entrenched regimes was a serious development for all Near Eastern states, however, because so many Arabs lived in that country. Egyptian president Hosni Mubarak's initial refusal to step down after thirty years of rule hardly surprised his allies, the chief of which was the United States, although Washington was quick to advise a positive engagement with the protesters. Whereas the 1.5 billion dollar programme of American foreign aid obviously helped to sustain Mubarak in office, Saudi Arabia's own oil wealth always gave it a financial independence second to none in the Arab world. Despite protests, the ability of this traditional kingdom to continue along its own separate path never seemed in doubt.

In most places, however, the Arab Spring demonstrations were met with violent responses from the existing governments. Numerous factors stood behind these protests, ranging from unemployment, official corruption, extreme poverty, and the increased numbers of young people in each country's population. Inspired by the uprising in Tunisia, the Egyptians by February 2011 forced President Mubarak to resign his office. Yet his later sentence to life imprisonment did not please everybody. And his successor, Mohammed Morsi, Egypt's first democratically elected president, soon precipitated a crisis by appointing only members of the Muslim Brotherhood to key positions in his administration. Established in the late 1920s by Hassan al-Banna, a schoolteacher working in the city of Ismailia, its aim was the revival of Islam in Egyptian society. A certain imprecision in al-Banna's reform programme probably assisted the growth of the Muslim Brotherhood, since it allowed people to associate their own ideas and aspirations with the movement. Between 1920 and 1940 membership reached 450,000 Egyptians.

Following the Arab–Israeli War of 1948, leading members of the Muslim Brotherhood spread across the modern Near East and took the call for an Islamic revival to other Arab countries. The murder of Hassan al-Banna in 1949 put the movement on the back foot, as did Nasser's military coup three years later. Since the republican regime which Nasser founded was positively secular, a confrontation with the Muslim Brotherhood was unavoidable. Its prominent members ended up in prison or exile abroad. Learning from this experience, the Muslim Brotherhood eschewed confrontation elsewhere. In Jordan, for instance, King Hussein was willing to cooperate with its objectives, not least because they resonated with both Palestinian refugees who had lost their homes in the 1948 war between Israel and its Arab neighbours as well as the traditionally pious Jordanians themselves. After all, King Hussein could trace his own ancestry back to the Prophet Muhammad, a cornerstone of his justification to rule.

As times changed in Egypt, the Muslim Brotherhood came to terms with Anwar Sadat, Nasser's successor. Instead of confrontation, its strategy was to build an economic support system for Egypt's poor, which would provide in due course the votes it needed to challenge the secular order. Mohammad Morsi's short-lived triumph in 2012 stemmed from this initiative. That he overplayed his hand in the changes he swiftly made to the government was most evident in his sacking of Egypt's defence minister, who had held the post for two decades. Morsi was of course exercising his prerogative as the country's elected president to form an administration of his own choosing, but his choice of new ministers appeared very much as cronyism. He overlooked key secular figures who had played a prominent role in the 2011 uprising against Mubarak, and therefore raised fears that he would usher in a permanent Islamic regime in Egypt. When the president issued a constitutional declaration by which he granted himself unlimited authority to enact legislation, without judicial oversight or review of his acts, it was clear that Morsi was attempting to put the Muslim Brotherhood above the law. Protests erupted across Egypt in 2013 calling for the president's resignation, and he was overthrown by the Egyptian army, which then cracked down on the Muslim Brotherhood.

Libya's descent into chaos was even more brutal, with Gaddafi's overthrow after forty-two years in power. An armed uprising against his regime split the country into warring tribal factions and gave a huge opportunity to the jihadists. No less disruptive was the situation in Syria, once President Bashar al-Assad ordered troops to subdue protesters. By 2012 the county was engulfed in a full-scale civil war. An especially provocative action was that of Syrian security forces in the city of Homs, who fired on protesters from inside ambulances. Eleven people were killed there. Syria's version of the Arab Spring gradually became a sectarian confrontation between Sunni and Shia Muslims, during the course of which former members of the radical Islamist group al-Qaeda established the Islamic State of Iraq and Syria.

From the start, the Islamic State behaved in a manner that suggested it intended to develop as the core country of the Muslim world. In the

The destruction of the Syrian civil war visited upon Homs

areas that it controlled, fighters and their families were accommodated, their children offered an education, hospitals set up, and subsidized food provided. Tapping into the oil pipelines which ran through its territory, the Islamic State found the means to finance its religious war. International alliances against it were weak, so that Russian–American rivalry once again gave the Islamic State enough time to strengthen its position. Bombings and shootings caused consternation in western Europe, but conspicuously failed to rouse its nations to engage in a long-term and exacting ground war.

CONFLICT IN IRAQ AND SYRIA

An undoubted factor behind the rise of the Islamic State was the disintegration of Iraq as a consequence of the Second Gulf War. After the end of hostilities, the United States purged Ba'ath party members from Iraq's army and civil service, with the result that the balance of political power moved from the Sunni Iraqis to the Shia Iraqis. This gave the Shias, who constitute the majority of the country's population, the first chance in decades to achieve an influence commensurate with their numbers. Many of Iraq's new establishment figures were in fact Shia refugees or political dissidents, who had fled from Saddam Hussein's regime. Arguably the United States must shoulder much of the responsibility for the Iraqi civil war which raged after the overthrow of Saddam Hussein. Determination to achieve regime change was only matched by a failure to anticipate the post-battle impact of its invasion. It did not help Iraq either that so many qualified people despaired of the situation and moved abroad with their families.

Similar developments happened in Lebanon in 2005: after the assassination of Prime Minister Rafik Hariri that year, the various militias representing Sunni, Shia and Christian communities squared up for a civil conflict which threw up Hezbollah as the most powerful force in the country. For years Hezbollah, or 'the party of Allah', had vacillated between remaining an independent Islamist movement or acting as an agent of Iranian foreign policy. Because Iran had always opposed the existence of Israel, Hezbollah was bound to be drawn into its sphere of

2009 Baghdad car bombs killed ninety-five people

influence. Rather like the Muslim Brotherhood in Egypt, it had staked a claim to power by the development of health, education, transportation, security and social services which dwarfed those provided by the Lebanese state. Most of all, Hezbollah reaped the harvest of Arab anger over the inability of secular government to ameliorate widespread poverty. Another factor in its appeal was improved media communications which allowed the leaders of Hezbollah to reach target audiences in Lebanon and indeed around the Muslim world.

For Hezbollah, Israel was 'Little Satan' and 'Great Satan' the United States, which explains its focus on the city of Jerusalem and the need to liberate it from Israeli control. Jerusalem is of course Judaism's holiest city, but it is also Islam's third holiest, after Mecca and Medina. Yet from the beginning Hezbollah was staunchly anti-Zionist, which is the reason for its total opposition to any negotiations with Israel, because they would be tantamount to recognizing its right to exist, a much sterner stance than that adopted by either the Palestine Liberation Organization or the Palestinian Authority. Although Hezbollah revealed deep concern over the plight of the Palestinians, it never replaced Hamas as the main opponent of Israel in the Gaza Strip. Hamas, 'the Islamic resistance movement', had emerged from the Muslim Brotherhood as an alternative to the more conventional, secular-minded politics of the Palestine Liberation Organization. The equivalent of Hezbollah and Hamas in Iraq was the Islamic State.

It was Saddam Hussein's invasion of Kuwait in 1990 that led to the conflict raging in Iraq today. The First Gulf War drove the Iraqis out of Kuwait, but this did not stop Saddam Hussein from using chemical weapons against subsequent uprisings in the north of Iraq by the Kurds and in the south by the Marsh Arabs. Perhaps as many as 100,000 died, notwithstanding the imposition of no-fly zones. The United Nations also tried to compel Saddam Hussein to destroy his stockpile of chemical and biological weapons, whose continued existence would appear to have inspired the mistaken belief that Iraq possessed 'weapons of mass destruction'. Unreliable as reports were later proved to be about the nature of his arsenal, the United States and Britain were able to put together another coalition and invade Iraq itself in 2003. This Second Gulf War ended Saddam Hussein's hold on the Iraqi government and broke Sunni control of its institutions, including the armed forces. Almost immediately an insurgency against the invaders tore Iraq apart, as Sunni ex-soldiers and policemen joined guerrilla units. Within another year, both Sunni and Shia guerrilla forces were fighting the coalition army of occupation, as well as each other.

The election of a new Iraqi government made little difference to the rising level of violence, which reached a peak in 2006 with the execution of Saddam Hussein, and the killing of the local al-Qaeda leader by American troops. But the Iraqi government's request for a gradual withdrawal of coalition forces gave hope to many Iraqis that a return to peace was still possible. The last American detachment crossed the border into

Kuwait, the original launching pad for the invasion, at the end of 2011. In spite of continued civil unrest, stimulated by Arab Spring-style protests, the Iraqi government did not fall from power. More significant than these protests, however, was the involvement of both Sunni and Shia fighters in the Syrian civil war. In 2014 Sunni members of the Islamic State also seized large areas in northern Iraq, including several major cities such as Tikrit and Mosul. So intense did the conflict become that the idea was floated of splitting Iraq into three autonomous regions: Kurdistan in the north, Sunnistan in the west and Shiistan in the south. This division would have returned the country to almost the same administrative arrangements which were in place during Ottoman rule.

The advent of the Islamic State scuppered any such plan, because its Sunni-inspired ambitions aimed at the restoration of the caliphate and sharia law. Although the majority of its fighters were Iraqi and Syrian nationals, the international appeal of Islamic State to young Muslims resulted in the recruitment of volunteers from western European countries, Britain included. An important difference between the Islamic State and other jihadist movements, including al-Qaeda, was its emphasis on the Last Judgement. Recruits were attracted by the idea of being, as it were, on the spot when this actually happened. Behind the Islamic State were the *salafists*, scholars who based their views and conduct on the righteous followers of Muhammad, whose outlook was almost unaffected by the modern world. As far as the *salafists* were concerned, women should not be seen in public and should be segregated from men; education should reflect Islamic theology and place emphasis on reciting the Qur'an; and in the visual arts there should be only decorative design. Muslim tradition was all that counted; everything else was unworthy of attention. In 1992, salafist leaders in the Arabian peninsula condemned the Saudi King Fahd's decision to allow US forces to be based in his kingdom during the war to eject Saddam Hussein from Kuwait, on the grounds that it would be an insult to the holy cities of Mecca and Medina.

Naming Abu Bakr al-Baghdadi as caliph in 2014 marked the final separation of the Islamic State from other terrorist groups. The forty-four-year-old al-Baghdadi had originally claimed that suicide attacks and car bombings in Iraq were a response to the death in 2011 of Osama bin Laden, the al-Qaeda leader. But links between the Islamic State and al-Qaeda were formally severed two years later. Al-Baghdadi was born in northern Iraq shortly after Saddam Hussein usurped power, at a time when the country was steadily moving towards war with Iran. After the 1979 referendum converted Iran into an Islamic Republic, Ayatollah Ruhollah Khomeini called for the spread of an Islamic revolution and supplied arms to Shia and Kurdish opponents of Saddam Hussein. Where al-Baghdadi and the Iranian mullahs never saw eye to eye was in the nature of the proposed revolution, because as a convinced Sunni he looked upon the Shia faith of Iran as nothing more than a deviant form of Islam. Hardly surprising then was Iranian backing of the Shia in Iraq, where even Revolutionary Guards arrived from Iran to take the fight to the Islamic State.

Holding its own in Iraq, the Islamic State was able to dispatch experienced guerrilla fighters to Syria from 2011 onwards. Their numbers were soon enhanced by veteran insurgents, who were freed from Iraqi prisons through surprise attacks. It was not long before the Islamic State gained a foothold in war-torn Libya and farther south in Africa, where an alliance was formed with Boko Haram, an extremist group in northern Nigeria.

Boko Haram leader Abubakar Shekau at first pledged his support for the Islamic State's caliph in a 2014 video, but then he set up his own caliphate. He declared that the prime objective of Boko Haram was 'to gain revenge on Nigeria's ruling Christian community', although its violence also spread into neighbouring Chad. An indifference to the fate of captive girls similar to that shown by Islamic State fighters in Iraq and Syria made Boki Haram the terror of Nigeria's northern provinces, where official corruption and government weakness gave it plenty of scope to operate without interference. The Nigerian army succeeded in releasing some captives in late 2015 and early 2016, but its progress against the well-entrenched terrorist group enjoying local support has been limited.

When the Arab Spring reached Syria and an uprising began in 2012 against the Assad regime, it came as no surprise that President Bashar al-Assad used force to crush the rebels. Thirty years earlier his father, Hafez al-Assad, had unleashed the Syrian army at Hama, a town situated on the Orontes river. According to the Assad government, security forces only swung into action then because the rebels killed 'women and children, mutilating the bodies of the martyrs in the streets, driven, like mad dogs, by their black hatred'. Few Syrians believed this explanation for shelling Hama over the period of a month, and leaving at least 20,000 of its inhabitants dead. Sensing the danger involved for political stability in the modern Near East through a Syrian collapse, Bashar al-Assad was pledged the support of both Russia and Iran. In 2013 Iran-backed Hezbollah fighters took to the field; and two years later Russian aircraft commenced a bombing campaign. Already Bashar al-Assad was deploying heavy artillery against rebel strongholds, but he received international condemnation when he added biological weapons and barrel bombs to his armoury. A problem for those opposing the Assad government was the number of competing rebel groups, which soon encompassed the Kurds and the Islamic State as well.

Damascus and Aleppo witnessed bitter fighting and large-scale destruction, as whole sections of these cities were reduced to rubble. Even though joint Hezbollah and Syrian army offensives recovered territory, the strength of the rebellion thwarted widespread advances. The official reason for Hezbollah operating in Syria was a determination 'not to allow Syrian militants control of areas that border Lebanon'. That the Islamic State managed to establish itself at Raqqah, Syria's sixth largest city, only served to complicate a confused military situation. Weapons acquired during campaigns in Iraq facilitated the capture of Raqqah, which was then used as a centre to organize suicide attacks and car bombings throughout Syria. Fearful of this jihadist advance, the United States began attacking Islamic State positions from the air. France and Britain also joined the bombing offensive, but it failed to prevent Palmyra's destruction. Several ceasefire attempts failed to slow down the conflict for any length of time, and were never going to contain the territorial ambitions of the Islamic State anyway.

GAZA AND ISRAEL

With Egypt's frustration of the 1956 Suez venture by Britain and France, the Palestinians bottled up in the Gaza Strip looked to Nasser as their saviour. But the Egyptian president's overwhelming priority was in fact to avert any provocation of Israel, so that nothing would stand in the way of his post-Suez political gains. Egypt was fortunate in that nearly all of those Palestinians committed to an armed struggle for the liberation of Palestine had quit Gaza, while the Muslim Brotherhood leadership in Egypt found refuge in Saudi Arabia. An Egyptian administration in Gaza deliberately kept Palestinian activism in check, at least until the founding of the Palestine Liberation Organization in the early 1960s. Then Nasser had to agree that Sinai and the Gaza Strip could be used by Yasser Arafat for training his armed forces. Born in Cairo, the son of an Arab merchant, Arafat lived in Jerusalem from 1933 to 1937 before returning to Egypt to complete his education. Although he was caught up in the general excitement of agitation against the British, Arafat did not take part in any fighting in either Palestine or Egypt.

Palestinians called the 1948 Israeli victory over its Arab neighbours a *nakba*, or 'catastrophe'. Gaza was almost submerged by waves of displaced Palestinians, so that it soon contained a quarter of the old mandated territory's Arab population. For them Gaza was always looked upon as a temporary refuge, a kind of Noah's Ark that preserved the Palestinian heritage, wedged as it was between the Israeli army and the Mediterranean shore. Barely 360 square kilometres in area, at its widest point along the border with Egypt it is only 13 kilometres across. Even though Cairo did as much as possible to ease the lot of overcrowded Gaza, the Muslim Brotherhood accused the Egyptian government of having sidelined jihad in Palestine. There were border incidents between the Israelis and the Palestinians, but these were never enough to cause an Israeli takeover of the Strip. Not until the Six-Day War in 1967 between Israel and Egypt did an Israeli occupation take place and the idea of removing the Palestinian refugees was considered.

Dealing with Gaza was soon discovered to be far from an easy proposition. In Rafah a civilian disturbance led to the killing of ten people, including a small girl. It was followed by unrest in the city of Gaza after a Palestinian mine exploded near the port. Yasser Arafat was unable to check the belligerence of his followers, who executed 'informers' allegedly working for the Israelis. Nor could he prevent in 1970 the hijack of three commercial airliners—one American, one Swiss and one British—before forcing these planes to fly to a Jordanian airstrip. Subsequently they were all destroyed on the ground. No matter how hard Israel endeavoured to find a working arrangement within the Gaza Strip, so deep seated was Palestinian hatred of the Israelis that all the efforts of Tel Aviv came to nothing. And the establishment of Israeli settlements hardly helped, since they involved the dispossession of Arab owners. Leaving the Strip to its own devices was not a solution either, because although the territories of Gaza and the West Bank both fall under the jurisdiction of the Palestinian Authority, Gaza has since 2007 been ruled by Hamas. The Oslo Accords of 1993 between the Palestine Liberation Organization and Israel had set up the Palestinian Authority as a starting point for the development of a fully independent Palestinian state, but Hamas regarded the agreement as a total betrayal of the Palestinian people.

Israel's occupation of the Gaza Strip during the Six-Day War immediately shattered the calm imposed there by the Egyptians, and the Oslo Accords were a belated attempt to put Israeli–Palestinian relations on a new footing, despite the first Hamas suicide bombing in Gaza. Yet it could not be expected to be much of an improvement when Israel always saw the Gaza problem in terms of its own security, which prompted heavy-handed operations by the Israeli army. And Hamas, along with other jihadist groups, were adept at using densely populated areas to cloak their activities, such as firing missiles. Ironically, it was Israel's occupation of Gaza in 1967 that stimulated the rise of Islamism. By 2011, most of the Palestinian activists in the Strip had acknowledged Hamas' leadership, thereby blocking any possibility of a permanent peace agreement. Without the cooperation of the people living in the Gaza Strip, no Palestinian state could ever become fully independent. Only then would the controversial security barrier raised by the Israelis around its own territory become surplus to requirements.

THE GULF STATES

The inhabitants of the Gulf states enjoyed a high standard of living, especially compared to their neighbours in the rest of the Arab world and

Iran. In return, they were expected to accept the rule of their leading families, whose ability to survive without imposing taxation arose from enormous oil revenues. With the exception of Kuwait, the rulers of the Gulf states have therefore been able to manage their affairs without the bother of elected parliaments, or indeed any oversight of their administrations. Legitimacy rested upon a religious–tribal mandate sanctioned by Islamic authorities. An obvious example of this was the establishment of Abdulaziz al-Saud as the king of Saudi Arabia. A tribal prince from central Arabia, he defeated his opponents in battle and was then confirmed by Sunni clerics as an absolute ruler, after allowing the strict Wahhabi sect almost exclusive control over the kingdom's religion. The Commission for the Promotion of Virtue and the Prevention of Vice, with its religious police force, was the agency that the Wahhabis used to dominate Saudi Arabian society.

Elsewhere in the Persian Gulf, it was Britain that had played a major role in the creation of its Arab states. On a visit in 1903, Lord Curzon, then viceroy of India, let slip the reality of the political position there. The sovereignty accorded to some of the Gulf sheikhdoms, Curzon commented, was no more than the other side of a coin on which the supremacy of British power was stamped. In India the same kind of quasi-independence enjoyed by Arab rulers was allowed to native princes, in recognition of their loyalty during the Indian Mutiny of 1857. Understandable then was the deliberate association of Gulf ruling families with the Umayyad and Abbasid dynasties, which had ruled Muslims from the seventh to the eleventh centuries. The Umayyad-Abbasid idea of an hereditary monarchy with religious responsibilities expressed though the caliphate exactly suited traditional Gulf politics, before the Arab Spring began to impact upon the region. Reference to the caliphate also seemed to offer protection against the charge that the Gulf royal families were mere pawns of Europe and the United States.

What undermined this assumption, as much as the notions generated by the Arab Spring, was rapid population growth. Between 1990 and 2010, the Gulf population doubled from 20 million to 40 million. The overthrow of Ben-Ali in Tunisia, then Mubarak in Egypt, frightened the Gulf authorities as neither the United States nor Britain opposed these regime changes. When at the start of 2011 Bahrainis took to the streets in an attempt to limit the privileges of the al-Khalifa family, rulers of Bahrain for two centuries, it was transparent how modern times had arrived at last in the Persian Gulf. A fundamental difficulty for the Sunni al-Khalifas was that the majority of the island's inhabitants were Shia, who believed themselves to be treated as second-class citizens. During demonstrations they waved banners depicting the face of Hussein ibn Ali, the younger son of Ali ibn Abi Talib, Muhammad's son-in-law. A Shia icon, Hussein had been killed by the Umayyads in 680. Faced with the possibility of a successful Shia uprising sponsored by the Iranians, troops from Saudi Arabia and the United Arab Emirates stepped in and ended the disturbances.

A similar anxiety caused Saudi Arabia to become involved in Yemen's civil war. Again Iranian backing of the Shia community in Yemen seemed no more than a blatant attempt at regional hegemony. What Tehran's foreign policy triggered was alarm. In the same way that Khomeini's revolution had scared his neighbours, so this new Islamism galvanized Iran's opponents. Saudi Arabia and Abu Dhabi combined to confront the threat, backing Sunni politicians in Iraq and the rebels fighting Assad's regime in Syria. Even Jordan's king Abdullah II warned of a 'Shia crescent' reaching from Iran to Iraq, to Syria and Lebanon. A more conciliatory Iran, following the election of Hassan Rouhani as president in 2013, may defuse the Near Eastern conflict which has troubled nearly every state except Oman.

Fearful of an Arab Spring takeover of the Arab world, the Gulf ruling families bolstered the monarchies in Jordan and Morocco. They also introduced welfare reforms in their own countries. Qatar, whose total population was less than 300,000, announced a massive welfare package worth billions of US dollars. In Oman, on the other hand, political uncertainty derived not from popular unrest but rather power struggles within the ruling family.

FURTHER READING

Part One: Lost Civilizations

Bacon, Edward (ed.), *The Great Archaeologists and their discoveries as originally reported in the pages of The London Illustrated News*, London, 1976.

Bang, Peter F. and Walter Scheidel (eds), *The Oxford Handbook of the State in the Ancient Near East and Mediterranean*, Oxford, 2013.

Bermant, Chaim and Michael Weitzman, *Ebla. An Archaeological Enigma*, London, 1979.

Blacker, Carmen and Michael Loewe (eds), *Ancient Cosmologies*, London, 1975.

Cotterell, Arthur, *The Minoan World*, London, 1979.

—— (ed.), *The Penguin Encyclopedia of Ancient Civilizations*, London, 1988.

Dalley, Stephanie, *Mari and Karana. Two Old Babylonian Cities*, London, 1984.

Evans, Sir Arthur, *The Palace of Minos*, London, 1921.

Finkel, I. L. and M. J. Seymour, *Babylon. Myth and Reality*, London, 2009.

Hopkins, Clark, *The Discovery of Dura-Europos*, ed. B. Goldman, New Haven, CT, 1979.

Horowitz, Wayne, *Mesopotamian Cosmic Geography*, Winona Lake, IN, 2011.

Karageorghis, V., *Kition*, London, 1962.

Kramer, Samuel N., *History Begins at Sumer*, London, 1958.

Layard, A. H., *Nineveh and its Remains*, London, 1850.

—— *Discoveries in the Ruins of Nineveh and Babylon*, London, 1853.

Lloyd, Seton, *The Archaeology of Mesopotamia. From the Old Stone Age to the Persian Conquest*, London, 1978.

Oates, Joan and David, *Nimrud. An Assyrian Imperial City Revealed*, London, 2001.

Radner, Karen and Eleanor Robson (eds.), *The Oxford Handbook of Cuneiform Culture*, Oxford, 2011.

Sartre, Maurice, *The Middle East Under Rome*, trans. C. Porter and E. Rawlings, Cambridge, MA, 2005.

Schliemann, H., *Troja*, London, 1884.

Woolley, Sir Leonard, *Ur of the Chaldees*, London, 1929.
—— *Excavations at Ur. A Record of 12 Years' Work*, London, 1954.
Yon, Marguerite, *The City of Ugarit at Tell Ras Shamra*, Winona Lake, IN, 2006.

Part Two: The Ancient Near East

Aubet, Maria Eugenia, *The Phoenicians and the West. Politics, colonies and trade*, trans. M. Turton, Cambridge, 1993.
Barton, John, *Ethics in Ancient Israel*, Oxford, 2014.
Birley, Anthony, R., *Hadrian. The Restless Emperor*, London, 1997.
Black, Jeremy et al., *The Literature of Ancient Sumer*, Oxford, 2004.
Borgeaud, Philippe, *Mother of the Gods. From Cybele to the Virgin Mary*, trans. L. Hochroth, Baltimore, MD, 2004.
Bottero, J., *Religion in Ancient Mesopotamia*, trans. T. L. Fagan, Chicago, IL, 2001.
Briant, P., *From Cyrus to Alexander. A history of the Persian Empire*, trans. P. T. Daniels, Winona Lake, IN, 2002.
Brinkman, J. A., *A Political History of Post-Kassite Babylonia*, Rome, 1968.
Brown, Peter, *The Making of Late Antiquity*, Cambridge, MA, 1978.
Bryce, Trevor, *The Kingdom of the Hittites*, Oxford, 1998.
—— *Life and Society in the Hittite World*, Oxford, 2002.
—— *The Trojans and their Neighbours*, London, 2006.
—— *The World of the Neo-Hittite Kingdoms. A Political and Military History*, Oxford, 2012.
—— *Ancient Syria. A Three Thousand Year History*, Oxford, 2014.
Burkert, Walter, *Babylon, Memphis, Persepolis. Eastern Contexts of Greek Culture*, Cambridge, MA, 2010.
Casson, Lionel, *Travel in the Ancient World*, 1974.
Charpin, Dominique, *Reading and Writing in Babylon*, trans. J. M. Todd, Cambridge, MA, 2010.
—— *Hammurabi of Babylon*, London, 2012.
Clifford, Richard J., *The Cosmic Mountain in Canaan and the Old Testament*, Eugene, OR, 1972.
Cotterell, Arthur, *Chariot. The Astounding Rise and Fall of the World's First War Machine*, London, 2004.
Crawford, Harriet, *Ur. The City of the Moon God*, London, 2015.
Culican, W., *The First Merchant Adventurers*, London, 1964.
Curtis, John and Neil MacGregor, *The Cyrus Cylinder and Ancient Persia. A New Beginning in the Middle East*, London, 2013.
Dalley, Stephanie, *Myths from Mesopotamia. Creation, The Flood, Gilgamesh and Others*, Oxford, 1989.
—— *The Mystery of the Hanging Garden of Babylon*, Oxford, 2013.

Dick, Michael B. (ed.), *Born in Heaven, Made on Earth. The Making of the Cult Image in the Ancient Near East*, Winona Lake, IN, 1999.

Dodson, Aidan, *Amarna Sunset. Nefertiti, Tutankhamun, Ay, Horemheb, and the Egyptian Counter-Reformation*, Cairo, 2009.

Finkel, Irving, *The Ark before Noah. Decoding the Story of the Flood*, London, 2014.

Foster, Benjamin R, and Karen P. Foster, *Civilizations of Ancient Iraq*, Princeton, NJ, 2009.

George, A. R., *House Most High. The Temples of Ancient Mesopotamia*, Winona Lake, IN, 1993.

—— *The Babylonian Gilgamesh Epic. Introduction, Critical Edition and Cuneiform Texts*, Oxford, 2003.

Gibson, J. C. L., *Canaanite Myths and Legends*, London, 1956.

Grayson, A. K., *Assyrian and Babylonian Chronicles*, Locus Valley, NY, 1975.

—— *Assyrian Rulers of the Early First Millennium BC II (858–745 BC)*, Toronto, 1996.

Gurney, O. R., *The Hittites*, London, 1952.

Hammond, N. G. L., *Alexander the Great. King, Commander and Statesman*, London, 1981.

Hoffner, Harry A., *Hittite Myths*, Atlanta, GA, 1990.

Horbury, William, *Jewish War under Trajan and Hadrian*, Cambridge, 2000.

Jacobsen, Thorkild, *The Treasures of Darkness. A History of Mesopotamian Religion*, New Haven, CT, 1976.

Kramer, Samuel N., *Sumerian Mythology. A Study of Spiritual and Literary Achievement in the Third Millennium BC*, Philadelphia, PA, 1961.

—— and John Maier, *Myths of Enki. The Crafty God*, New York, 1989.

Lee, A. D., *From Rome to Byzantium AD 363 to 565. The Transformation of Ancient Rome*, Edinburgh, 2013.

Liverani, Mario, *Uruk: the first city*, trans. Zainab Bahrani and Marc Van De Mieroop, Sheffield, 2006.

Ma, John, *Antiochus III and the Cities of Western Asia Minor*, Oxford, 1999.

Macqueen, J. G., *The Hittites and their Contemporaries in Asia Minor*, London, 1975.

Marinatos, Nanno, *Minoan Kingship and the Solar Goddess. A Near Eastern Koine*, Urbana and Chicago, IL. 2010.

Markus, R. A., *Christianity in the Roman World*, London, 1974.

—— *The End of Ancient Christianity*, Cambridge, 1990.

Millar, F., *The Roman Empire and its Neighbours*, London, 1951.

Nigosian, S. A., *From Ancient Writings to Sacred Texts. The Old Testament and Apocrypha*, Baltimore, MD, 2004.

Oates, Joan, *Babylon*, London, 1979.

Olmstead, A. T., *History of Assyria*, London, 1923.

Pardee, Dennis, *Ritual and Cult in Ugarit*, Leiden, 2002.

Postgate, Nicholas, *The Land of Assur and the Yoke of Assur. Studies on Assyria: 1971–2005*, Oxford, 2007.

Rahe, Paul A., *The Grand Strategy of Classical Sparta. The Persian Challenge*, New Haven, CT, 2015.

Redford, Donald B., *Egypt, Canaan and Israel in Ancient Times*, Princeton, NJ, 1992.

Ringgren, Helmer, *Israelite Religion*, trans. D. Green, London, 1966.

—— *Religions of the Ancient Near East*, trans. J. Street, London, 1973.

Rogers, Guy Maclean, *The Mysteries of Artemis of Ephesos. Cult, Polis, and Change in the Greco-Roman World*, New Haven, CT, 2012.

Sandars, N. K., *The Sea Peoples. Warriors of the Ancient Mediterranean*, London, 1978.

Sherwin-White, S. and A. Kurt, *From Samarkhand to Sardis. A New Approach to the Seleucid Empire*, London, 1993.

Stoneman, Richard, *Xerxes. A Persian Life*, New Haven, CT, 2015.

Taylor, Joan E., *The Essenes, the Scrolls, and the Dead Sea*, Oxford, 2012.

Thonemann, Peter (ed.), *Roman Phrygia. Culture and Society*, Cambridge, 2013.

Vanstiphout, Herman, *Epics of the Sumerian Kings. The Matter of Aratta*, ed. J. S. Cooper, Leiden, 2004.

Vermes, Geza, *Christian Beginnings. From Nazareth to Nicaea (AD 30–325)*, London, 2012.

von Soden, W., *The Ancient Orient. An Introduction to the Study of the Ancient Near East*, trans. D. G. Schley, Grand Rapids, MI, 1994.

Wilhelm, Gernot, *The Hurrians*, trans. J. Barnes, Warminster, 1989.

Wolkstein, Diane and Samuel N. Kramer, *Inanna. Queen of Heaven and Earth, Her Stories and Hymns from Sumer*, Philadelphia, PA, 1983.

Yamada, Shigeo, *The Construction of the Assyrian Empire. A Historical Study of the Inscriptions of Shalmaneser III (859–824 BC) Relating to his Campaigns in the West*, Leiden, 2000.

Zaehner, R. C., *The Dawn and Twilight of Zoroastrianism*, London, 1967.

Part Three: The Medieval Near East

Abulafia, David, *Frederick II. A Medieval Emperor*, London, 1988.

Alatas, Syed Farid, *Ibn Khaldun*, New Delhi, 2013.

Amitai-Preiss, Reuven, *Mongols and Mamluks. The Mamluk-Ilkhanid War, 1260–1281*, Cambridge, 1995.

Avni, Gideon, *The Byzantine-Islamic Transition in Palestine. An Archaeological Approach*, Oxford, 2014.

Barber, Malcolm, *The New Knighthood. A History of the Order of the Temple*, Cambridge, 1994.

—— *The Crusader States*, New Haven, CT, 2012.

FURTHER READING

Bennison, A. K., *The Great Caliphs. The Golden Age of the Abbasid Empire*, London, 2009.

Bowersock, G. W., *Mosaics as History. The Near East from Late Antiquity to Islam*, Cambridge, MA, 2006.

—— *The Throne of Adulis. Red Sea Wars on the Eve of Islam*, Oxford, 2013.

Cobb, Paul M., *The Race for Paradise. An Islamic History of the Crusades*, Oxford, 2014.

Cohn, Norman, *The Pursuit of the Millennium. Revolutionary Millenarians and Mystical Anarchists of the Middle Ages*, London, 1957.

Comolli, Virginia, *Boko Haram. Nigeria's Islamist Insurgency*, London, 2015.

Cook, Michael, *Muhammad*, Oxford, 1996.

Dale, S. F., *The Orange Trees of Marrakesh. Ibn Khaldun and the Science of Man*, Cambridge, MA, 2015.

Edmondson, Jonathan et al. (eds), *Flavius Josephus and Flavian Rome*, Oxford, 2003.

Elias, Jamal J., *Aisha's Cushion. Religious Art, Perception, and Practice in Islam*, Cambridge, MA, 2012.

Enan, Mohammad Abdullah, *Ibn Khaldun: His Life and Works*, Kuala Lumpur, 2007.

Findley, C. V., *The Turks in World History*, Oxford, 2005.

Fletcher, Richard, *Moorish Spain*, London, 1992.

France, John, *Hattin*, Oxford, 2015.

Frankopan, Peter, *The First Crusade. The Call from the East*, London, 2004.

Goody, Jack, *Islam in Europe*, London, 2004.

Harris, Jonathan, *The Lost World of Byzantium*, New Haven, CT, 2015.

Hildinger, Erik, *Warriors of the Steppe. A Military History of Central Asia, 500 BC to 1700 AD*, Cambridge, MA, 2001.

Hillenbrand, C., *Turkish Myth and Muslim Symbol. The Battle of Manzikert*, Edinburgh, 2007.

Holt, P. M., *The Age of the Crusades. The Near East from the Eleventh Century to 1517*, Harlow, 1986.

Howard-Johnson, James, *Witnesses to a World Crisis. Historians and Histories of the Middle East in the Seventh Century*, Oxford, 2010.

Hoyland, Robert G., *In God's Path. The Arab Conquests and the Creation of an Islamic Empire*, Oxford, 2015.

Ibn Khaldun, *The Muqaddimah. An Introduction to History*, trans. F. Rosenthal, Princeton, NJ, 1967.

Imber, Colin, *The Ottoman Empire*, Basingstoke, 2002.

Kaegi, Walter E., *Byzantium and the Early Arab Conquests*, Cambridge, 1992.

—— *Heraclius. Emperor of Byzantium*, Cambridge, 2003.

Kennedy, Hugh, *The Prophet and the Age of the Caliphates*, Harlow, 1986.

—— *The Court of the Caliphs. The Rise and Fall of Islam's Greatest Dynasty*, London, 2004.

Khatibi, A. and M. Sijelmassi, *The Splendour of Islamic Calligraphy*, London, 1996.

Kreutz, Barbara M., *Before the Normans. Southern Italy in the Ninth and Tenth Centuries*, Philadelphia, PA, 1991.

Lowney, Chris, *A Vanished World. Muslims, Christians and Jews in Medieval Spain*, New York, 2005.

Luttwak, Edward N., *The Grand Strategy of the Byzantine Empire*, Cambridge, MA, 2009.

Marozzi, T., *Tamerlane. Sword of Islam, Conqueror of the World*, London, 2004.

Mohring, Hannes, *Saladin. The Sultan and his Times, 1138–1193*, trans. D. S. Bachrach, Baltimore, MD, 2008.

Odahl, Charles M., *Constantine and the Christian Empire*, New York, 2004.

Quataert, Donald, *The Ottoman Empire, 1700–1922*, Cambridge, 2000.

Riley-Smith, Jonathan, *The Crusades, Christianity and Islam*, New York, 2008.

Runciman, Steven, *The First Crusade*, Cambridge, 1951.

—— *The Fall of Constantinople 1453*, Cambridge, 1965.

—— *Lost Capital of Byzantium. The History of Mistra and the Peloponnese*, London, 1980.

Smail, R. C., *Crusading Warfare, 1097–1193*, Cambridge, 1956.

Starr, S. Frederick, *Lost Enlightenment. Central Asia's Golden Age from the Arab Conquest to Tamerlane*, Princeton, NJ, 2013.

Treadgold, Warren, *Byzantium and its Army, 284–1081*, Stanford, CA, 1995.

Tyerman, C., *Fighting for Christendom. Holy War and the Crusades*, Oxford, 2004.

Wilkinson, John, *Jerusalem Pilgrims. Before the Crusades*, Oxford, 2002.

Part Four: The Modern Near East

Allawi, Ali A., *Faisal I of Iraq*, New Haven, CT, 2014.

Bruce, Anthony, *The Palestine Campaign in the First World War*, London, 2002.

Filiu, Jean-Pierre, *Gaza. A History*, London, 2012.

Gilbert, M., *Israel. A History*, London, 1998.

Gleis, Joshua L. and Benedetta Berti, *Hezbollah and Hamas*, Baltimore, MD, 2012.

Hanioglu, M. Sukru, *Preparation for a Revolution: The Young Turks, 1902–1908*, Oxford, 2001.

—— *Ataturk. An Intellectual Biography*, Princeton, NJ, 2011.

Hinnebusch, R. A., *Authoritarian Power and State Formation in Baathist Syria*, Boulder, CO, 1990.

Hulsman, J. C., *To Begin the World Again. Lawrence of Arabia from Damascus to Baghdad*, New York, 2009.

Klein, Menachem, *Lives in Common. Arabs and Jews in Jerusalem, Jaffa and Hebron*, London, 2014.

Lapidus, Ira M., *A History of Islamic Societies*, Cambridge, 1988.

Lawson, F. H. (ed.), *Demystifying Syria*, London, 2002.

Louis, Wm. Roger, *Ends of British Imperialism. The Scramble for Empire, Suez and Decolonization*, London, 2006.
Macleod, Jenny, *Gallipoli*, Oxford, 2015.
Mackesy, Piers, *British Victory in Egypt, 1801. The end of Napoleon's conquest*, London, 1995.
Mango, A., *Ataturk*, London, 1999.
Menoret, P., *The Saudi Enigma. A History*, trans. P. Camiller, London, 2003.
Meyer, K. E. and S. B. Brysac, *Kingmakers. The Invention of the Modern Middle East*, New York, 2008.
Morris, Benny, *The Birth of the Palestinian Refugee Problem, 1947–1949*, Cambridge, 1981.
Nissen, Hans J. and Peter Heine, *From Mesopotamia to Iraq. A Concise History*, Chicago, IL, 2009.
Osman, Tarek, *Islamism. What it Means for the Middle East and the World*, New Haven, CT, 2016.
Robins, P., *A History of Jordan*, Cambridge, 2004.
Rogan, Eugene, *The Fall of the Ottomans. The Great War in the Middle East, 1914–1920*, London, 2015.
Rubin, Barry and Wolfgang G. Schwanitz, *Nazis, Islamists and the Making of the Modern Middle East*, New Haven, CT, 2014.
Russell, Gerard, *Heirs to Forgotten Kingdoms. Journeys into the Disappearing Religions of the Middle East*, London, 2015.
Schlaim, A., *The Politics of Partition. King Abdullah, the Zionists, and Palestine. 1921–1951*, Oxford, 1988.
Stone, Norman, *Turkey. A History*, London, 2012.
Yapp, M. E., *The Making of the Modern Near East, 1792–1923*, Harlow, 1987.
—— *The Near East since the First World War. A History to 1995*, Harlow, 1996.
Zurcher, Erik Jan, *Turkey: A Modern History*, London, 1993.

LIST OF ILLUSTRATIONS

THE NEAR EAST

LIST OF ILLUSTRATIONS

THE NEAR EAST

Chapter 5: The Biblical Lands

SYRIA

PHOENICIA

Chapter 6: Greco-Roman Domination

MACEDON

AFTER ALEXANDER

EARLY CHRISTIANITY

THE NEAR EAST

HOLDING OFF THE ARABS

ICONOCLASTIC CONTROVERSY

A LIMITED REVIVAL

Chapter 9: The Crusades

THE FIRST CRUSADE

CRUSADER STATES

ADVENT OF SALADIN

FOURTH AND FIFTH CRUSADES

Chapter 10: The Ottoman Empire

TURKISH RESCUE OF ISLAM

LIST OF ILLUSTRATIONS

THE NEAR EAST

INDEX

INDEX